# CONTENTS

Canadian Silver & Silverplate ................... 5
Hallmarked Silver .......................... 80
Glossary — Silver ............................ 82
George V & Queen Mary Silver Jubilee ........... 97
Glass ....................................... 99
Glossary — Glass ............................ 100
Art Glass ................................... 104
Cut Glass — American ........................ 110
Cut Glass — Canadian ........................ 114
Canadian Container Manufacturers and Their Marks .. 116
Trade Marks on Glass — Canadian ............... 122
Trade Marks on Glass — Various ................ 125
Trade Marks on Glass — Miscellaneous ........... 142
Ceramics ................................... 145
Types of Marks Found on Ceramics ............. 146
Dating — Clues............................... 147
Glossary — Ceramics ........................ 150
Ceramics, England - Europe - Japan, etc. ........... 155
Nineteenth Century Majolica ................... 187
Canadian Potters ............................ 241
American Potters ............................ 253
Furniture Styles & Periods .................... 269
British Registry Mark ........................ 276
British Monarchs ............................ 278
Its A Fake! ................................. 280
Reference Books ............................. 282
Index ...................................... 286

# Editors' Note

"Unitt's Book of Marks on Antiques and Collectalbes" has been compiled to fill a need: we have received many requests from collectors and dealers to put together a book which contains marks on antiques and collectables likely to be available in North America, with an emphasis on Canadiana. Therefore, we include known Canadian silver marks as well as British hallmarks. The silverplate marks are confined to known Canadian manufacturers.

Marks on glass include art glass, cut glass, bottles and other containers.

Under ceramics we show a wide selection of marks on china, pottery and porcelain.

It is our hope that this handbook will prove useful and informative.

The Editors, 1973.

The above "Editors' Note" appeared in the first (1973) edition of "Unitt's Book of Marks on Antiques and Collectables" and the hope was expressed that it would prove "useful and informative."

In the 20 years that have passed since those words were written this book has never been "out of print" and sales both in Canada and the U.S.A. have far exceeded expectations.

Many changes have been made in this new, expanded and revised edition. It remains our hope that this handbook will prove useful and informative.

The Editors, 1995.

# Canadian Silver & Silverplate

---
**Abbreviations Used**
b. BORN   d. DIED   Kn. KNOWN
L. LISTED   W. WORKING
---

## CANADIAN MARKS

Are arranged alphabetically in order of province, town and maker's name.

### NEW BRUNSWICK

### FREDERICTON

SPAHN, JUSTIN  b. 1803 - 1856

Born in Fredericton, established himself as working silversmith. Spahn with Pseudo hallmarks used identical to those of Josiah Allen, Halifax, N.S.

WOLHAUPTER, BENJAMIN  Kn. 1771 - 1857

Refused a Land Grant in 1821, was granted Block 2 on Regent Street in 1826. Became Sheriff of Fredericton 1847. Gold and Silversmith. Teaspoon on display Fredericton Museum.

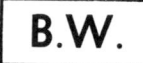

### MILLTOWN

Y.S. & CO  c 1815

Table Fork on Display in Fredericton Museum.

| Y.S.&CO |
|---|

### SAINT JOHN

AGNEW, JAMES  Kn. 1834 - 1850

Situated on Dock Street. Lost business through fire 1837. Last heard of in Eastport, Maine. Understood to have disappeared whilst on a visit there in 1850.

BARRY, JOHN  Kn. 1838 - 1867

Working Silversmith, purchased stock from John Munro. Situated on Germain Street, later on King. Prince William Street 1865. Also used BARRY with Leopard Head and Anchor & Lion.  *See top - opposite page.*

BOOTH, JOHN  Kn. 1770 - 1813

Working gold and silversmith from England. Known to have repaired jewellery. Teaspoon with his mark on display Fredericton Museum.

BROTHERS, Wm.  L. 1785

BURNS, JAMES  Kn. 1810 - 1870

Also English, worked for a time in Halifax then settled in Saint John.

FAIRBANKS, WHITCOMB          Kn. 1851
Dessert spoon on display Fredericton Museum.

W.F. WITH PSEUDO HALLMARKS.

GARD, THOMAS DAPLETON        Kn. 1856
Working silversmith situated at 25 Germain Street. Also used pseudo hallmarks similar to those of James Burns and John Barry.

HARWOOD, ARTHUR           Kn. 1871
Was successor to William Norris Venning when he retired in 1871.

HAY, A. & J.                  Kn. 1869 - 1922
Partnership of Albert Stephen Hay and John Hay. Albert in business on own account 1859-1869. Joined John Hay that year and continued in business as active partner until shortly before his death in 1922.

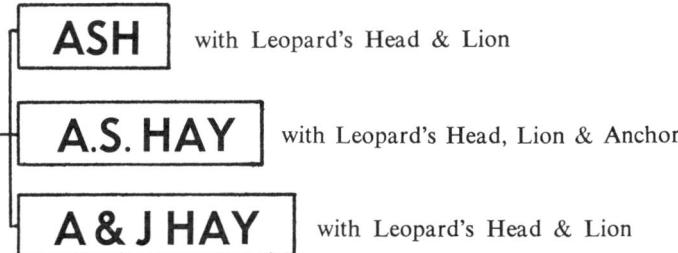

| ASH | with Leopard's Head & Lion |
| A.S. HAY | with Leopard's Head, Lion & Anchor |
| A & J HAY | with Leopard's Head & Lion |

HERSEY, JOHN A.           Kn. 1823 - 1864
Working silversmith advertised extensively.

J.A.H

HUTCHINSON, GEORGE G.      Kn. 1819 - 1864
In business on own account 1819-1931 was joined by Willian Hutchinson. Son George Hutchinson Jnr. succeeded to the business in 1864 but lost everything in fire of 1877.

HUTCHINSON
ST. JOHN N.B.

GH

**KERR & THORNE**  Kn. 1878 - 1885

The late Senator W. H. Thorne refers to Kerr & Thorne as hardware merchants in an article written in 1917 for the Magazine HARDWARE & METAL. The partnership was dissolved in 1885. Believed to have had silver made for them by Hendery & Leslie. Spoons found bearing their name Kerr & Thorne, also some with K&T.

**KERR & THORNE**

**LORD, DANIEL**  L. 1840

Silversmith, pieces bearing his mark have been found in New Brunswick.

**MELICK, JAMES GODFREY**  b. 1802 - d. 1885

Long established Watchmaker, Jeweller & Silversmith. Prince William Street 1856. Had premises in Market Square 1885.

**MUNRO, ALEX**  b. 1754 - d. 1828

Freeman of Saint John 1813. Advertised extensively. Working Jeweller & Silversmith. Advertised Engraving Service. Bought old gold and silver.

**MUNRO, JOHN**  Kn. 1813 - 1864

According to Profesor Traquair the mark of John Munro was almost certainnly "JM" "NB" in separate cartouches, with a Lion passant, Anchor and Sovereign's Head which might face either way. The marks shown may be those of James Munro, who was working in New Glasgow in the 'sixties.  *For marks - see top page 10.*

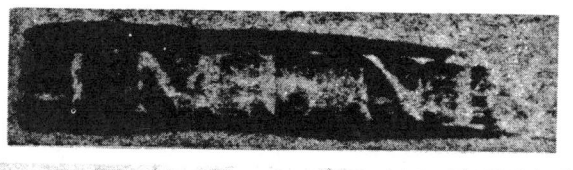

PAGE BROS.   Kn. 1850 - 1870

Sons of Amos Page of Amherst, N.S. Richard and Clement Page partners. When Clement retired in 1870 the firm became PAGE, SMALLEY & FERGUSON. Richard's son Henry Page, and Ferguson (brother-in-law of Richard and Clement) in business together with another silversmith, Smalley. Continued business till 1880, then Ferguson retired and name of firm again changed. This time it became FERGUSON & PAGE.

PAGE, SMALLEY & FERGUSON   Kn. 1870 - 1880
See above.

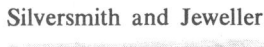

THOMPSON, RICHARD   Kn. 1842 - 1844

VENNING, J. H.   Kn. 1850 - 1877
Was an apprentice of John Munro and became his successor. Silversmith and Engraver. Mark small J.H.V. with Lion.

VENNING, WILLIAM NORRIS   Kn. 1813 - 1871
Silversmith and Jeweller.

WARLOCK, DANIEL O. L.　　　Kn. 1819 - 1880

Irish silversmith, born in Killarney. Was situated on King Street, Saint John, 1858, corner of King and Charlotte 1880.

| D.W. | NB | with Lion |

# NOVA SCOTIA
## AMHERST

PAGE, AMOS　　　　　　　b. 1803　d. 1895

Born August 4, 1803 in Truro, N.S. Son of David Page, and Jean Fraser Page, natives of Haverhill, Massachusetts. Silversmith. Brothers David, John and Thomas all silversmiths. His brother Benjamin became a doctor with a practice in Truro. Listed in the 1864 Nova Scotia Directory. He and his brother Thomas were partners for a brief period. Died on December 4th, 1895 in Amherst.

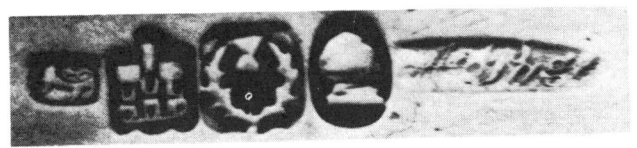

PAGE, THOMAS　　　　　　　　　　L. 1840

Brother of Amos Page, known to have been a partner of Amos for brief period. Moved to Pugwash.

# HALIFAX

ALLEN, JOSIAH                                    L. 1786
Was acquitted of counterfeiting silver coins Halifax 1786.
Occupation given as 'silversmith'. Used pseudo hallmarks.

BESSONETT, J. S. B.                        Kn. 1827 - 1832
Believed to have been partner in BESSONETT &
BROWN, 1834. November 1834, *Acadian Recorder*.

J.B.   with pseudo hallmarks

BLACK, WM. A. & S.                         Kn. 1814 - 1832
William and Samuel advertised their business 1814 through
1832. Wm. A. was well known as the Hon. W. A. Black
in the Legislative Council

BLACK & PARKER                                   L. 1809
Recorded as Engravers; also advertised themselves as
'working silversmiths'.

BLACK, PARKER & BLACK                      Kn. 1810 - 1812
*Halifax Chronicle* of June 30th, 1811 carried advertisement. Silversmiths. Manufacturing jewellers. Partnership
dissolved April, 1812.

BOLTON, THOMAS                             Kn. 1809 - 1847
With F. Meyer as partner. Firm known as 'MEYER &
BOLTON.' Silversmiths and Jewellers. Partnership ended
on death of Mr. Meyer, December 11th, 1847.

BAUME, GUSTAVE LA              Kn. 1835 d. 1838
Advertised himself as maker of silver and jewellery in
the *Acadia Recorder* (1853). Address Granville Street,
Halifax. His tools were auctioned by Deblois & Merkel:
October 30th, 1838. Gustavè La Baume drowned September 30th, 1838.

BECKER & CORNELIUS  Kn. 1869 - 1870
John Becker and Robert Cornelius partners at 81 Granville Street. Silversmiths and Jewellers.

BENNETT, JOHN B.  L. 1877
65 Barrington Street.

BRAUN, F. B.  Kn. 1858
46 Hollis Street.

BROWN, GEORGE STAIRS  Kn. 1844
Working silversmith, moved to Yarmouth.

BROWN, MICHAEL SEPTIMUS  b. 1818  d. 1886
Son of William Brown. Apprenticed to Peter Nordbeck. Established himself in business 1840 at 3 Granville Street. Moved to 106-108 Granville. Did not marry, was succeeded by his nephew Thomas Brown whom he had taken as an apprentice in 1851. Also apprenticed to M. S. Brown, David Hudson Whiston and Henry Wentworth Tully. Died November 28th, 1886.

BROWN & CO., M.S.  Kn. 1886 - 1919
This was the name given to the firm by Thomas Brown when he succeeded to the business of his uncle Michael Septimus Brown in 1886.

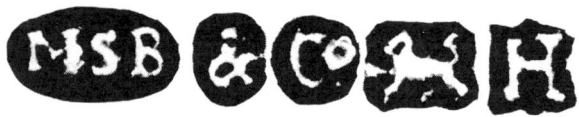

BROWN, THOMAS           b. 1837    d. 1920

Nephew of Michael, Septimus Brown. Established M. S. Brown & Co. which was taken over by William J. Stewart on the retirement of Thomas. In 1919 the business was in the hands of Col. I. W. Vidito who sold it to Henry Birks & Sons. Col. Isaac Vidito is listed as a Director of Birks, Halifax, January 11th, 1920 to May 1920.

BROWN, T. B.                      L. 1800
Four marks ascribed. One having T.B. intertwined.

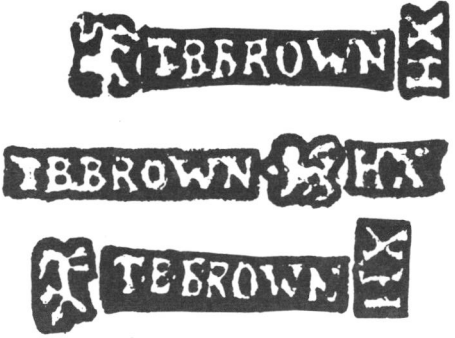

BUTLER, JAMES                  L. 1750
Working silversmith arrived with Lord Cornwallis.

CORNELIUS, JULIUS          b. 1825   d. 1916

Born July 4th, 1825, Prenzlau, Brandenburg, Prussia. Won prize for design Berlin Art School. Served apprenticeship under manufacturing jeweller named Rhode. Travelled extensively. Worked for Tiffany & Co., New York 1853-54. Settled in Halifax 1855. Married 1856. Wife, Henrietta Blackader of Pictou, her father was Henry Blackader, member of the Provincial Legislature. Store at 97 Barrington Street 1864, situated at 99 Granville Street during 1870 to 1878, two locations known. He was one of the finest craftsmen in Canada. He and his highly trained workmen designed and made exquisite jewellery from Nova Scotia Gold delicately set with precious gems. He applied his very special skill and artistic talent to the making of gold brooches with applied mayflowers and foliage — hairwork jewellery was made by him with meticulous care. Handed business over to Herman Cornelius in 1905 when he decided to retire. Died September 20th, 1916.

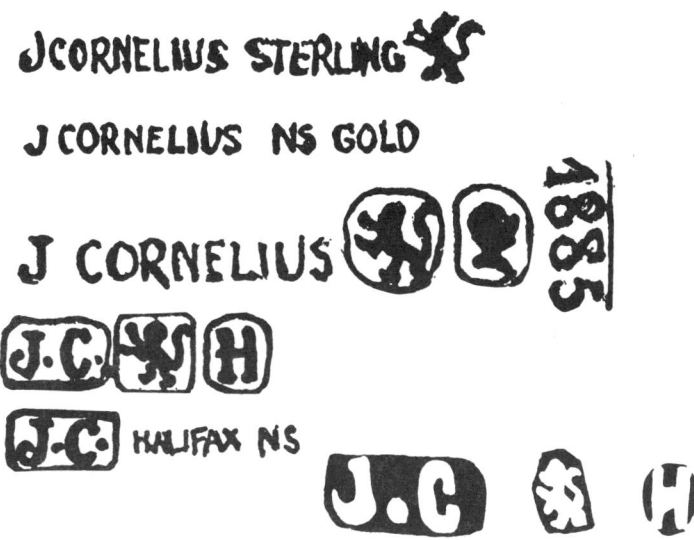

CORNELIUS & CO.                          Kn. 1905

Herman Cornelius succeeded to his father's business and established the firm of Cornelius & Co.

CRAWFORD, WILLIAM            Kn. 1816 - 1867

1827-47 member of North British Society. 1831, advertised as silversmith and watchmaker. 1841, his advertisement says, jeweller and watchmaker. 1863-64 situated at 153-5 Barrington Street.    *For marks - see top page 16*

ETTER, BENJAMIN               b. 1763      d. 1827
Born in Braintree (Quincy) Massachusetts. Apprenticed Berne, Switzerland. 1783, arrived in Halifax. 1787, took over store of Peter Etter (brother). 1813, business taken over by son-in-law Thomas Hosterman and B. B. Etter (son). During the interim period he had James Tidmarsh (1789-1799), then Thomas Hosterman (1806-1813) as partners. 1827, died on the 28th of September.

ETTER, B. B.                  Kn. 1813 - d. 1838
Son of Benjamin Etter. 1813, was partner of Thomas Hosterman. 1815, partnership dissolved. 1816, situated at 26 George Street. 1823, died April 21st at Margaret, Cape Breton.

GRIGG, WILLIAM                Kn. 1765 - 1797
1765 worked in Albany, New York. Advertised in *Nova Scotia Gazette* September 30, 1783. Believed to have arrived in Halifax around 1787. Returned to New York 1796, died the following year 1797. Serving Spoon with his mark on display Nova Scotia Museum, Halifax.

16

HALL, GEORGE A.                          Kn. 1830
Situated at 6 Granville Street. Advertisement *Acadian Recorder*. Working silversmith. Sugar tongs bearing mark on display Nova Scotia Museum, Halifax.

HAMMAN, THOMAS                Kn. 1774 - 1829
Sugar tongs bright cut on display Nova Scotia Museum, Halifax.

HOSTERMAN & PARKER            Kn. 1813
Partnership dissolved December 11th, 1813. Hosterman joined B. B. Etter that year.

HOSTERMAN, THOMAS             Kn. 1802 - 1816
See B. B. Etter.

HULSMAN, LOUIS                  Kn. 1799 - 1815
Served apprenticeship in Europe. 1799 situated on Duke Street according to advertisement in *Royal Gazette* February 26th. Death reported in *Acadian Recorder* December, 1815.

HUNT, WILLIAM                    Kn. 1806 - 1810
Teaspoon on display Nova Scotia Museum, Halifax.

HURD, BENJAMIN                                    b. 1739
Church silver marked B Hurd (name engraved) in collection of Church Silver, Public Archives, Halifax. Date inscribed on bowl October 25, 1769. He was the younger son of Jacob Hurd, brother of Nathaniel Hurd. Hurd family listed as American Silversmiths by G. S. C. Ensko. Nathaniel believed to have worked in Canada around 1777. It is possible some of the silver bearing the Hurd marks was brought into Canada by Loyalist families.

Mark of Jacob Hurd

HURD, NATHANIEL                                   Kn. 1777
Teaspoon on display Nova Scotia Museum, Halifax. N. Hurd in oblong or N. Hurd very small in cartouche.

JOHNSON, THOMAS CHARLES         Kn. 1853 - 1923
Apprenticed to John McCulloch. Working silversmith, situated at Duke and Barrington Streets. Two sons, Charles E. and Albert G. became partners in February 1890 firm became JOHNSON & SONS LTD., T. C., Silversmiths and Jewellers.

TCJ&S STERLING

T·C JOHNSON & SONS

LANGFORD, JAS. I.                Kn. 1815 - d. 1847

Originally from London. 1841, entered into partnership with Franz F. Meyer whom he had trained. Gold and silversmiths. 1847, died in Halifax on February 6th. the business of LANGFORD & MEYER was acquired by William James Veith and George Witham. VEITH & WITHAM advertised that they had taken over the business as of March 20th, 1847. 1848, partnership dissolved.

*NOTE*
*All silver marks are greatly enlarged — see below.*

MARSTERS, R. U.                  Kn. 1817 - 1845

Teaspoon on display Nova Scotia Museum, Halifax. Also made medals and insignia for militia.

| R·U·MARSTERS |

McCULLOCH, JOHN                  b. 1821 - d. 1875

Originally from Scotland. Learned his skills from Peter Nordbeck, 1844. Started business on own account. Clockmaker, jeweller, silversmith. Made lovely jewellery in gold. Thomas C. Johnson one of his apprentices. 1858, married Mary Jane Kerr. A prominent citizen, alderman and school commissioner. Continued in business until 1875. Died Nov. 29th. Believed to have been connected with Arthur W. Carten of Liverpool, N.S. - *see top page 20*

McDONALD, DANIEL    Kn. 1822 - 1828
Dissolved partnership with David Ross June 5th, 1822. Working silversmith.

MELROSE, GEORGE    Kn. 1839
Teaspoon on display Nova Scotia Museum, Halifax

MEYER, FRANZ F.    b. 1809 - d. 1847
1841, partner of Jas. I. Langford, partnership dissolved 1843 joined Thomas Bolton as partner. 1847, died on December 11th.

MIGNOWITZ, HENRY    Kn. 1826
Situated at 234 Water Street, goldsmith, also importer of jewellery and silver gilt from England. Offered new silver in exchange for old gold and silver.

NEWMAN, WILLIAM HERMAN   b. 1826 - d. 1894
1863, situated 92 Granville Street. 1873, corner of George and Granville. Working silversmith, clock and watchmaker, also jeweller. Made fine jewellery and Masonic jewels. 1894, died. Business continued by son until 1905.

NORDBECK, PETER   b. 1789 - d. 1861
1789, born in Germany, received his training there as gilder, jeweller and silversmith. Known to have used the mark N.S. for Nova Scotia. 1815, was in the West Indies. 1819, situated at 40 Duke Street. Entered into partnership with Henry Mignowitz and a Mr. Clark, this partnership was dissolved in 1827. Established Nordbeck & Co. in that year. 1832, wife Caroline died, age 37. 1833, moved to 4 Granville Street. Michael Septimus Brown was apprenticed to Nordbeck. Married widow of Jas. I. Langford sometime after 1847. Had three daughters and a stepdaughter. Died 1861.

ROSS, ADAM   Kn. 1813 - d. 1843
1818, had shop adjoining gunmaker Henry Watkey. 1822, partnership of Ross & McDonald dissolved, June 5th. 1826, advertised that he had restarted business, situated on Granville Street. 1828, offered a saving of 10 per cent in manufacturing for those supplying their own silver. 1828, announced the discovery of molasses. 1840, umbrella repairing service advertised. 1841, situated second corner above Northrup's Country Market. Died 1843.

ROSS, J.                                                    L. 1818
Listed as silversmith.

SPIKE, EDMUND LLOYD          Kn. 1837 - 1900
1863, Situated 78 Granville Street moved to 102 Granville Street, there from 1864 to 1867. 1868, proprietor of "Ophir House". Made jewellery from Nova Scotia gold. Also made emblems for various organizations. He and his brother Thomas Daniel Spike were both apprenticed to J. Cornelius, silversmith. The brothers were partners about 1867. Moved to town somewhere near New York. Died at beginning of century.

SPIKE, THOMAS DANIEL         b. 1840 - d. 1926
Carried on business after his brother Edmund Lloyd Spike had decided to move to New York area. Died, 1926.

STEPHANIS, GOTHELF           Kn. 1787 - 1795
1787. Advertised *Nova Scotia Gazette,* November 12th. Silversmith and engraver. 1791. (Okie) New York City. 1793-1795 located in New York (Ensko).

STERNS, EDWIN                      Kn. 1832 - 1839
1832. Situated 12 Barrington Street. 1839. Situated at Barrington and Buck Street. Gold and silversmith.

TOLER, JOSEPH                              Kn. 1831

Sugar Tongs Nova Scotia Museum, Halifax.

TROOP, ALEXANDER              b. 1776 - d. 1856

1843, situated on Argyle Street. Silversmith and watchmaker. 1856, died December 30th.

TROOP, JR. ALEXANDER          b. 1806 - d. 1873

Situated at 45 Duke St. in 1868-69, business taken over by James Carr. 1873, died in Halifax, October 8th.

TULLY, HENRY WENTWORTH     b. 1863 - d. 1944

1880, apprenticed to D. H. Whiston. Trained as silversmith and jeweller. Foreman of the jewellery manufacturing department for M. S. Brown and Co. 1894, went into partnership with his brother Thomas, firm name, Tully Bros. Manufacturing and repairing jewellery. Died April 14th, 1944.

          *Tully Bros. Trademark*
                     *Used Principally On Gold Work*

VEITH, WILLIAM JAMES           b. 1827 - d. 1900

1827, born Halifax February 3rd. 1847, acquired business of Jas. I. Langford with a partner George Witham. Gold and silversmiths. 1848, partnership dissolved November 11th. Continued business at 10 Granville Street. Lost store in Granville Street fire 1854. Retired. Started entirely different type of business, stage coach and stables, gave this up in 1863. Became farmer. Died Aug. 8th, 1900.

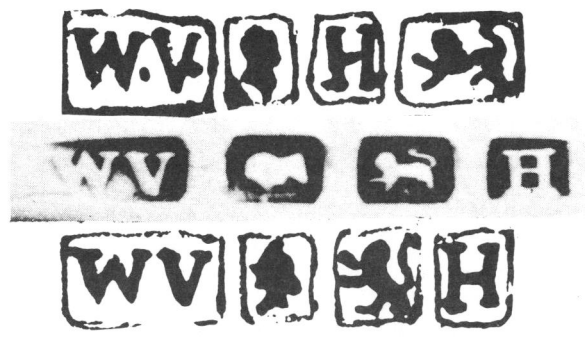

VEITH & WITHAM                          Kn. 1848
Mustard Spoon Nova Scotia Museum, Halifax.

WALLACE & BALCOM                        Kn. 1876
Teaspoon on display Nova Scotia Museum, Halifax.

WHISTON, DAVID HUDSON          b. 1834 - d. 1917
1834, born Halifax April 23rd. Was apprenticed to Michael Septimus Brown. Foreman of silversmithing department for many years. 1864-68, situated 26 Buckingham Street. 1870-77, situated 149 Granville Street. 1884, shared store with R. T. LePine at 181 Barrington Street. Made silverware for T. C. Johnson. Marked it TCJ-H. Killed in Halifax explosion December 6th, 1917.

WITHAM, GEORGE                  b. 1825 - d. 1875
Partner of William James Veith in 1847. Father a General Merchant. George became a Stage Coach Operator after 1848.

## NEW GLASGOW

EASTWOOD, JAMES                         Kn. 1875 - 1914
Advertised as manufacturer of Jewellery and Rolled Plate. *The Trader* 1900. Large manufacturing firm. Introduced rolled gold plate into Canada. The firm employed about 50 men and women in the factory. Gold and silversmiths included HILTZ, a native of Nova Scotia, who left and started "CRESCENT JEWELLERY"; GRIMNER (German); PARSONS (English); DES JARDINS (American) and OLAF LARSEN who worked in Halifax after 1904. Larsen used this mark.      *For marks - see page 25.*

*Olaf Larsen*

*James Eastwood*

## NEW MINAS

BISHOP, HENRY                      L. 1864

Mark H.G.B. in oblong pseudo English hallmark.

## PICTOU

FLETCHER, W.S.                   L. 1840

GEDDIE, JOHN             b. 1778 - d. 1843

## SHELBURNE

BRUFF, CHARLES OLIVER     b. 1735 - d. 1817

Recorded as having come from New York with other Loyalists. Jeweller, Goldsmith & Silversmith. Moved to Liverpool 1793. Died there in 1817.

GANO, DAVID               Kn. 1783 - 1786

Spoon on display Nova Scotia Museum, Halifax.

## TRURO

MORGAN, C. P.               Kn. 1865 - 1891

1891, listed in Nova Scotia Directory as silversmith, also as an engraver. Situated on Prince Street.    *-see page 26.*

C. P. Morgan

PAGE, DAVID  b. 1770 - d. 1840
Originally from Haverhill, Massachusetts. 1793, settled in Onslow, N.S. later made his home in Truro. Sons David Jr., Thomas, John and Amos were trained as watchmakers and silversmiths. 1840, died January 22nd.

## WINDSOR

ANDERSON, ROBERT  L. 1816

## WOLFVILLE

HERBIN, JOHN FREDERIC  Kn. 1869 - d. 1923
Mark a fleur de lis. Fine goldsmith, no silver work traced. Situated at 191 Hollis St. 1871.

The fleur de lis of Herbin is on a number of historic pieces.
(*see Nova Scotia Gold & Silversmiths by Harry Piers and D. McKay*)

TWEEDELL, RICHARD HENRY  Kn. 1878 - d. 1906

## R. H. TWEEDELL

NOVA SCOTIA SILVER C. B. & CO.  C. 1883
Location not known. Several spoons found bearing trade mark. M. S. Brown was believed to have manufactured for the trade but B. M. Co. might be his choice of mark.

CORNELIUS BECKER & CO. another possibility.

## MERIDEN BRITANNIA CO. LTD.   Kn. 1879 - 1912

It was in 1879, the year Sir John A. MacDonald with the National Policy came into power that 1847 Rogers Bros. made its debut before the Canadian public, in the City of Hamilton, as the Canadian branch of the Meriden Britannia Co. of Meriden, Conn. The first Canadian manager was John E. Parker, with James A. Watts as sales manager. Mr. Watts remained only a short time. The business progressed steadily, additional factory space was added from time to time, and in 1900 the original branch was incorporated as the Meriden Britannia Co., Ltd.

It was in 1880 that J. W. Millard came to Hamilton as assistant to Mr. Parker. These positions were held respectively by the two senior officers till June 1907 when Mr. Parker — a man of sound judgment, sterling integrity and a progressive citizen — passed away. He was succeeded as Manager by Mr. Millard.

In December 1924 the International Silver Co. of Canada, Ltd. was incorporated to further the best interests of three firms — Meriden Britannia Co.; Standard Silver Co.; and Wm. Rogers & Son. George Wilcox was the first President. Today these three companies operate as separate units in the company as 1847 Rogers Bros.; Factory E. C. Hamilton, makers of silverplated nickel silver and white metal holloware, 1847 Rogers Bros. silverplate and sterling silver flatware; Wm. Rogers & Son, Factory H. C. Niagara Falls; and Standard Silver Co., Factory S.C. Toronto.

Copy from the Trader & Canadian Jeweller - 1929
Written by Mr. J. W. Millard

Pages 27 to 33 show marks of these various companies

*Organized in 1894 as part of Meriden Britannia Company*

..........Sections 8 and 10 of "The Trade Mark and Design Act" of 1879 which they verily believe is theirs on account of having been the first to make use of the same.

The said Specific Trade Mark consists of,

a Conventional Bird with neck, head and wings pointing upwards mounted on a bar over the word "Sterling," the letter "M" (in old English) immediately over the Bird's head, as fully and clearly shown in the accompanying wood cut illustration; and we hereby request the said Specific Trade Mark to be registered in accordance with the law.

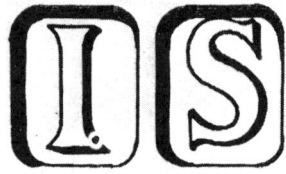

INTERNATIONAL  STERLING

INTERNATIONAL  STERLING

INTERNATIONAL  STERLING

INTERNATIONAL SILVER COMPANY

INTERNATIONAL  STERLING

*Wilcox*

**INTERNATIONAL SILVER CO.**

I.S.CO.

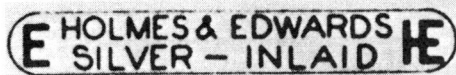

E. G. WEBSTER & SON bought by
International Silver Co. 1928

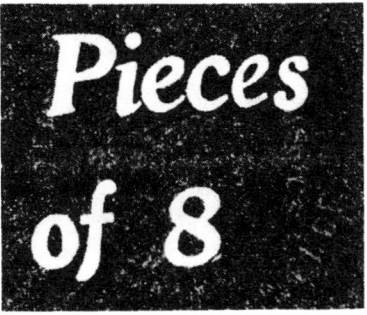

DERBY SILVER CO.

*A promotion trademark for chest containing eight place settings — a best selling idea.*

# ONTARIO
## BELLEVILLE
DINGMAN, JAMES F.                    Kn. 1894
Situated at 1 Front Street

   With Pseudo Hall Marks

## CARLETON PLACE
BREADNER, S.            1900 - 1904. See page 55.
Advertised in The Trader as manufacturing jewellers.

   Moved to Hull, Quebec. Manufacture
                       Souvenir Spoons

## GUELPH
SAVAGE, DAVID                    Kn. 1847 - 1869
Situated on Market Square. Worked in Montreal 1847.

   MARKS — Leopard Head in Shield and
                       Uncrowned Head in Octangle
                       GUELPH.

SMITH, S. W.                          1864 - 1881
Advertised as silversmith, jeweller in The Trader, worked for Savage, father and son 17 years.

JUDGE, MICHAEL                    Kn. 1853 - 1854
Gunsmith, engraver, Market Square. Worker in gold and silver.

MALONE, WILLIAM                   Kn. 1853 - 1854
Watchmaker and jeweller.

## HAMILTON
BEEMER & NEWBURY                  Kn. 1853 - 1854
Clocks, gold and silver jewellery and watches — watches, clocks and jewellery repaired.

CAMPBELL, A.                           Kn. 1880
Entry in The Trader August 1880, Davis & McCollough practical workmen have bought out A. Campbell, jeweller.

CARTER, J. F.                     Kn. 1853 - 1854
Jeweller, King St.        *For marks - see opposite page.*

**J.F.C** *With Pseudo Hall Marks*

CLARINGBOWL, FRED     Kn. 1835 - 1890
Situated at 140 King Street E. Advertised in The Trader January 1890. Jeweller.

LEES, GEORGE H.     Kn. 1885
Situated 47 Main Street. Advertised in The Trader as Gold & Silver refiners, and Jewellery manufacturers.

OSBORNE, ROBERT     Kn. 1851 - 1869
Situated on James Street. Watchmaker, jeweller.

 or  with pseudo hallmarks including Beaver

RAMAGE, JOHN     Kn. 1851 - 1869
Situated on Brock Street. Listed 1853-1854 Canadian Directory.

| J. RAMAGE |

RUSSELL, RICHARD     Kn. 1851 - 1885
Situated at 15 King Street W. Later at James Street opposite Fountain in 1869.

WARE, T. P. & CO.     Kn. 1853 - 1854
Clocks, watches, jewellery, fancy goods, temperance regalia and emblems. Situated on King Street.

## KINGSTON

SPANENBERG, GEORGE     Kn. 1845 - 1870
Situated at 30 King Street in 1857, sold business to Frederick Spanenberg in 1870.

𝒮 or 𝒮 — *Sometimes with Pseudo Hallmarks, sometimes with KINGSTON.*

SPANENBERG, FREDERICK W.   Kn. 1870 - 1887
See above. Situated at 347 King Street East 1885-1887. Pieces found bearing his mark and also the mark of R. W. & Co. and R. W. & S. The R. W. marks are unlike the marks ascribed to Robert Wilkes. George Spanenberg was connected with Rossin Bros. but this cannot be their mark.

SPANENBERG, S. A.   Kn. 1885
Pieces found bearing mark S. A. S. and pseudo hallmarks.

STENNET, Wm.   Kn. 1822 - 1847
Watchmaker, Jeweller and Silversmith. Known to have been in Kingston in 1822. Later moved to Toronto (York) was there from 1832 through to 1847. Believed to have come from London via Bermuda.

## LONDON

BAKER, T. H.   Kn. 1881 - 1970
Manufacturing Jewellers established in 1881. Now owned by T. W. Baker & W. S. Brown.

DAVIS, HENRY   Kn. 1853 - 1854
Watchmaker, Ridout Street.

DEWEY, WILLIAM   Kn. 1853 - 1854
Working gold and silversmith. Jeweller from London, England, 6 doors East of Robinson Hall — "all kinds of repairs neatly executed."

JEANNERET, J.   Kn. 1853 - 1854
Watchmaker, Dundas Street.

WARE, D. T. & CO.   Kn. 1853 - 1854
Watchmakers and jewellers, 31 Dundas Street — wholesale and retail, watches, clocks, jewellery and silver plate.

# NIAGARA FALLS

NIAGARA SILVER CO.
See Wm. A. Rogers.
NIAGARA FALLS SILVER CO.
Wm. A. Rogers Mark.

ROGERS, WM. A.  Kn. 1899 - 1929
According to the history of the Oneida Silversmiths The Wm. A. Rogers Ltd. had originated in Ontario, Canada and had factories in Niagara Falls, Ontario, New York and North Hampton, Massachusetts. Wm. A. Rogers had taken over the Niagara Silver Company about 1903, Simeon L. & Geo. H. Rogers Co. in 1918 and the Toronto Silver Plate Co. in the 1920s. The (R) ROGERS (R) trademark was first used in 1900, the 1881 (R) ROGERS (R) in 1910. There are many variations of the Rogers mark and Wm. A. Rogers Ltd. added their share. When the Wm. Rogers Mfg. Co. of Meriden, Connecticut decided to open a Canadian branch Wm. A. Rogers already owned the Niagara Silver Co. In 1914 the company name was changed to CANADIAN ROGERS COMPANY LIMITED. This was opposed and the name was changed to "CANADIAN WM. A. ROGERS LIMITED". Oneida purchased the business in 1929.

NIAGARA FALLS CO., 1877

N. F. NICKEL SILVER

WM. A. ROGERS A1
WM. A. ROGERS

## ONEIDA LTD.    Kn. 1847 - 1970

The founder of the Oneida Community of Perfectionists, John Humphrey Noyes, studied at the Yale Theological Seminary, and many of the early converts were lawyers, doctors, clergymen and teachers and their families. The members of this deeply religious group not only shared work and wordly goods but also practiced a kind of group marriage and mating under the community's direction. Their communal rearing of children prefigured the modern Israeli kibbutzim.

Originally Oneida Community Limited included five manufacturing enterprises. The name first appeared on bottled fruits. The Oneida label being put on one thousand jars of home preserves and to the "delighted surprise" of the group found a very ready market. The packing of fruit and vegetables continued for seventy years. 1847-1916.

The second enterprise was the manufacturing of traps. Started in 1852, within five years the orders for the Newhouse trap were coming from all over the world including Australia, Canada and Russia. In 1896 a factory was built in Canada to help meet the demand of the Canadians for this highly successful and popular product. The trap business lasted until 1925.

Silk manufacturing was started by three of the "Community members in 1865, by 1900 the business had an anunal return of $300,000. This business was not as profitable as the Newhouse Trap. It was sold in 1913 to M. Hemingway & Son.

Chain manufacturing was started in 1880 and continued until 1912 then sold to The American Chain Company.

In 1877 the Oneida Community began to manufacture tableware. A branch of the Community had been formed at Wallingford, Connecticut on the farm of Henry Allen. It was there that two iron spoons changed the fortunes of a great many people. "Lily" and "Oval" were the first patterns of what was eventually to become "COMMUNITY PLATE". 1880, the silver business had grown to such an extent that it was moved to Niagara Falls. 1895, Dr. Theodore Noyes became president of Oneida Community Ltd. Pierrepont Noyes was appointed superintendent of the company's three departments at Niagara Falls.

1901, the first 'silver' COMMUNITY PLATE pattern was made and shown at Buffalo Exposition. Designed by Pierrepont Noyes, who took the bowl from one spoon, the top from a second, the side ornaments from a third, the whole adapted to the contours of a fourth and the result "AVALON".

The next pattern was "FLOWER DE LUCE" which was designed by Grosvenor Allen with the help of professional artist Julia Bracken. Other designs which followed were the work of Allen in consultation with artists, who were put on the payroll.

1910, The Coles Phillips Girl" appeared in Oneida advertisements. At the same time International Silver launched their "1847" Girl". This started the 'pretty girl' trend in advertising.

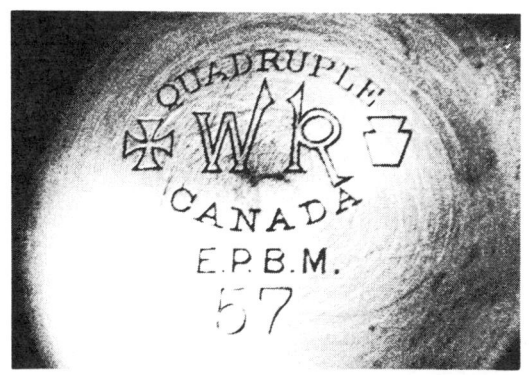

ONEIDA SILVERSMITHS

Oneida Sterling

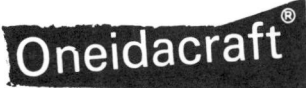

## Oneida

HEIRLOOM
ONEIDA
RELIANCE
SILVER METAL
REX PLATE
TUDOR PLATE
ONEIDA COMMUNITY
COMMUNITY
COMMUNITY SILVER
COMMUNITY PLATE
N. F. NICKEL SILVER 1877

*Trademark on Stainless Steel*

**BURKE & WALLACE LIMITED**
234 BELFIELD ROAD, REXDALE, ONTARIO
Registered Manufacturers and Distributors
WM. A. ROGERS AND 1881 (R) ROGERS (R)

Silverware manufacturers advertised Wm. A. Rogers lines in Canadian Jewellery Directory, 1969.

## OTTAWA

ADDISON, CHARLES                 Kn. 1882 - 1892
Situated at 117 Sparks Street for a period of at least ten years. Mark used included in the Robert Hendery and Hendery & Leslie punch marks.

LESLIE, JOHN                     Kn. 1845 - 1895
Situated on Rideau Street in 1848. Had a jewellery store and repaired silver. Was on Sparks Street in 1869, moved to 62 Sparks in 1876. 1895, died in Ottawa on November 19th. Two of the punch marks bearing his name are those used by Robert Hendery and Hendery & Leslie on his behalf.

  OTTAWA
with Lion & head

J. LESLEY

MARKS, N. M.                     Kn. 1876
Situated at 85 Sparks Street, also had silver marked by Robert Hendery and Hendery & Leslie.

N. M. MARKS

OLMSTED, C. A.            Kn. 1890 - 1903
Situated at 97 Sparks Street, was joined in partnership by Mr. Hurdman in 1902. Business sold to Henry Birks & Sons in 1903.

**C.A.O**     OLMSTEAD

**O & H**     STERLING

ROSENTHAL, A. J.          Kn. 1882 - 1903
Situated at 87 Sparks Street. Business became part of Henry Birks & Sons in 1903.

**ROSENTHAL**

TRACY, WILLIAM H.          Kn. 1851 - 1892
Watchmaker jeweller, Rideau St.

| W. H. TRACY |

## SIMCOE

DARLING, GEORGE          Kn. 1852 - 1899
Had silver made by Hendery & Leslie, Montreal. Clock, Watchmaker, jeweller, Rideau St.

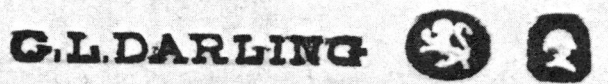

## TORONTO

ACME SILVER CO. THE          1885-1895
Situated at 9-11 Church Street. Manufactured quadruple plated ware. Advertised spoons and forks with the G. Rodgers A.1 trademark and G. Rodgers 12 DWT mark on knives. The firm moved to a new factory 31-41 Hayter Street in 1890. 1895, sold out to W. K. George and others who formed the Standard Silver Company Toronto Ltd. which later became part of International Silver Company of Canada Ltd.          *For mark - see page 42*

ARMS & QUIGLEY                    Kn. 1879 - 1882
Manufacturing Jewellers. Won the award for Gold and Silver watch cases exhibit at the first Toronto Exhibition. Office 10 King Street E. Advertised in The Trader. December 1879 had moved to factory, 33-35 Adelaide Street. Listed in the February 1882 edition of The Trader as manufacturers of cuff buttons and watch cases in gold & silver.

BELL, WM.                                    1835 - 1861
Situated in Niagara 1835. Moved to Church Street Toronto 1840. 172 Yonge Street 1846. Address given as 123 Yonge St. in 1853. Succeeded by John Wanless Snr.

CANADA MFG. CO.                                  1890
Known both in Toronto and Montreal.

CANADIAN WM. A. ROGERS LTD.          1914-1929
This firm came into being after Wm. A. Rogers Co. had purchased The Toronto Silver Plate Co. Wm. A. Rogers later sold out to Oneida, Niagara Falls and Sherrill, New York. Canadian Rogers Company Limited 1914 see Wm. A. Rogers.

CROWN SILVER PLATE CO.          1909 - 1920

Listed in Jewellers' Circular - Keystone. Mark well known in Canada.

DERBY SILVER CO.          1881 - 1884

Factory at 31 Adelaide Street E. The Trader October 1884 reports Derby Silver Co. closed. Trade Mark advertised March 1900 by Standard Silver Company which at that time had become part of the International Silver Company of Canada.

EAGLE BRAND

Advertised in The Trader by Simpson, Hall, Miller & Co. Toronto and Montreal. Made in Montreal factory. See Simpson, Hall, Miller & Co.

ELLIS & COMPANY. P. W.   Kn. 1852 - 1928

Situated at 4 Toronto Street 1879. Awarded first prize Goldsmiths Work at Industrial Exhibition, Toronto. Jewellery manufacturers, also made badges, medals and presentation articles. The Trader September 1879 carried an advertisement which stated "First home made jewellery ever exhibited in this country." 1880, R. Y. Ellis and Brothers Hardware Store, Ingersoll, dissolved partnership. A. H. Ellis continued business independently. P. W. Ellis & Co. admit R. Y. Ellis as partner. The partners were Phillip W. Ellis and Matthew C. Ellis (nephews of James E. Ellis.) A George Ellis joined the firm in 1890. The Trader 1882 (Feb.) lists 8 manufactures, cuff buttons and watch cases in gold and silver. P. W. Ellis & Co. headed list. 1918, Matthew C. Ellis became the first president of "The Canadian National Jewellers Association". Company liquidated 1928. Soverign Plate trademark for silver plate made by the firm. P. W. Ellis married the daughter of Goodham, manager Toronto Silver Plate Company.

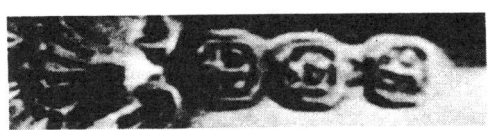

ELLIS, JAMES E. 1848 - 1881

Came from England 1848. 1852, situated at 30 King St. Bought part of business of Rossin Bros. on retirement. 1881, retired. Son who had joined the firm in 1862 carried on in partnership with M. T. Cain. Firm became ELLIS & CO. J. E. 1881-1901.

GOLDSMITH'S STOCK COMPANY OF
CANADA LTD. Kn. 1880 - 1922

Partners Henry Smith and Harris Fudger, formerly senior partners in Robert Wilkes & Co. Situated at 48 Yonge Street in 1890. Advertised in The Trader as Manufacturers agents. Acted as agents for Roden Bros. who produced Flatware, Hollow ware, Enamelled Souvenir ware, Sterling Silver and Cut Glass. The Goldsmith Company also had silver stamped with their trade mark made for them by Robert Hendery and Hendery and Leslie. Listed in J. C.K 1915-22.

HILL & HOUGHTON. Kn. 1879 - 1882

Listed as one of 8 manufacturers of cuff buttons and watch cases in gold and silver in The Trader Feb. 1882.

HOLMES & EDWARDS
See International Silver Co. of Canada.

**HOLMES & EDWARDS**
**INLAID**

INLAID SILVER CO. Kn. 1889 - 1890

Advertised in The Trader, April that they had purchased the rights to manufacture Inlaid Silver Spoons and Forks. The advertised wares were stamped Inlaid Silver Patd.

| INLAID SILVER Patd. |
|---|

JACKSON, HENRY                     Kn. 1837 - 1869
Situated at several addresses on King St. East, during the
32 years known to be in business. Silversmith, watchmaker
and jeweller. Manufacturer of silver plate.

JOSEPH & CO., J. G.                Kn. 1857 - 1877
Situated 56 King Street E. 1857. 35 Front Street 1877.
Silversmith, watchmaker and jeweller. Had silver made
by Robert Hendery and Hendery & Leslie. Used a variety
of marks. Some pieces stamped Toronto. Included every
type pseudo Hallmark.

KENT BROS.                         Kn. 1867
Situated at 116 Yonge Street 1867. 166 Yonge Street in
1878. Indian Clock Palace, 168 Yonge Street in 1887.
Issued annual catalogue with "The Sign of the Indian
Clock" on cover. Importers and manufacturers. Made fine
jewellery and emblems of every kind. Specialized in hand
enamelled work of highest quality.

KENT BROS.

KENT & SONS LTD., AMBROSE          1894 - 1946
Situated at 156 Yonge Street in 1894. Fairweather Ltd.
amalgamated in 1946 and firm became KENT-FAIR-
WEATHER LTD. Kent sold his interest in 1953. Firm
now FAIRWEATHER LTD.

STERLING

LASH, J. B.                        Kn. 1865 - 1887
Lash of Lash & Co., King St. 1865. In business on own
account at 13 King St. E. in 1887. Silversmith & Jeweller.
Listed as Secretary Toronto Silver Plate Company 1879.

LEE & CHILLAS                          Kn. 1879 - 1889
Partnership of Thomas H. Lee and George Chillas. Situated at 4 Wellington Street. The partnership was dissolved and T. H. Lee advertised in The Trader January 1890 from 1 Wellington Street. Was joined in business by son and name changed to T. H. LEE & Son, Wholesale Jewellers.

LOWE, WM. G. H.                              1879 - 1904
1879, Principal in the firm of ZIMMERMAN, McNAUGHT & CO. 1884, Partner in the firm of McNAUGHT & LOWE, other partners were Wm. K. Zimmerman and Wm. G. H. McNaught. This partnership formed after the retirement of Joseph Zimmerman of ZIMMERMAN & McNAUGHT & CO., manufacturers of gold chain, cuff buttons, watch cases. Importers and Jobbing Jewellers. 1885, formed partnership with A. C. Anderson after a short period of business on own account. Firm then became LOWE & ANDERSON. 16 Wellington St. East. 1888, partnership dissolved upon the retirement of William Lowe.

### Z. McN & Co
*with pseudo hallmarks*

LOWE & ANDERSON                     Kn. 1885 - 1888
See Wm. G. H. Lowe.

### L&A   with pseudo hallmarks

McNAUGHT & LOWE                          1884 - 1885
See Wm. G. H. Lowe.

MERIDEN SILVER PLATE CO.                 1881 - 1884
This branch of the American Company had plating rooms in Toronto which were transferred to Hamilton in 1884, having been taken over by the Meriden Britannia Company.

MONARCH
SILVER PLATE CO.

See Standard Silver Co.

MORPHY, EDWARD M.　　　　kn. 1847 - 1882
Situated at 98 Yonge St. 1847. Morphy Bros. listed at same address 1851-1856 and as Morphy Son & Co. E. M. at 141 Yonge St. in 1897. Morphy Bros. were listed at 141 Yonge St. in 1859. Also E. Morphy with pseudo hall-

E.M.M.

OLIVER, RICHARD KESTELL　　　Kn. 1843 - 1860
1843, Situated on Duchess Street. Moved to Parliament Street 1847. Had several addresses on King Street being at 213 East in 1853 and at 296 in 1860. Working silversmith.

RKO

POST, JORDAN　　　　b. 1770 - d. 1853
The Trader referred to Jordan Post as the pioneer watchmaker of Toronto who advertised that he kept "a complete assortment of watch furniture". It is considered that he was the first silversmith in Toronto having arrived with his father from Connecticut in 1787. He was a prominent figure and two streets were named as a tribute to him and his family, Jordan Street and Melinda (his wife) nee Woodruff. He owned considerable property. He started on the corner of King and Bay Streets. In 1833 he was situated at 221 King Street. C. Clinkunbroomer who died in 1881 at the age of 82 served his apprenticeship with Jordan Post.

 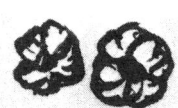

ROBINSON & CO., JOSEPH　　　Kn. 1859 - 1880
Partner with brother Charles at 15 King Street. Retired in 1880, the firm then became ROBINSON & BRO.

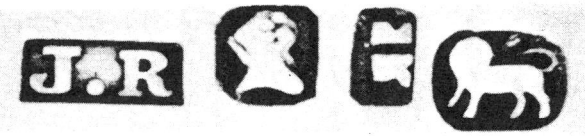

RODEN BROS., LTD.                Kn. 1891 - 1922
1900 moved to Royal Opera House Building, King St., Silverware and Cut Glass Manufacturers. Workers for the trade. Goldsmiths Stock Company of Canada were sole selling agents from 1900 to 1922. Thomas Roden, Honorary President of Canadian Jewellers Association. Factory on Carlaw Avenue 1917. Made silver for other firms putting trademarks as required. Makers of Duchess Plate, Sterling Silver, Cut Glass Signed.

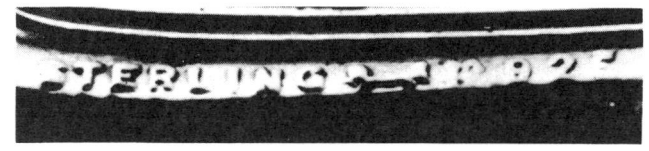

RODGERS, G.
See Standard Silver Co.

ROSENTHAL, ABRAHAM         b. 1866 - d. 1965
This business started in 1895. Abraham Rosenthal died February 8th, 1965.

RYRIE BIRKS         Kn. 1905 - 1925
Henry Birks & Sons consolidated with Ryrie Bros. in Toronto in the year 1905, name of business not changed until 1924.

RYRIE, JAMES         b. 1854 - d. 1933
Ryrie Brothers contributed a great deal to the growth of the jewellery business in Canada. James had a business at 113 Yonge Street from 1879. Joined Harry in 1882, the firm became RYRIE BROS. in 1897. Opened a new store on Yonge Street & Adelaide in 1890, where they had six men engaged for repair work in the watchmaking department. J. Ryrie was apprenticed to John Segsworth in 1870. See Robert Hendery and Hendery & Leslie mark for RYRIE. Used this plus pseudo hallmarks.

SARGANT, S. J.         Kn. 1879
"Manufacturer of Masonic and Society Regalia, Jewels, &C., &C., A.O.U.W. Badges. Send for price list. Box 1152. Toronto." Series of advertisements in The Trader 1879.

SAUNDERS, LORIE & CO.         Kn. 1897 - 1920
Manufacturing jeweller. Situated 35 Adelaide Street W. 1897 and at 114 Bay Street 1900. Still advertiseing in The Trader in 1920 offering platinum and gold jewellery.

| SAUNDERS, LORIE & CO. |

SAUNDERS, S. & A.                Kn. 1848 - 1900
Advertised in THE TRADER. January 1900 issue states "established 1848" Silversmiths, jewellers, manufactured all kinds of jewellery. Situated at 20 and 22 Adelaide Street.

> S & A SAUNDERS

SAVAGE, GEORGE                   Kn. 1829 - 1854
Son of George Savage, Montreal. Was in business with father 1829-1845. (George Savage & Son). A branch in Toronto at 3 Wellington Buildings King St. 1853. Listed under silversmiths (Canadian Directory). Importer and manufacturer of watches, clocks, gold and silver ware. Address 57 Victoria Row, King St. E. See George Savage & Son.

> G.S.

SAXTON, JOHN                     Kn. 1851 - 1854
Situated at 17 Church St. Listed as silversmith in The Canadian Directory 1853-1854.

SOVEREIGN PLATE
Trademark for silver plate made by P. W. Ellis & Co. Ltd.

STANDARD SILVER CO.              Kn. 1895 - 1925
Meriden Britannia. One of the companies taken over by Meriden Britannia Company of Hamilton, Ontario and Meriden Connecticut. Name was continued for some years afterwards. Standard used several trade marks, some of which had been acquired in the takeover of the ACME PLATE COMPANY. Monarch being one of the more popular, this mark is found on many of the items in antique stores. They also made the HOLMES & EDWARDS 'inlaid silver flatware 'under licence.

INTERNATIONAL SILVER COMPANY OF CANADA
Absorbed Standard Silver Company, Toronto; Simpson, Hall, Miller & Company, Toronto and Montreal; Meriden Britannia Company, Hamilton.

STANLEY & AYLWARD LTD.     Kn. 1920
This company used a trade mark of their own but have not traced a factory. Wholesalers of plated hollow ware.

NORMAN PLATE
See Stanley, Aylward.

STERLING CRAFT LTD.     Kn. 1920 - 1927
Situated at 107 Richmond St. East in 1927. Working silversmiths and repairers.

STERN, SAMUEL     Kn. 1879 - 1882
Advertised as "The Largest Clock House in Canada" in 1879 The Trader. In 1882 listed as one of 14 jobbing jewellers.

TAGGART, FRANK     Kn. 1886 - 1887
Previously general manager for Charles Starke Co. Opened own store at 87-89 King Street, first catalogue offered sterling silver souvenir spoons of Sir John A. Macdonald and Miss Canada. Made gold and silver thimbles.

TORONTO SILVER PLATE COMPANY 1882-1914
Founded in 1882 by J. A. Watts, formerly manager Meriden Britannia Co., Hamilton. All Canadian company. Won awards for silverware. Bought by W. A. Rogers Co. Ltd. (Canada) c. 1914. The following were directors in 1888.

Directors:
GEO. GOODERHAM,   H. W BEATTY.
W. H. PARTRIDGE,   WM. THOMPSON.
E. G. GOODERHAM,   JAMES WEBSTER
FRANK TURNER, C.E.

## STERLING

TORSIL E. P.—N. S.

TORSIL METAL

TORSIL STEEL

WANLESS, JOHN            b. 1830 - d. 1905
Born in Scotland John Wanless moved to Canada 1851. Worked with Wm. Bell who had moved from Niagara in 1840. Suceeded to the business in 1861. Joined by his son John Jnr. in 1890. Firm became WANLESS & CO. In 1920 John Wanless Jnr. was elected Treasurer of The Canadian Jewellers Association. Also had silver made by Roden Bros.

 with Lion, Beaver and Crowned Head

## JOHN WANLESS & CO.,
Established 1840.
## TORONTO.

*Manufacturers of Rings, Brooches, Watch Chains, Medals, Class Pins, Lockets, Cuff Links, and Fine Diamond and Pearl Jewellry.*

VIKING PLATE — is a registered trade mark of Lipman-Levinter Industries Limited, 41 Peter Street, Toronto.

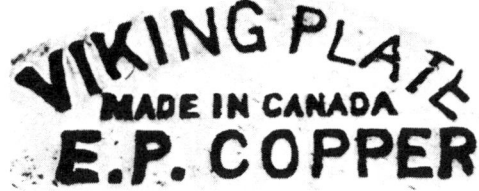

WELCH & TROWERN              Kn. 1880 - 1886

Manufacturing Jewellers. Advertisement in The Trader, September 1880, offers Silver lockets, Napkin rings, Masonic Jewels, Trowels, Stick heads, Silver Prize Cups, etc. 1882, mentioned as manufacturers of cuff buttons and watch cases in gold and silver. 1886, A. H. Welch retired.

| WELCH & TROWERN |

WHITE & SON, T.              Kn. 1879 - 1885

Advertisers in The Trader 1879. Manufacturing Jewellers, situated at 12 Melinda Street. Were listed in The Trader Feb 1882 edition as one of 8 manufacturers of cuff buttons and watch cases in gold and silver.

## TRENTON

BENEDICT PROCTOR MFG. CO.    Kn. 1920 - 1970

Manufacturers of quality plated silverware. Sheffield reproductions.

Trade Mark of Benedict Proctor

BREADNER, S. b. 1870 - d. 1948. see Carlton Place pg. 34
Samuel Breadner commenced manufacturing silverware in Carlton Place c. 1900.

BREADNER MANUFACTURING CO.　　　Kn. 1900 -
Mr. Breadner moved to Ottawa in 1904 and formed the Breadner Manufacturing Co. and built a factory in about 1910.

The firm specialized in souvenir jewellery for the tourist trade and the business acquired a collection of spoon dies from a Montreal firm that went bankrupt and these spoons became a background of the souvenir line.

In 1930 the business was reorganized as the Breadner Company Limited and continued to feature souvenir jewellery along with badges and emblems. During World War two the company made insignia for the armed forces and at the end of the war resumed the manufacture of souvenir jewellery. By this time the company had developed their own die making facilities and many new spoons were added to the line.

Samuel Breadner died in 1948 and his son Jack Breadner took over the presidency of the company.

In 1956 the company moved to Hull, Quebec where they continue to specialize in the production of fine quality souvenir jewellery and sterling spoons and is probably now the largest Canadian manufacturer of these items.

STERLING *BMCo* MADE in CANADA

sTERLING
B M Co

# MONTREAL

ALLAN, THOMAS & CO.          b. 1839 - d. 1899

1839, born in England. 1857, apprenticed to Savage & Lyman, Henry Birks also entered the firm that year as a junior. Joseph Savage at that time the "Old Man" of the firm, resting much of the time on a sofa in the back office. Thomas Allan was partner with Wood & Wood. 1866-67, operated as Wood & Allen with Wood as partner. Acquired business of W. Learmont, changed business name to T. ALLAN & CO. 1869, situated at 375 Notre Dame Street. 1881, 167 St. James Street. 1888, bought business of T. A. Adkins. 1891-92, situated on St. Catharine Street. Died February 1899.

ARNOLDI, JOHN PETER          Kn. 1769 - 1808

Son of Peter Arnoldi believed to have settled in Montreal before 1769. Brothers, Charles Arnoldi and Michael Arnoldi. Worked with John Oakes, leased workshop from brother Michael in 1792. Wife, Margaret Cayley. Those known to have served under him as apprentices include John Glatter and H. Morand.

ARNOLDI, CHARLES          b. 1779 - d. 1817

1779, born in Montreal, September 23rd. 1805, married Ann Brown, October 5th. 1806, succeeded to the business of John Irish. Benjamen Comins entered into partnership with him at 16 Notre Dame Street. Dissolved 1807. 1810, mentioned in poll book, Western Ward, Montreal as silversmith, made silver for Indian trade. 1812, became postmaster at Lavaltrie. Died in Montreal Dec. 17th, 1817.

ARNOLDI, MICHAEL        b. 1763 - d. 1807

1763, born in Montreal June 19th. 1784, dissolved partnership with Robert Cruickshank November 1st. 1792, made agreement with brother Peter and partner John Oakes to lease them his workshop in return for board, lodging, laundry and to provide him with a suit of fine cloth each year for a period of two years. 1793, bought property at Trois Rivieres. 1802, returned to Montreal, took John Justus Diehl, his nephew into apprenticeship. Died at Trois Rivieres August 27, 1807.

BARLOW, EDOUARD        Kn. 1829 - 1837

1829, situated on Craig Street. 1837, listed in Notre Dame Church records.

    *Leopard's Head & Lion*

BEAN, JOHN        Kn. 1819 - 1823

Originally from London, England. 1819, situated at 41 Notre Dame Street. 1820, worked with Alex. McNaughton at 5 St. Joseph Street. 1823-26, working at 13 Mountain Street. Advertisement for Old Gold, Silver and Silver Lace appeared in his name in the Quebec Gazette of August 25th, 1823.

 *with pseudo hallmarks*

BEAUDRY, NARCISSE        Kn. 1856 - 1880

1856-58, partner of E. P. Boivin at 116 Notre Dame St.

**N. BEAUDRY** *Lion and Head* **STERLING**

BIRKS, HENRY & SONS

*Canada's first Silver Marks*
*Granted to*
*Henry Birks & Sons Ltd.*

BOHLE, DAVID　　　　　　　Kn. 1831 - d. 1870

Partner with brother Peter Bohle for short period. Partner, George C. Denman 1863-66, employed W. H. Denham at that time. Partnership dissolved. Carried on own business till 1870. Drowned, Montreal Harbour.

BOHLE, PETER　　　　　　　b. 1786 - d. 1865

1800, apprenticed to Robert Cruickshank till 1807. 1851-56, partner with Robert Hendery. Were silversmiths to the trade. Customers included Savage & Lyman. 1862, worked for Maysenhoelder & Baddley.

 *with Leopard's Head and Lion*

BOHLE, FRANCIS　　　　　　　Kn. 1843 - 1867

1843, worked independently till 1849. 1849, partner with D. Maysenhoelder. 1859-1868, partner with Albert Desroches. Working silversmiths.

**F.B** *with Repeated Lions*

BOIVIN, LOUIS PHILLIPE　　　　　　　Kn. 1842 - 1856

1842, situated corner of Notre Dame and St. Vincent Sts. 1844-45, 80 St. Paul Street. 1850-51, 88 Notre Dame St. Working silversmith.

**L P B** *with Lion and sometimes with Montreal*

CAMIRAND J. D. & C0.　　　　　　　Kn. 1920

Manufacturers of silver, also plated silver.

**MADE BY
J. D. CAMIRAND
& CO.
MONTREAL**

CARON BROS.　　　　　　　Kn. 1920

Manufacturers of silver, silver plate and jewellery. Situated 233-239 Bleury St., Montreal.　*For mark - see page 59.*

CANADIAN JEWELLERS LTD.          L. 1920
Manufacturers of Jewellery and silver deposit ware.

CRUICKSHANK, ROBERT          b. 1767 - d. 1809

DENMAN & BOHLE          Kn. 1863 - 1866
Partnership of George C. Denman and David Bohle. Made silver for Savage & Lyman. Geo. Denman carried on business on own account after partnership dissolved.

DESROCHES, ALFRED.          Kn. 1858 - 1890
1859, partner with Frances Bohle. After partnership dissolved worked independently. 1860, listed at 99 Sanquinet Street.

DWIGHT, JAMES ADAMS          Kn. 1818 - 1847
1818, partner of George Savage. Situated at 56, St. Paul Street. Associated with Martin Cheney and the Twiss Brothers, American Clockmakers who had settled in Montreal. 1844, partner with son at 151 Notre Dame Street.

DWIGHT & SAVAGE          Kn. 1818 - 1819
See Above.

**HEMMING MANUFACTURING CO.**  Kn. 1909 - 1915
Listed in Jewellers' Circular as manufacturers of Sterling silverware and jewellery. Also in Trader as manufacturers of boxes and jewel cases.

**LEARMONT, WILLIAM**  Kn. 1841 - 1870
1843-1854, situated at 147 Notre Dame Street. Moved to several different sites on the street during the following 20 years. Seven marks attributed to this firm. The Learmont Estate managed the business in 1870. Professor Ramsay Traquair refers to him as a jeweller who sold plate "probably not a working silversmith".

 *with varying pseudo hallmarks*

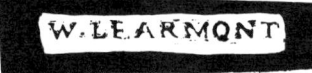 *also with pseudo hallmarks*

**LIDO JEWELLERS CO.**  Kn. 1867 - 1970
Manufacturers of jewellery.

**MEVES, OTTO**  Kn. 1858 - 1871
1860, situated at 10 Lambert Hill. Had been associated with John Maysenholder at 159 Notre Dame Street. 1862, Moved to Kingston, Ontario.

**O. MEVES** *with pseudo hallmarks. sometimes KINGSTON*

**MILLER & BREMNER**  Kn. 1880 - 1900
1880, situated 191 St. James Street. Partners David Miller and James Bremner. 1890, situated 35 Bleury Street and 2325 St. Catharine Street in 1900.

## MILLER BREMNER  *with pseudo hallmarks*

PEACOCK, HENRY                    Kn. 1847 - 1890
Advertised in The Canada Directory 1853-54 from 67 St. Paul Street offering watches, clocks, and jewellery, etc. for sale at a small advance on cost. 1890, situated at 194 St. George Street.

ROGERS SONS & CO., HENRY    Kn. 1909 - 1915
Listed in Jewellers' Circular under plated silver. Address given as Montreal, Quebec. Usual mark - flag over crown over H. R. S. & Co. This mark on blade of knife.

SAVAGE, GEORGE            b. 1767 - d. 1855
Born in Huddersfield, England. Listed in "Watch and Clockmakers of the World" G. H. Baillie.

SAVAGE.
George, Huddersfield and London 1808-23. Went to Canada and died 1855. A very able watchmaker. Patented a remontoir in 1808, and gained award of Soc. Arts for a detached escapement for watches, desc, in Trans. Soc. Arts, Vol. 40, 1823."

1818, partner of Adams Dwight at St. Paul Street and St. Diziere Lane. Carried on independently after one year, in business there until 1840. 1823, opened a West End Store with Mr. Wood in charge, had a very large stock of English Key Wind Lever Watches. Peter Bohle made silver spoons etc., for him at this time. Robert Hendery joined Bohle in 1840. George Savage was joined by his eldest son in the business. Name changed to *George Savage & Son*. Uptown store opened at 1612 Notre Dame Street, which later became 40 Notre Dame St. East, due to renumbering. Business carried on at this address till May 1858. In 1850 the name of the firm was changed to *Savage & Lyman* (Joseph married Abigail Lyman sister of Major (later Lt. Col.) Theodore Lyman). The partners were Theodore and Joseph.

1857, Henry Birks entered Savage & Lyman, Montreal, as a junior. It was considered the finest retail store in Canada and was lit by three sperm oil lamps. 1867, Henry Birks and Chas. W. Hagar joined Savage & Lyman as partners Name changed to *Savage, Lyman & Co.* 1878, depression caused by withdrawal of British troops from Montreal in 1870, seriously affected business and the firm went into bankruptcy. Henry Birks remained on as manager whilst the assets were liquidated.

A branch of the business was carried on in Toronto at 3 Wellington Buildings first as *George Savage* then as *Savage and Lyman.*

SHARPLEY, RICE     Kn. 1835 - 1880

Situated at 131 Notre Dame Street, 1851-54. Advertised in the Trader and The Canadian Directory. Judging by his advertisements Rice Sharpley had an interesting business being an importer, and wholesale and retail dealer of fancy goods, silver, jewellery, guns, rifles, swords, and pistols, etc. Did not claim to make or manufacture any of the lines offered. Two sons carried on the business when he retired. He lived in England in the year 1880.

## R. SHARPLEY

SHARPLEY & SONS, RICE     1870 - 1890

Fred and William Sharpley, sons of Rice. First at 281 Notre Dame St.

SIMPSON, HALL, MILLER & CO.     Kn. 1879 - 1898

Canadian branch of Wallingford, Connecticut company. Advertised in The Trader November 1879. Zimmerman McNaught their sole agents in Ontario. Manufactured silver plate in the Montreal factory. In September 1882 advertised "The Wm. Rogers goods sold by us are made under the supervision of Mr. Wm. Rogers, formerly of Hartford and West Meriden. Son of the old original Wm. Rogers who died in 1873. Please do not associate us with goods made in Hartford, Connecticut, with which we have no connections. We make all the goods we sell and have our own special patterns. 1896, advertised their address as 50 Bay Street, Toronto. Also advertised Sterling Silverware, Fine Electroplate, Flat & Hollow ware. 1899, became part of The International Silver Co. Canada. Two Canadian patterns, "St. James" and "Geneva".

## BIRKS & SONS, HENRY     1840 - 1970

1832, John Birks and his wife Anne, nee Massey, arrived in Montreal from Barnsley, Yorkshire, England.

1840, Henry Birks born at 84 Little St. James Street on November 30. 1857, Henry Birks becomes Junior in the firm of Savage & Lyman, April 22nd. 1866, Henry Birks travels to Europe as a Buyer for his Firm. 1868, salary that year $1,000.00 per annum. Married Harriet Phillips Walker, (born Brantford, Ont., December 5th, 1847.) Marriage took place in Toronto on January 16th, 1868.

1868, son, William Massey Birks, born on Mansfield Street, October 25th.

1870, John Henry Metcalfe Birks born in Metcalfe Cottages, August 31st.

1872, Gerald Walter Birks born at 108 University Street.

1877, Henry Birks sells his interest in Savage Lyman & Co. to make good a note for $1,000.00 (equal to his annual income) which he had endorsed for a brother.

(It is understood that members of the family in the business have, since that time, on their 21st birthday signed an agreement not to sign any negotiable paper without the consent of the Directors.)

Henry Birks remained with Savage, Lyman & Co. as Store Manager.

1878, Company failed, Henry carried out liquidation of company on behalf of the liquidator.

1879, Henry Birks & Co., established at 222 St. James Street, staff beside himself numbered three — Bertram Cox, watchmaker, George C. Robinson, bookkeeper-salesman and William H. Lavers, messenger boy. The space rented was 15 ft. x 50 ft. this included a wrapping area at the rear of his store. Capital was $3,000, plus $1,000, which was a gift to his wife from an uncle. He also had an advance shipment of clocks from Germany, to be paid for as they were sold. Various firms with which he had dealt as Store Manager of Savage, Lyman & Co. gave him agencies, Gorham, Nardin Watches, Reed & Barton, etc.

His business policies were unusual — cash for all purchases, one price for all and no haggling — He turned over his inventory seven and one-half times in the first year, his sales $30,000.

1885, moved business to 235-7 St. James St. Floor space 1500 square feet. Staff ten. Added three new departments — china, crystal and leather goods. Son graduated from Montreal High School and enters the business.

1887, first factory opened - jewellery only. James Davidson from Hamilton, manager, seven employees.

RIDEAU PLATE
a Henry Birks
& Sons
Trademark

Canada's first Silver Marks
Granted to
Henry Birks & Sons Ltd.

1888, Gerald W. Birks starts in business, graduated from Montreal High School.

1890, reported in The Trader, that "Henry Birks & Co., one of the leading retail jewellery houses of Montreal have just completed some alterations to their establishment which have improved its appearance very much."

1891, John H. Birks, graduated from Massachusetts Institute of Technology with B. Sc. Enters the family business.

1893, Henry Birks admits his three sons as equal partners — name of the partnership — Henry Birks & Sons.

1894, moved to Phillips Square. New premises had 90 ft. frontage on St. Catharine Street and 55 ft. on Phillips Square, in all 4950 sq. ft. 1895, staff 56.

1895, Hendery & Leslie dissolve partnership. Mr. Leslie sole owner of the business, Robert Hendery died in 1897 and in 1898 an agreement is made that Hendery & Leslie will confine their Montreal sales to Birks only. 1899, Henry Birks & Sons buy Hendery & Leslie. John Leslie continues as head of the factory until 1925. 1900, factory moved from 134 St. Peter Street to the Birks Building, Phillips Square. Factory staff of Hendery & Leslie, 20. In 1904 the staff of Henry Birks & Sons numbered 221 plus the four seniors. Seniors 4, Glass Cutters 11, Silversmiths 47, Ottawa 13, Watchmakers 13, Goldsmiths 44, Winnipeg 17, Stationery Factory 9, Salesmen 36, Office and Mail Order 31.

1905, Henry Birks & Sons Ltd. incorporated. The first directors were the four partners and Wm. H. Lavery (the original messenger boy 1879.)

1907, sold Glass Cutting Factory to Phillips Glass Co. Bought the Gorham Co. of Canada Ltd. Acquired dies of Chantilly and Louis XV. Gorhams pledge to remain out of Canada for ten years.

In 1907 staff of 453 increased at Christmas to 793. Absorbed various business right across Canada, open branches in all major cities, expansion rapid in every direction.

1912, The Birks Chair Metallurgy at McGill University established by Gift of $100,000 from the four seniors.

1925, registration of Trade Marks (1) Garb of Wheat; (2) Birks' Coat-of-Arms; (3) Canada Lynx Standant. 1926, own date letter on silver started (on London Key) — retarded one year in 1967.

April 16th, 1928, Henry Birks died. Taken ill in Florida and brought back to Montreal General Hospital.

1935, William M. Birks admitted as liveryman to Goldsmiths Guild, London, England. Henry G. Birks, liveryman, 1949 and Drummond Birks in 1955.

## HENDERY, ROBERT     b. 1814 - d. 1897

Born in Scotland, Robert Hendery emigrated sometime before 1837. Worked with Peter Bohle, partnership of & Hendery 1837-1840. Worked for the firm of George Savage & Son and Savage & Lyman. Established himself in business on his own account in 1840.

1850, Situated at 62 Lagauchetiere Street. Peter Bohle partner 1850-56. Their customers numbered many watchmaker-jewellers. These had their own initial or names along with the Hendery "hallmarks" punched on the articles ordered. As the demand for electroplated articles grew the work of the skilled silversmith producing quality sterling silver was concentrated in the hands of a few firms. 1864, John Leslie became an apprentice to Hendery. 1867, by this time Robert Hendery had become the leading silversmith in Quebec. Only a few independent silversmiths remained in Montreal.

Peter Bohle had died in 1865. Francis Bohle and David Smillie in 1867. Otto Meves had gone to Kingston. William Learmont for whom Hendery was making silver had died. There remained only three firms of note in the city. John Street (known for plated wear bearing the beaver mark). John Wood & Son and Savage & Lyman. In Quebec City there remained only Ambroise LaFrance and Pierre Lesperance as active silversmiths. Robert Hendery had already begun to make silver for Gustavus Seifert of Fabrique Street. In the years following Hendery manufactured for many well known firms adding M. S. Brown & Co. and Julius Cornelius of Halifax to his customers in the late 1870's.

1887, John Leslie became a partner, the name of the firm was changed to Hendery & Leslie. Factory at 134 St. Peter Street, Montreal. 1895, dissolved partnership with John Leslie leaving John sole owner of the business — which was sold by him to Birks in 1899. 1897, Robert Hendery died after 67 years in the silver business (Names of firms for whom he made silver and whose touch marks were acquired by Henry Birks & Sons Ltd. in 1899 follow.

R$^H$    *with Pseudo Hallmarks*

    *also with Pseudo Hallmarks*

**H & L**
   *with Pseudo Hallmarks*

*Hendery & Leslie used*

**H & L STERLING**

| Year | Mark | Year | Mark |
|---|---|---|---|
| 1898 | a | 1901 | d |
| 1899 | b | 1902 | d |
| 1900 | c | 1903 | d |

## 1904-1924 BIRKS STERLING

| Year | Mark | Year | Mark |
|---|---|---|---|
| 1925 | 🐎 ♞ k | 1945 | G 🐎 K |
| 1926 | 🐎 ♞ l | 1946 | G 🐎 L |
| 1927 | 🐎 ♞ m | 1947 | G 🐎 M |
| 1928 | 🐎 ♞ n | 1948 | G 🐎 N |
| 1929 | 🐎 ♞ o | 1949 | G 🐎 O |
| 1930 | 🐎 ♞ p | 1950 | G 🐎 P |
| 1931 | 🐎 ♞ q | 1951 | G 🐎 Q |
| 1932 | 🐎 ♞ r | 1952 | G 🐎 R |
| 1933 | 🐎 ♞ s | 1953 | G 🐎 S |
| 1934 | 🐎 ♞ t | 1954 | G 🐎 T |
| 1935 | ● 🐎 ♞ u | 1955 | G 🐎 U |
| 1936 | 🐎 ♞ A | 1956 | G 🐎 a |
| 1937 | G 🐎 B | 1957 | G 🐎 b |
| 1938 | G 🐎 C | 1958 | G 🐎 c |
| 1939 | G 🐎 D | 1959 | G 🐎 d |
| 1940 | G 🐎 E | 1960 | G 🐎 e |
| 1941 | G 🐎 F | 1961 | G 🐎 f |
| 1942 | G 🐎 G | 1962 | G 🐎 g |
| 1943 | G 🐎 H | | |
| 1944 | G 🐎 I | | |

## FIRMS WHICH BECAME PART OF HENRY BIRKS & SONS

1899, Hendery & Leslie, situated at 134 St. Peter Street. John Leslie remained as manager until 1925. Director of Henry Birks & Sons Ltd. from March 11th, 1925-1939.

1903, Olmstead & Hurdman, Ottawa, Charles Olmstead, manager. Replaced by Howard S. Porter in 1914.

1905, Ryrie Bros., Toronto. Harry Ryrie Director of Henry Birks & Sons, 1906-1917. James Ryrie elected first Hon. Treasurer of "The Canadian National Jewellers Association" on September 25th, 1918. J. H. Birks was elected 1st. Vice-President.

1907, George E. Trorey, Vancouver (b. 1861 - d. 1946). Director to 1931.

1907, Gorham Co. of Canada Ltd., silver plate factory situated on Vitre Street, west of Beaver Hall Hill.

1919, M. S. Brown & Co., Halifax.

1920, D. E. Black & Co., Calgary. David E. Black, Director to 1953.

1927, D. A. Kirkland, Edmonton.

1928, N. C. Maynard, Hamilton. Mr. Maynard resigned his position as Managing Director Birks Toronto in 1923. Started with Ryrie Bros.

1929, J. E. Wilmot, Ottawa, closed out this store, 1931.

1930, G. Seifert & Co. Gustavus Seifert b. 1831 d. 1909. Quebec.

1931, Firm of Birks-Ellis-Ryrie formed.

1933, Firm of Birks-Dingwall formed.

## TOUCH MARKS ACQUIRED BY HENRY BIRKS & SONS

| NAME OF FIRM | DATE | MARK |
|---|---|---|
| C. & J. Allen<br>Toronto | 1870-1887 | C. & J. ALLEN<br>C. & J. A |
| Lowe & Anderson<br>Toronto | 1885-1888 | L & A |
| C. Addison<br>Ottawa | 1882-1892 | C.A. |
| T. Allen & Co.<br>Montreal | 1862-1900 | T A & CO |
| Messrs. H. Birks & Co.<br>Montreal | 1849-1893 | BIRKS (five sizes) |
| Messrs. H. Birks & Co.<br>Montreal | 1894- | H. B. & CO |
| Bilsky & Son<br>Ottawa | 1885 | BILSKY & SON |
| N. Beaudry, Jeweller<br>Montreal | 1880 | N. BEAUDRY |
| W. Bramley<br>Montreal | 1890-1891 | *W. BRAMLEY |

| NAME OF FIRM | DATE | MARK |
|---|---|---|
| M. S. Brown & Co. Halifax | 1886-1919 | M. S. B. & CO |
| A. Beauchamp, Jeweller Montreal | 1865-1880 | A. B |
| Geo. B. Bailey Montreal | 1880 | *G. B. |
| Smith Bros. Kingston | 1885 | S. Bs |
| M. Cochenthaler, Jeweller Montreal | 1885-1931 | M. COCHENTHALER M.C |
| Canada Manufacturing Co. Montreal and Toronto | 1890 | CANADA M'FG. Co STERLING SILVER |
| J. Cornelius Halifax | 1825-1916 | J. CORNELIUS (two sizes) |
| Lee & Chillas Toronto | 1881-1889 | L. & C. |
| John C. Copp Montreal | (possibly) 1892 | *J. C. C. |
| G. L. Darling Simcoe | 1852-1899 | G. L. DARLING |
| J. E. Ellis & Co. Toronto | 1871-1901 | J. E. E. & Co. |
| J. Froland Kingston | 1865-1885 | J. FROLAND J. F. |
| Matthew Gage Kingston | 1851-1879 | M. GAGE |
| M. L. Gurd, Jeweller Montreal | | M. L. GURD |
| J. R. Harper & Co. Montreal | 1880 | J. R. H. & CO |
| R. Hendery Montreal | 1814-1895 | R. HENDERY R. H |
| Hendery & Leslie Montreal | 1887-1899 | HENDERY & LESLIE H & L |
| Olmstead & Hurdman Ottawa | 1892-1903 | O & H |
| J. G. Joseph & Co. Toronto | 1857-1877 | J. G. J. & Co |
| A. C. Johnson & Bros. Kingston, Montreal Believed sold to Mappin | 1894-1913 | A. C. J. & B. |
| J. H. Jones & Co.   & Webb Montreal | 1880-1890 | *J. H. J. & Co. |
| W. H. Kearney Toronto | 1880 | W. H. KEARNEY |
| W. H. Kirk Toronto | 1885 | W. H. K. |
| Kent Bros. Toronto | 1867-1882 | KENT BROS |
| Ambrose Kent & Son Toronto | 1894-1897 | A. K. & S. |

| NAME OF FIRM | DATE | MARK |
|---|---|---|
| John Leslie | 1845-1895 | J LESLIE |
| Ottawa | | (two sizes) |
| Lowe & Co. | 1885 | LOWE & Co. |
| Toronto | | |
| J. W. Millar & Co. | 1882 | J. W. M. & Co. |
| Toronto | | |
| Simpson Hall Miller & Co. | 1879-1890 | S. H. M. & Co. |
| Montreal | | |
| N. Marks | 1876 | N. MARKS |
| Ottawa | | |
| E. M. Morphy | 1847-1882 | E. M. M |
| Toronto and London, Ont. | about | |
| Miller & Bremner | 1880-1890 | M & B |
| Working Jewellers, Montreal | | |
| W. C. Morrison | 1846-1886 | *W. C. M. |
| Toronto | | |
| Zimmerman McNaught & Co. | 1882-1885 | Z. McN & CO |
| Toronto | | |
| Hugh S. Murray | 1869 | *H. S. M. |
| London | | |
| D. Miller | | D. MILLER |
| Montreal | | |
| David McPherson | 1849-1903 | *D. M M |
| Montreal | | |
| C. A. Olmstead | 1890-1903 | OLMSTEAD |
| Ottawa | | C. A. O. |
| P. E. Poulin | 1867-1869 | POULIN |
| Quebec, Ottawa | | P. E. P. |
| Pelton | 1885 | PELTON |
| Montreal | | |
| George G. Robinson & Co. | 1890 | G. G. R. & CO |
| Montreal | | |
| A. J. Rosenthal | 1882-1903 | ROSENTHAL |
| Ottawa | | A. J. R |
| C. E. Redfern | 1874-1900 | C. E. R |
| Victoria | | |
| Ryrie Bros. | 1882-1905 | RYRIE |
| Toronto | | |
| Savage | | SAVAGE |
| Montreal | | |
| Savage & Lyman | | *SAVAGE & LYMAN |
| Montreal | | SAVAGE & LYMAN |
| Savage & Lyman & Co. | 1767-1885 | |
| Montreal | | *S. L. & CO |
| George Savage | | |
| Montreal | | G S |
| W. H. Savage | | |
| Montreal | | W. H. S |

| NAME OF FIRM | DATE | MARK |
|---|---|---|
| Gustavus Seifert<br>Quebec<br>Used with Seifert's mark. | 1857-1930 | G. SEIFERT<br>SEIFERT<br>*QUEBEC |
| R. Sharpley & Sons<br>Montreal | 1837-1900 | R. SHARPLEY<br>& SONS |
| T. B. Steacy<br>Brockville | 1860-1966 | T. B. STEACY |
| H. & A. Saunders, Jewellers<br>Toronto, Montreal | 1869-1885 | H & A. S |
| F. W. Spanenberg<br>Kingston | 1870-1887 | F. W. S.<br>*F. W. S. |
| S. A. Spanenberg<br>Kingston | 1885 | S. A. S<br>*S. A. S |
| F. W. Sark & Bros.<br>Napanee | 1885 | F. W. S & B |
| Tasker & Sons<br>Toronto | 1882 | TASKER & SONS |
| Toronto Silver Plate Co.<br>Toronto | 1882-1920 | TORONTO SILVER<br>PLATE Co |
| W. H. Tracy<br>Ottawa | 1851-1892 | W. H. TRACY |
| Kerr & Thorne<br>Saint John | 1878-1885 | K & T |
| G. Warren<br>Toronto | 1880 | G. WARREN |
| Watson<br>Montreal | 1870 | WATSON |
| Watson & Pelton<br>Montreal | 1880 | W. & P. M |
| W. S. Walker<br>Montreal | 1855-1890 | WALKER<br>W. S. W |
| J. Wanless<br>Toronto | 1865-1905 | WANLESS |
| R. Wilks & Co.<br>Montreal & Toronto | 1847-1880 | R W & Co. |
| J. B. Williamson<br>Montreal | 1885 | *J. B. W |
| William Walker<br>Montreal | 1855-1890 | W. W |
| S. B. Windrum<br>Toronto | 1882-1885 | S. B. W |
| W. G. Young<br>London, Ont. | 1890 | W. G. YOUNG |
| J. Zimmerman<br>Toronto | 1882 | J. ZIMMERMAN |

Most of the marks are incised. Those which have letters in relief on a sunk panel are marked *

*Pseudo-English "Hall" and Combined Marks Used by Hendery and Leslie*

These marks, individually, or in various combinations, were used on silver manufactured for the trade. The date letters conform to the London date letters up to 1903. "a" is 1896-1897 and the others follow in annual succession. These letters serve to date pieces by Hendery & Leslie up to 1903. J.R. & Co. was John Round & Co.

DATE LETTERS

1896-1897
1898-1899
1900-1901
1902-1903

JOHN ROUND & CO.

NOT IDENTIFIED

NOT IDENTIFIED

GOLDSMITHS STOCK COMPANY OF CANADA

NOT IDENTIFIED

TORONTO SILVER PLATE COMPANY

# QUEBEC CITY

**AMIOT, JEAN NICOLAS**      Kn. 1750 - 1821

Apprenticed to Joseph Schindler 1767. Repaired silver for the Notre Dame de la Victoria Church. Father of Laurent Amiot. Died March, 1821.

**AMIOT, LAURENT**      b. 1764 - d. 1838

Born in Quebes., father of Jean Joseph Amiot, brother of Augustin and Jean Amiot Jnr. One of twelve children. Apprenticed to I. F. Ranvoyze. Studied in France. Worked in Quebec for many years. His apprentices included Paul Morin. Made beautiful silver for the church. His punch was later used by Ambroise Lafrance who sometimes added a 'Napoleonic' head.

**BEGUAY, JEAN BAPTISTE**      Kn. 1786 - 1815

Recorded as working goldsmith.

**BEWES, DANIEL**      Kn. 1844 - 1852

Watchmaker, Jeweller and Gold and Silversmith. Believed to be the same man as Daniel Bews known in Toronto in 1856.

 *with Lion, Leopard's Head Letter & Fleur de lis*

**BOURE, NARCISSE**      Kn. 1854 - 1865

Listed at several addresses in Quebec.

| N.B | *Lion and Head of Man* |

**CHRISTMAS, D. S.**      Kn. 1836 - 1854

Listed as Silversmith. Situated at 58½ St. John Street, 1854.

**COUTURE, PIERRE**      Kn. 1844 - 1854

Listed as silversmith. Situated at 25 Mountain Street. Wife believed to have taken over business at that time.

**ELLIS, JAMES**      Kn. 1820 - 1822

Working Silversmith situated at 20 St. Ursule Street.

| J. ELLIS | *With Other Marks Similar to Those Used by James Adams Dwight of Montreal* |

GATIEN, M.                                    Kn. 1762
Made silver for the Church of St. Jean Deschaillons.

GENDRON, P.                         Kn. 1852 - 1865
Partner and brother of Hector Gendron. Advertised in Canadian Directory 1853-1854.

GROTHE, Z.                          Kn. 1849 - 1850

HANNA, JAMES                      Kn. 1763 - 1807
Believed to be an Irishman, originally from Dublin. In business in Quebec about forty years. Succeeded by son James Godfrey Hanna.

HANNA, JAMES GODFREY         Kn. 1803 - 1819
Clock and Watchmaker as well as gold and silversmith. Succeeded to his father's business in 1807 and worked with him as partner for the previous four years. F. Delagrave his partner 1816-18.

HANNA & DELAGRAVE           Kn. 1816 - 1818
See above. This partnership disolved when Hanna went into bankruptcy.

HARDY, ANSELM            Kn. 1853 - 1854
Situated at 18 St. Peter Street. L.T.

 with Lion

HARRIS, E. B.            Kn. 1853 - 1854
Situated at 7 Notre Dame Street.

HULL, MRS. E.            1853 - 1854
Listed in Canadian Directory at 13 Buade Street U.T.

HUNTER, WILLIAM          Kn. 1805
Partner with brother Francis Hunter 1804. Silver with Laurent Amiot mark plus W.H. would suggest that Amiot made silver for Hunter.

INNES, WILLIAM           Kn. 1848 - 1864
Situated on St. John Street 1848 - 54. Address 12 Palace Street 1864. Listed in the directory of 1853 at St. John Street.

 with Leopard's Head and Man's Head

LAFRANCE, AMBROISE       Kn. 1822 - 1908
See Laurent Amiot.

LAMBERT, PAUL            b. 1691 - 1749
Born in Quebec. Considered one of the more outstanding silversmiths of the French Period.

LAMONTAGNE, MICHAEL      Kn. 1833 - 1871
Silversmith, Jeweller and Watchmaker. 3 St. John Street 1853 to 1864. Moved to Coulliard St.

LANDRON, JEAN FRANCOIS   Kn. 1686 - 1759
Church silversmith.

LESPERANCE, PIERRE    Kn. 1819 - 1882

Trained by his Uncle Francois Sasseville. Became his partner then his successor. Laurent Amiot's tools came to him from his uncle. Made church silver.

LUCAS, JOSEPH    Kn. 1775

Listed as silversmith.

MARTYN, MRS. JOHN    Kn. 1853 - 1854

Situated at 45 St. Peter Street. Specialized in the repairing and regulating of chronometers, listed as silversmith.

MORIN, PAUL    1775 - 1805

Church silversmith, apprenticed to Laurent Amiot.

   *also with Pseudo Hallmarks*

McLAUGHLIN, SAMUEL    Kn. 1853 - 1854

Clockmaker and Silversmith. Situated at St. Peters Street.

ORKNEY, JAMES    Kn. 1791 - 1826

Working silversmith. Partner of Joseph Sasseville around 1800. Listed as juryman in 1797.

PAGE, JACQUES    Kn. 1686 - 1742

One of the outstanding early silversmiths. Apprenticed to Levasseur. Was in Paris 1713-1715. Returned to Quebec. Died 1742.

PARADIS, ROLAND

Made a great deal of Church silver.

Kn. 1696 - 1754

POULIN & CO., P. E.  Kn. 1888
Situated at 40 Fabrique Street. Silver made for this firm by Hendery & Leslie.

**P. E P**
*or* With Pseudo Hallmarks
**POULIN**

POWIS, THOMAS  Kn. 1781
English goldsmith and jeweller. Believed in advertising. Made silver for Indian trade, all manner of jewellery and much flatware.

RANVOYZE, IGNACE FRANCOIS  Kn. 1739 - 1819
Church silversmith. Served in the Militia. Worked three years as locksmith.

SASSEVILLE, FRANCOIS  Kn. 1797 - d. 1864
Son of Joseph Sasseville, silversmith and brother of Geo. Sasseville, silversmith. Francois succeeded Laurent Amiot Was in partnership with Pierre Lesperance 1854-56. Situated 17 Mountain Street. 1853-54. Made silver for the church.

SASSEVILLE, JOSEPH  Kn. 1776 - 1831
Father of Francois and George Sasseville. Made Indian trade silver and ceremonial pieces as well as other silver items.

SASSEVILLE & ORKNEY  Kn. 1800
Partnership of Joseph Sasseville and James Orkney.

 With Lion

SCHINDLER, JONAS           Kn. 1760 - 1786
Made trade silver.

SEIFERT, GUSTAVUS          Kn. 1831 - 1909
A firm of long standing 1857 - 1930 acquired by Henry Birks & Sons, Montreal. Used a variety of marks. Some silver made for him by Hendery & Leslie.

 **G. SEIFERT**

*Sometimes With STERLING*
*or Pseudo Hallmarks and*
*Some Pieces Marked QUEBEC*

SHEFFIELD, HOUSE           Kn. 1867
Listed in Quebec 1867.

# Hallmarked Silver

### Standard Mark
Denoting the minimum silver or gold content.

| Mark | Standard | Minimum Percentage |
|---|---|---|
| | Sterling silver Marked in England | 92.5 |
| | Sterling silver Marked in Scotland | 92.5 |
| | Britannia silver | 95.84 |
| | 22 carat gold Marked in England | 91.66 |
| | 18 carat gold Marked in England | 75.0 |
| | 14 carat gold | 58.5 |
| | 9 carat gold | 37.5 |

### Assay Office Mark
Showing which assay office tested the article.

| Mark | Office | Standard |
|---|---|---|
| | London | Sterling silver & gold |
| | London | Britannia silver |
| | Birmingham | Silver & gold |
| | Sheffield | Silver |
| | Sheffield | Gold |
| | Edinburgh | Silver & gold |

\*\*There were formerly Assay Offices at other towns, each having its own distinctive mark.

## Look for the HALL-MARK

A hallmark on a gold or silver article shows that it has been accurately tested or assayed at one of the four official assay offices and that the metal conforms to one of the legal standards of purity.

A hallmark consists of several symbols:

Maker's       Standard      Assay         Date
                            Office        Letter

The **Maker's Mark** nowadays consists of the initials of the person or firm submitting the article to the assay office. It takes the form of the symbol NM in the above example.

The **Date Letter** indicates the year in which the article was hallmarked. It consists of a shield enclosing a letter of the alphabet. The letter is changed in May each year at the London office, in July at Birmingham and Sheffield and in October in Edinburgh. To determine the date of the marking of an article it is necessary first to identify the particular assay office from the assay office mark and then to refer to a published list of date letters. This is because each assay office uses different alphabetical cycles.

Lion Passant   Lion Passant Guardant   Lion Rampant

# Glossary Silver

**ASSAY:**
A test for standard of purity and quality of silver and gold.

**ASSAYER:**
An officer appointed by an Assay Office. Responsible for testing silver and gold to check standards.

**BRITANNIA STANDARD:**
Compulsory standard for silverware, set 1697-1720 in Britain. Only 10 dwts. of copper were allowed to each pound weight of silver. The figure of Britannia was the mark used to denote this standard. Replacing the leopard head previously used. 1720, Sterling standard was again used. Higher Britannia standard continued to be used by some silversmiths.

**DATE MARK:**
Consists of a cycle of twenty letters of the alphabet omitting j, v, w, x, y, z in various type and shields. Used to denote year.

**HALLMARK:**
The distinguishing mark of a British Assay Office. Plural — Denotes group of marks, giving maker, date, standard and hall at which assayed.

**MAKER'S MARK:**
Stamp or punch used by maker, to imprint with device or initials all pieces leaving his workshop. The distinguishing mark of the workshop not always the mark of the actual maker. (In Canada, trade silversmiths marked pieces with the name of the vendor, as in the case of Robert Hendery and Hendery and Leslie.)

**PLATE:**
Term used in Europe for items of wrought silver or gold. Now used to describe Sheffield or Electroplate.

**PSEUDO HALLMARKS:**
Punch marks sometimes used by early smiths to denote silver and indicate standards. Used in countries where silversmiths had no established guilds or Assay Offices.

**SHEFFIELD PLATE:**

Copper coated with silver by a special process invented by Thomas Boulsover of Sheffield, 1743. It was hard to distinguish it from Silver, so alike was it in appearance, it could be identified best by its weight being heavier than silver. It was made by sandwiching the copper between two layers of silver and fusing the three layers together before manufacturing into various articles.

**SILVERPLATE:**

A base metal, usually either nickel silver or copper, coated with a layer of pure silver by electroplating.

**TOWN MARK:**

The mark applied to denote the location of Assay Office.

## BIRMINGHAM MARKS 1773 - 1861

Assay office established in 1773 for the marking of silver. The anchor is the mark of the office. Date letter changed each July. Sovereign's head duty mark 1874 - 1890.

| Year | Mark | Year | Mark | Year | Mark | Year | Mark | Year | Mark |
|---|---|---|---|---|---|---|---|---|---|
| 1773 | ⚓♛ | 1796 | ⚓♛☉Y | 1818 | ⚓♛☉u | 1840 | ♛⚓☉R | | |
| 1774 | B | 1797 | Z | 1819 | V | 1841 | S | | |
| 1775 | C | | | 1820 | W | 1842 | T | | |
| 1776 | D | | | 1821 | X | 1843 | U | | |
| 1777 | E | 1798 | ⚓♛☉a | 1822 | Y | 1844 | V | | |
| 1778 | F | 1799 | b | 1823 | Z | 1845 | W | | |
| 1779 | G | 1800 | c | | | 1846 | X | | |
| 1780 | H | 1801 | d | | | 1847 | Y | | |
| 1781 | I | 1802 | e | 1824 | ⚓♛☉A | 1848 | Z | | |
| 1782 | K | 1803 | f | 1825 | B | | | | |
| 1783 | L | 1804 | g | 1826 | C | | | | |
| 1784 | M | 1805 | h | 1827 | D | 1849 | A | | |
| 1785 | N | 1806 | i | 1828 | E | 1850 | B | | |
| 1786 | O | 1807 | j | 1829 | F | 1851 | C | | |
| 1787 | P | 1808 | k | 1830 | G | 1852 | D | | |
| 1788 | Q | 1809 | l | 1831 | H | 1853 | E | | |
| 1789 | R | 1810 | m | 1832 | J | 1854 | F | | |
| 1790 | S | 1811 | n | 1833 | K | 1855 | G | | |
| 1791 | T | 1812 | o | 1834 | L | 1856 | H | | |
| 1792 | U | 1813 | p | 1835 | M | 1857 | I | | |
| 1793 | V | 1814 | q | 1836 | N | 1858 | J | | |
| 1794 | W | 1815 | r | 1837 | O | 1859 | K | | |
| 1795 | X | 1816 | s | 1838 | ☉P | 1860 | L | | |
| | | 1817 | t | 1839 | Q | 1861 | M | | |

## BIRMINGHAM MARKS 1862 - 1968

| Year | Mark | Year | Mark | Year | Mark | Year | Mark |
|---|---|---|---|---|---|---|---|
| 1862 | [anchor] N | 1884 | [anchor] k | 1906 | [anchor] g | 1929 | [anchor] E |
| 1863 | O | 1885 | l | 1907 | h | 1930 | F |
| 1864 | P | 1886 | m | 1908 | i | 1931 | G |
| 1865 | Q | 1887 | n | 1909 | k | 1932 | H |
| 1866 | R | 1888 | o | 1910 | l | 1933 | [anchor] J |
| 1867 | S | 1889 | p | 1911 | m | 1934 | K |
| 1868 | T | 1890 | q | 1912 | | 1935 | L |
| 1869 | U | 1891 | r | 1913 | o | 1936 | M |
| 1870 | V | 1892 | s | 1914 | p | 1937 | N |
| 1871 | W | 1893 | t | 1915 | q | 1938 | O |
| 1872 | X | 1894 | u | 1916 | r | 1939 | P |
| 1873 | Y | 1895 | v | 1917 | s | 1940 | Q |
| 1874 | Z | 1896 | w | 1918 | t | 1941 | R |
| | | 1897 | x | 1919 | u | 1942 | S |
| | | 1898 | y | 1920 | v | 1943 | T |
| 1875 | a | 1899 | z | 1921 | w | 1944 | U |
| 1876 | b | | | 1922 | x | 1945 | V |
| 1877 | c | | | 1923 | y | 1946 | W |
| 1878 | d | 1900 | a | 1924 | z | 1947 | X |
| 1879 | e | 1901 | b | 1925 | A | 1948 | Y |
| 1880 | f | 1902 | c | 1926 | B | 1949 | Z |
| 1881 | g | 1903 | d | 1927 | C | 1950 Continuing thus: A |
| 1882 | h | 1904 | e | 1928 | D | 1952 C |
| 1883 | t | 1905 | f | | | 1968 Continuing thus: T |

## CHESTER MARKS 1701 - 1962

Gold and silver was assayed in Chester as early as the 15th century, but the marks were not regulated until about the end of the 17th century. Three wheatsheafs with sword were the assay office mark 1686 - 1700. Three wheatsheafs with sword was used again after 1779.

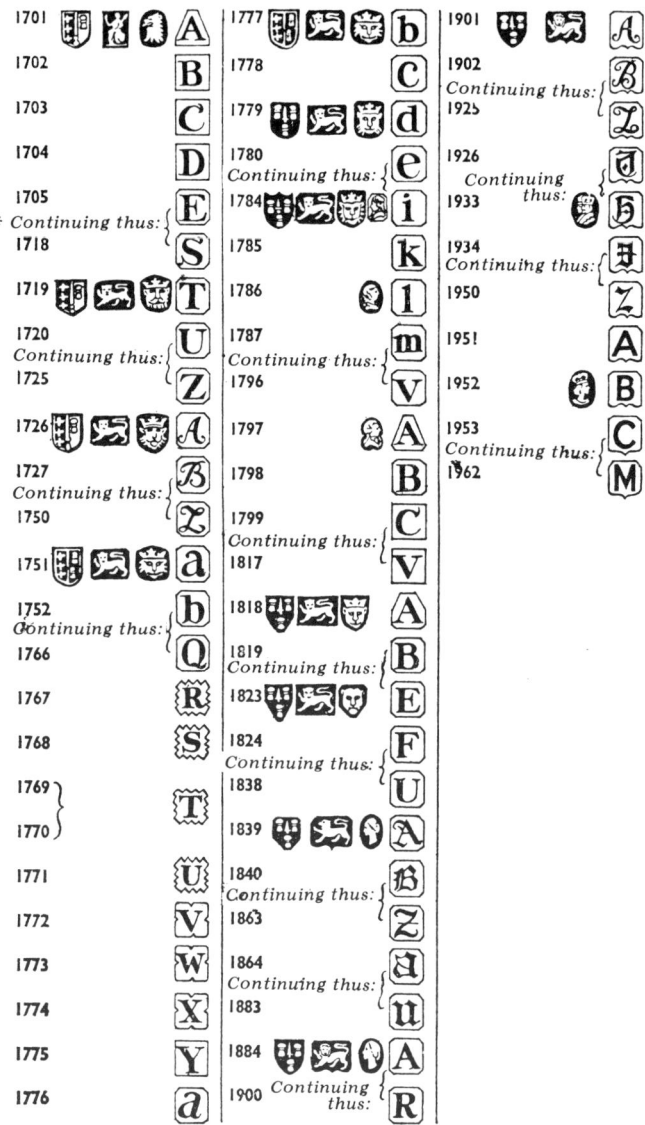

NOTE: * "continuing thus" i.e. 1705 - 1718 continued the same style of lettering from E to S on the same shape of shield and with other markings identical to those used 1701 to 1704. The words "continuing thus" have a similar meaning in every instance.

## EXETER MARKS 1701 - 1882

Wrought silver was made in Exeter during the middle ages. Roman X is the 16th and 17th century town mark. Three towered castle mark of assay office from 1701. Date letter changed in August each year.

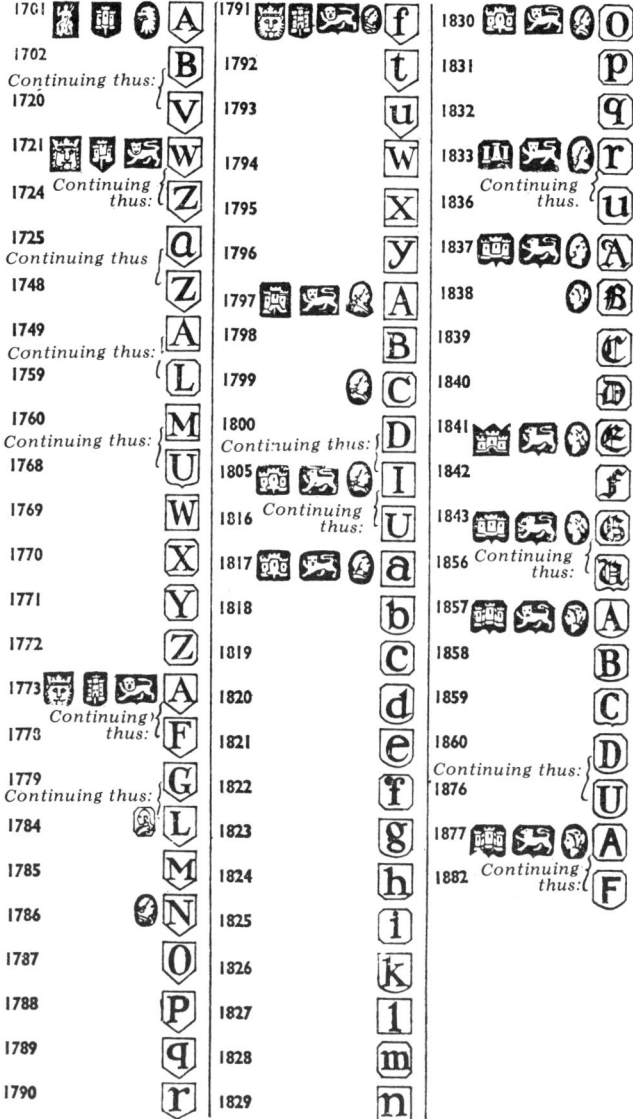

# LONDON MARKS 1658 - 1770

Gold and silver assayed and marked since 1327. Various styles of Leopard's head used as office mark, also note changes of lion mask which indicated sterling standard. Date letter changed in May each year.

| Year | Mark | Year | Mark | Year | Mark | Year | Mark |
|---|---|---|---|---|---|---|---|
| 1658 | 🦁 A | 1687 | 🦁 b | 1715 | 🦁 | 1743 | 🦁 H |
| 1659 | B | 1688 | l | | | 1744 | I |
| 1660 | C | 1689 | m | 1716 | A | 1745 | K |
| 1661 | D | 1690 | n | 1717 | B | 1746 | L |
| 1662 | E | 1691 | o | 1718 | C | 1747 | M |
| 1663 | F | 1692 | p | 1719 | 🦁 D | 1748 | N |
| 1664 | G | 1693 | q | 1720 | E | 1749 | O |
| 1665 | H | 1694 | r | 1721 | 🦁 F | 1750 | P |
| 1666 | I | 1695 | s | 1722 | G | 1751 | Q |
| 1667 | K | 1696 | t | 1723 | H | 1752 | R |
| 1668 | L | | | 1724 | 🦁 I | 1753 | S |
| 1669 | M | 1697 | 🦁 A | 1725 | K | 1754 | T |
| 1670 | N | | B | 1726 | L | 1755 | U |
| 1671 | O | 1698 | C | 1727 | M | | |
| 1672 | P | 1699 | D | 1728 | N | 1756 | 🦁 A |
| 1673 | Q | 1700 | E | 1729 | 🦁 O | 1757 | B |
| 1674 | R | 1701 | F | 1730 | P | 1758 | C |
| 1675 | S | 1702 | G | 1731 | Q | 1759 | D |
| 1676 | T | 1703 | H | 1732 | R | 1760 | E |
| 1677 | U | 1704 | I | 1733 | S | 1761 | F |
| | | 1705 | 🦁 K | 1734 | T | 1762 | G |
| 1678 | 🦁 a | 1706 | L | 1735 | V | 1763 | H |
| 1679 | b | 1707 | M | | | 1764 | I |
| 1680 | 🦁 c | 1708 | N | 1736 | 🦁 a | 1765 | K |
| 1681 | d | 1709 | O | 1737 | b | 1766 | L |
| 1682 | e | 1710 | P | 1738 | c | 1767 | M |
| 1683 | f | 1711 | Q | 1739 | d | 1768 | N |
| 1684 | g | 1712 | R | 1740 | e | 1769 | O |
| 1685 | h | 1713 | S | 1741 | f | 1770 | P |
| 1686 | i | 1714 | T | 1742 | g | | |

## LONDON MARKS 1771 - 1881

| Year | Mark | Year | Mark | Year | Mark | Year | Mark |
|---|---|---|---|---|---|---|---|
| 1771 | 👑🦁 O | 1799 | 👑🦁👤 D | 1827 | 👑🦁👤 m | 1855 | 👑🦁👤 U |
| 1772 | R | 1800 | E | 1828 | n | | |
| 1773 | S | 1801 | F | 1829 | o | 1856 | 👑🦁👤 a |
| 1774 | T | 1802 | G | 1830 | p | 1857 | b |
| 1775 | U | 1803 | H | 1831 | 👤 q | 1858 | c |
| 1776 | a | 1804 | I | 1832 | r | 1859 | d |
| 1777 | b | 1805 | K | 1833 | s | 1860 | e |
| 1778 | c | 1806 | L | 1834 | t | 1861 | f |
| 1779 | d | 1807 | M | 1835 | u | 1862 | g |
| 1780 | e | 1808 | N | | | 1863 | h |
| 1781 | f | 1809 | O | 1836 | 👑🦁👤 A | 1864 | i |
| 1782 | g | 1810 | P | 1837 | 👤 B | 1865 | k |
| 1783 | h | 1811 | Q | 1838 | C | 1866 | l |
| 1784 | 👤 i | 1812 | R | 1839 | D | 1867 | m |
| 1785 | k | 1813 | S | 1840 | E | 1868 | n |
| 1786 | 👤 l | 1814 | T | 1841 | f | 1869 | o |
| 1787 | m | 1815 | U | 1842 | G | 1870 | p |
| 1788 | n | | | 1843 | H | 1871 | q |
| 1789 | o | 1816 | 👑🦁👤 a | 1844 | J | 1872 | r |
| 1790 | p | 1817 | b | 1845 | K | 1873 | s |
| 1791 | q | 1818 | c | 1846 | L | 1874 | t |
| 1792 | r | 1819 | d | 1847 | M | 1875 | u |
| 1793 | s | 1820 | e | 1848 | N | | |
| 1794 | t | 1821 | 👑🦁👤 f | 1849 | O | 1876 | 👑🦁👤 A |
| 1795 | u | 1822 | g | 1850 | P | 1877 | B |
| | | 1823 | h | 1851 | Q | 1878 | C |
| 1796 | 👑🦁👤 A | 1824 | i | 1852 | R | 1879 | D |
| 1797 | B | 1825 | k | 1853 | S | 1880 | E |
| 1798 | C | 1826 | l | 1854 | T | 1881 | F |

## LONDON MARKS 1883 - 1968

| Year | Mark | Year | Mark | Year | Mark | Year | Mark |
|---|---|---|---|---|---|---|---|
| 1882 | 🦁 👤 🦁 G | 1910 | 👤 🦁 P | 1936 | 🦁 👤 A | | |
| 1883 | H | 1911 | q | 1937 | B | | |
| 1884 | I | 1912 | r | 1938 | C | | |
| 1885 | K | 1913 | s | 1939 | D | | |
| 1886 | L | 1914 | t | 1940 | E | | |
| 1887 | M | 1915 | u | 1941 | F | | |
| 1888 | N | | | 1942 | G | | |
| 1889 | O | | | 1943 | H | | |
| 1890 | P | 1916 | 👤 🦁 a | 1944 | I | | |
| 1891 | 👤 🦁 Q | 1917 | b | 1945 | K | | |
| 1892 | R | 1918 | c | 1946 | L | | |
| 1893 | S | 1919 | d | 1947 | M | | |
| 1894 | T | 1920 | e | 1948 | N | | |
| 1895 | U | 1921 | f | 1949 | O | | |
| 1896 | 👤 🦁 a | 1922 | g | 1950 | P | | |
| 1897 | b | 1923 | h | 1951 | Q | | |
| 1898 | c | 1924 | i | 1952 | 👤 R | | |
| 1899 | d | 1925 | k | 1953 | S | | |
| 1900 | e | 1926 | l | 1954 | T | | |
| 1901 | f | 1927 | m | 1955 | U | | |
| 1902 | g | 1928 | n | 1956 | a | | |
| 1903 | h | 1929 | o | *Continuing thus:* | | | |
| 1904 | i | 1930 | p | 1968 | n | | |
| 1905 | k | 1931 | q | | | | |
| 1906 | l | 1932 | r | | | | |
| 1907 | m | 1933 | 👤 s | | | | |
| 1908 | n | 1934 | t | | | | |
| 1909 | o | 1935 | u | | | | |

## NEWCASTLE MARKS 1702 - 1883

Silver and goldsmiths are recorded as working in Newcastle from the mid-thirteenth century. A single castle with lion passant was used prior to 1670. Three castles were used after that date. The assay office was re-established in 1702.

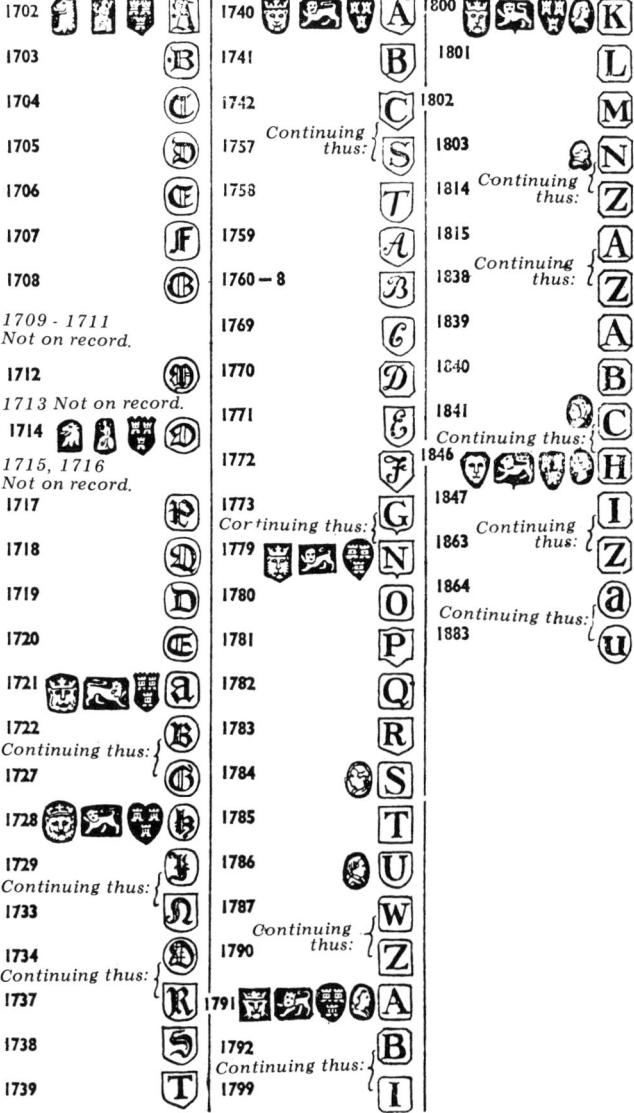

## SHEFFIELD MARKS 1773 - 1883

Assay Office established in 1773 for the marking of silver. The crown is the mark of this office. Date letter changed each July. From 1784 - 1890 a duty was levied on all silver in Britain and the sovereign's head was the duty mark.

| Year | Mark | Year | Mark | Year | Mark | Year | Mark |
|---|---|---|---|---|---|---|---|
| 1773 | 🦁 👑 E | 1800 | 🦁 👑 👤 N | 1828 | 🦁 👑 👤 e | 1856 | 🦁 👑 👤 N |
| 1774 | 👑 F | 1801 | H | 1829 | f | 1857 | O |
| 1775 | R | 1802 | M | 1830 | g | 1858 | P |
| 1776 | R | 1803 | F | 1831 | h | 1859 | R |
| 1777 | W | 1804 | G | 1832 | k | 1860 | S |
| 1778 | S | 1805 | B | 1833 | l | 1861 | T |
| 1779 | A | 1806 | A | 1834 | m | 1862 | U |
| 1780 | C | 1807 | S | 1835 | p | 1863 | V |
| 1781 | D | 1808 | P | 1836 | q | 1864 | W |
| 1782 | G | 1809 | K | 1837 | 👤 r | 1865 | X |
| 1783 | B | 1810 | L | 1838 | s | 1866 | Y |
| 1784 | 👤 I | 1811 | C | 1839 | t | 1867 | Z |
| 1785 | U | 1812 | D | 1840 | 👤 u | 1868 | A |
| 1786 | 👤 K | 1813 | R | 1841 | v | 1869 | B |
| 1787 | L | 1814 | 👤 W | 1842 | x | 1870 | C |
| 1788 | M | 1815 | O | 1843 | z | 1871 | D |
| 1789 | M | 1816 | T | 1844 | 🦁 👑 👤 A | 1872 | E |
| 1790 | Z | 1817 | X | 1845 | B | 1873 | 🦁 👑 👤 F |
| 1791 | P | 1818 | I | 1846 | C | 1874 | G |
| 1792 | u | 1819 | V | 1847 | D | 1875 | H |
| 1793 | o | 1820 | Q | 1848 | 🦁 👑 E | 1876 | J |
| 1794 | m | 1821 | Y | 1849 | F | 1877 | K |
| 1795 | q | 1822 | Z | 1850 | G | 1878 | L |
| 1796 | Z | 1823 | U | 1851 | H | 1879 | M |
| 1797 | 🦁 👑 👤 X | 1824 | 👤 | 1852 | I | 1880 | N |
| | | 1825 | b | 1853 | K | 1881 | O |
| 1798 | 🦁 👑 👤 V | 1826 | c | 1854 | L | 1882 | P |
| 1799 | E | 1827 | d | J855 | M | 1883 | Q |

On smaller objects a crown appears above the date letter. e.g. 1802.

## SHEFFIELD MARKS (1884 – 1968)

| Year | Mark | Year | Mark | Year | Mark |
|---|---|---|---|---|---|
| 1884 | R | 1911 | 👑 🦁 t | 1936 | 👑 🦁 t |
| 1885 | S | 1912 | u | 1937 | u |
| 1886 | T | 1913 | v | 1938 | v |
| 1887 | U | 1914 | w | 1939 | w |
| 1888 | V | 1915 | x | 1940 | x |
| 1889 | W | 1916 | y | 1941 | y |
| 1890 | X | 1917 | z | 1942 | z |
| 1891 | Y | | | | |
| 1892 | 🦁 👑 Z | 1918 | 👑 🦁 a | 1943 | A |
| | | 1919 | b | 1944 | B |
| 1893 | 👑 🦁 a | 1920 | c | 1945 | C |
| 1894 | b | 1921 | d | 1946 | D |
| 1895 | c | 1922 | e | 1947 | E |
| 1896 | d | 1923 | f | 1948 | F |
| 1897 | e | 1924 | g | 1949 | G |
| 1898 | f | 1925 | h | 1950 | H |
| 1899 | g | 1926 | i | 1951 | I |
| 1900 | h | 1927 | k | 1952 | 👑 🦁 😊 K |
| 1901 | i | 1928 | l | 1967 | Z |
| 1902 | k | 1929 | m | 1968 | A |
| 1903 | l | 1930 | n | | |
| 1904 | m | 1931 | o | | |
| 1905 | n | 1932 | p | | |
| 1906 | o | 1933 | 👑 🦁 😊 q | | |
| 1907 | p | 1934 | r | | |
| 1908 | q | 1935 | s | | |
| 1909 | r | | | | |
| 1910 | s | | | | |

Continuing thus: (1967 Z, 1968 A)

# YORK MARKS 1700 - 1856

Assay office existed from mid-16th century, but closed in 1717. Re-opened 1774 and closed again in 1856. Silver pieces from this area are rare.

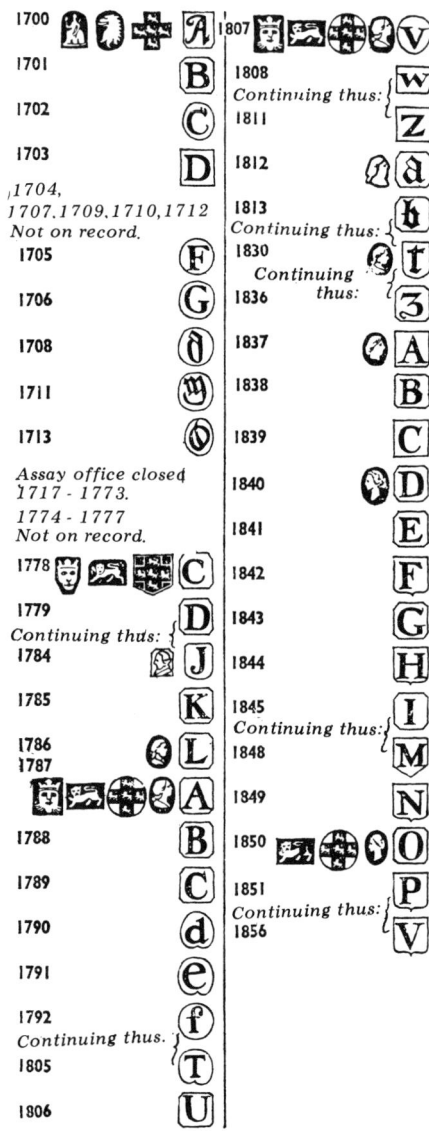

## DUBLIN DATE LETTERS

| | | | | | | | | | | | | | | |
|---|---|---|---|---|---|---|---|---|---|---|---|---|---|---|
| l | 1856–7 | A | 1871–2 | Q | 1886–7 | J | 1901–2 | A | 1916–7 | Q | 1932 |
| m | 1857–8 | B | 1872–3 | R | 1887–8 | G | 1902–3 | b | 1917–8 | R | 1933 |
| n | 1858–9 | C | 1873–4 | S | 1888–9 | H | 1903–4 | C | 1918–9 | S | 1934 |
| o | 1859–0 | D | 1874–5 | T | 1889–0 | I | 1904–5 | D | 1919–0 | T | 1935 |
| p | 1860–1 | E | 1875–6 | U | 1890–1 | K | 1905–6 | e | 1920–1 | U | 1936 |
| Q | 1861–2 | F | 1876–7 | V | 1891–2 | L | 1906–7 | F | 1921–2 | V | 1937 |
| r | 1862–3 | G | 1877–8 | W | 1892–3 | M | 1907–8 | S | 1922–3 | W | 1938 |
| s | 1863–4 | H | 1878–9 | X | 1893–4 | N | 1908–9 | h | 1923–4 | X | 1939 |
| t | 1864–5 | I | 1879–0 | Y | 1894–5 | O | 1909–0 | i | 1924–5 | Y | 1940 |
| u | 1865–6 | K | 1880–1 | Z | 1895–6 | P | 1910–1 | B | 1925–6 | Z | 1941 |
| v | 1866–7 | L | 1881–2 | A | 1896–7 | Q | 1911–2 | L | 1926–7 | A | 1942 |
| w | 1867–8 | M | 1882–3 | B | 1897–8 | R | 1912–3 | m | 1927–8 | B | 1943 |
| x | 1868–9 | N | 1883–4 | C | 1898–9 | S | 1913–4 | n | 1928–9 | From Jan 1st 1932 Assay Year and Calendar coincide. Used throughout 1931. |
| y | 1869–0 | O | 1884–5 | D | 1899–0 | T | 1914–5 | O | 1929–0 | |
| z | 1870–1 | P | 1885–6 | E | 1900–1 | U | 1915–6 | P | 1930–1 | |

## "IRISH REPUBLICAN SILVER"

It may be of interest to note that when a new set of laws was enacted for the Irish Free State, in 1922, the law relating to hall-marking was thought to have been overlooked and the occasion was used by silversmiths to mark articles with a special punch, using a design of a ship for the town mark. The ship forms part of the city arms of Cork. Ultimately the situation was adjusted, but in the meantime a certain amount of silver had been made and marked, and a quantity was sold. The mark illustrated is from a small tray now in possession of the Dublin Assay Office. Pieces bearing this mark will have a certain value as curiosities for collectors.

# GLASGOW DATE LETTERS

| | | | | | | |
|---|---|---|---|---|---|---|
| A 1819 – 0 | V 1840 – 1 | 𝕬 1861 – 2 | L 1882 – 3 | 𝒢 1903 – 4 | b 1924 – 5 |
| B 1820 – 1 | W 1841 – 2 | 𝕽 1862 – 3 | M 1883 – 4 | 𝓗 1904 – 5 | c 1925 – 6 |
| C 1821 – 2 | X 1842 – 3 | 𝕾 1863 – 4 | N 1884 – 5 | 𝒥 1905 – 6 | d 1926 – 7 |
| D 1822 – 3 | Y 1843 – 4 | 𝕿 1864 – 5 | O 1885 – 6 | 𝒥 1906 – 7 | e 1927 – 8 |
| E 1823 – 4 | Z 1844 – 5 | 𝖀 1865 – 6 | P 1886 – 7 | 𝒦 1907 – 8 | f 1928 – 9 |
| F 1824 – 5 | 𝕬 1845 – 6 | 𝖁 1866 – 7 | Q 1887 – 8 | 𝓛 1908 – 9 | g 1929 – 0 |
| G 1825 – 6 | 𝕭 1846 – 7 | 𝖂 1867 – 8 | R 1888 – 9 | 𝓜 1909 – 0 | h 1930 – 1 |
| H 1826 – 7 | 𝕮 1847 – 8 | 𝖃 1868 – 9 | S 1889 – 0 | 𝒩 1910 – 1 | i 1931 – 2 |
| I 1827 – 8 | 𝕯 1848 – 9 | 𝖄 1869 – 0 | T 1890 – 1 | 𝒪 1911 – 2 | j 1932 – 3 |
| J 1828 – 9 | 𝕰 1849 – 0 | 𝖅 1870 – 1 | U 1891 – 2 | 𝒫 1912 – 3 | k 1933 – 4 |
| K 1829 – 0 | 𝕱 1850 – 1 | A 1871 – 2 | V 1892 – 3 | 𝒬 1913 – 4 | l 1934 – 5 |
| L 1830 – 1 | 𝕲 1851 – 2 | B 1872 – 3 | W 1893 – 4 | 𝓡 1914 – 5 | m 1935 – 6 |
| M 1831 – 2 | 𝕳 1852 – 3 | C 1873 – 4 | X 1894 – 5 | 𝒮 1915 – 6 | n 1936 – 7 |
| N 1832 – 3 | 𝕴 1853 – 4 | D 1874 – 5 | Y 1895 – 6 | 𝒯 1916 – 7 | o 1937 – 8 |
| O 1833 – 4 | 𝕵 1854 – 5 | E 1875 – 6 | Z 1896 – 7 | 𝒰 1917 – 8 | p 1938 – 9 |
| P 1834 – 5 | 𝕶 1855 – 6 | F 1876 – 7 | 𝒜 1897 – 8 | 𝒱 1918 – 9 | q 1939 – 0 |
| Q 1835 – 6 | 𝕷 1856 – 7 | G 1877 – 8 | ℬ 1898 – 9 | 𝒲 1919 – 0 | r 1940 – 1 |
| R 1836 – 7 | 𝕸 1857 – 8 | H 1878 – 9 | 𝒞 1899 – 0 | 𝒳 1920 – 1 | s 1941 – 2 |
| S 1837 – 8 | 𝕹 1858 – 9 | I 1879 – 0 | 𝒟 1900 – 1 | 𝒴 1921 – 2 | t 1942 – 3 |
| T 1838 – 9 | 𝕺 1859 – 0 | J 1880 – 1 | ℰ 1901 – 2 | 𝒵 1922 – 3 | u 1943 – 4 |
| U 1839 – 0 | 𝕻 1860 – 1 | K 1881 – 2 | ℱ 1902 – 3 | a 1923 – 4 | SINCE 1914-5 |

## GEORGE V & QUEEN MARY
## SILVER JUBILEE 1935
### TWENTY-FIVE YEARS

From 1784 to 1890 the Sovereign's head always appeared as part of the legal hall-mark stamped by the Assay Office on silver to denote the payment of duty. Only on one occasion has the Assay Offices ever used the head of the Sovereign and his Queen, this was when it was agreed to commemorate the Silver Jubilee of their Royal Majesties King George V and Queen Mary. This mark was used from 1933/4 to 1935/6.

Arthur Tremayne, the well-known authority on clocks, watches, diamonds and silver was the originator of the idea and went to a great deal of trouble to get it put into effect. In fact before the mark could be used, the laws of England had to be changed and not only did the Goldsmiths' Company, provincial Assay Office, Board of Trade, The Mint and Treasury have to be convinced and give their approval, but the Home Office sanction had to be waited for. The original of the obverse side of the official Jubilee Medal (designed by Mr. Percy Metcalf) was used for the punch.

This was a very exciting event in the history of silver for in more than six centuries of hall-marking it had never been used as anything but a mark of high quality for precious metals; never before had it been linked with events of national importance. Certainly it was the first time two crowned heads appeared on any stamp used for marking silver articles.

This fact alone makes any piece with the Jubilee mark of considerable importance. Samples can be found today, as thousands of sets of spoons, six to the set, each bearing the mark of a different Assay Office, were made and sold. The British Industries Fair sold many pieces to both home and overseas buyers, so you can be certain that Canada received its share. Many items: tea-services, trays, coffee pots, vases, flatware, boxes etc., were so marked and are definitely worth looking for as an addition to a collection of silver or Royal Commemoratives.

## GEORGE V & QUEEN MARY SILVER JUBILEE
### Town Marks & Date Letters

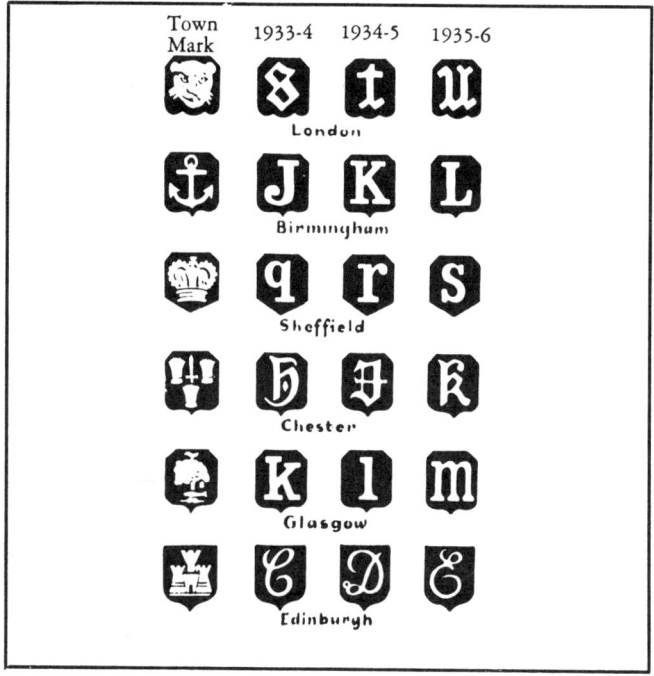

# GLASS

MOUNT WASHINGTON
1892

CROWN MILANO
1892

NEW ENGLAND
GLASS WORKS
1882

BACCARAT
current

MOUNT WASHINGTON PEACHBLOW
1885

ROSE AMBER
1884

KELVA
NAKARA
WAVE CREST
WARE

# Glass Glossary

AGATE: Opague glass resembling the stone agate. Colours: yellow, brown and tan.

AMBERINA: Transparent, used for tableware and ornamental pieces. Colours: vivid, shading from tones of pale amber to ruby.

ART GLASS: A generic term given to glass that came in elegant forms and diverse colour effects. Ornamental glass was often made to imitate other materials, such as satin, marble or porcelain etc.

AURENE: The trademark "Aurene" was registered by the Steuben Glass Works, 1904. A lustrous ornamental glass. Colours: rich, blue, gold or combination of colours.

BACCARAT: Fine glass ware produced by Compagnie des Cristalleries at Baccarat, France.

BOHEMIAN: The name is taken from Bohemia, a country which is now part of Czechoslovakia. Generally, the term refers to clear glass cased red and sometimes blue and yellow, cut into squares and lines. Copper wheel engraved scenes are also a feature of this glass. Still being made in Czechoslovakia. It is hard to distinguish the old from new in good quality pieces, but cheap copies, which are plentiful, are very obvious.

BRISTOL: Includes semi-opaque white glass painted in enamels. This glass was made in England at the numerous Bristol glass houses, the best work was in the mid-1700's. Also made in America during the Victorian era. In the late 1800's great quantities of "Bristol Blue" (bright translucent glass) was manufactured in Bristol, much of it for use as inserts in silverware.

BURMESE (AMERICAN): Mount Washington Glass Company, New Bedford, Mass. Pat. Dec 15th 1885. Developed by Frederick Shirley. Free blown and shaped with tools also blown moulded in quilted or stretched (expanded) diamond pattern. Soft mat finish, some polished pieces made, but not as lovely as those which are acid finished. Thin and very fragile in delicate yellows with blush rose overtones. No good reproductions made — uranium was used in the making and is not obtainable for glass production today.

BURMESE (ENGLISH) Made under a patent granted by Thomas Webb & Sons. Many pieces marked "Queen's Burmese" as it was made by arrangement with Queen Victoria, who admired the American Burmese, having been made a gift of some by Frederick Shirley.

CAMEO: Made in two or more layers of varying colours. By cutting or carving in cameo the outer layer/layers, the contrasting colour of the background is revealed.

CAMPHOR: Opaque, cloudy white.

CARAMEL: Opaque glass in a colour typical of its name.

CARNIVAL GLASS: Pressed glass made in vibrant and pastel colours, iridized to give it a rainbow effect. Produced by several American factories as well as factories in Australia, Britain, France and Germany. Carnival glass, a popular collectable today, came into fashion during the early 1900's, and was sold in stores, through catalogues and also was offered as prizes at fairs and carnivals.

CLAMBROTH: Grayish, semi-opaque.

CORALINE: Made by many factories in England and America. So-called because of designs. Thousands of very small glass beads placed on adhesive were used to simulate coral or seaweed patterns on acid etched forms, then fired. Usually yellow beads on lovely blues, greens and peachblow wares.

CRACKLE: Smooth interior with rough exterior. Colours: Clear and pastels.

CRANBERRY: Beautiful, wine-red glass.

CRYSTAL: Also known as flint glass or lead glass. Fine quality colourless glass containing a high proportion of lead oxide.

CROWN MILANO: Mat finish, with a texture similar to porcelain. Found in white and pastels elaborately decorated with enamel, gold or silver.

CUSTARD: Opaque, colour of a milk and egg custard.

CUT: Glass ornamented by cutting using a moving wheel.

DEPRESSION: Clear and coloured glassware made primarily during the Great Depression which began in 1929. This mass produced type of pressed glass was inexpensive to manufacture and available in a wide variety of designs. Some patterns made before and after the depression era are included in this category and "depression glass" is the term usually used to describe the many patterns and styles made from about 1925 to the late 1960's.

END-OF-DAY: (See spatter glass) So-called because pieces of this type were supposedly made after working hours using remnants of colours and odds and ends of glass remaining in the furnace pots. Most often referred to as spatter glass today.

FOVAL: This glass manufactured by the H.D. Fry Glass Co. and though seldom marked it can be easily identified. Wares have a opalescent body with brilliant coloured trim, e.g. white opal with blue handle; white to blue opal with brilliant amethyst handle. Most of this glass was produced during the 1920's. The letters FOVAL indicate Fry's Ovenware Art Line.

IRIDESCENT: An iridescent or lustered surface achieved by spraying the form while still hot with metallic salts. Found in a variety of colours. (see opalescent.).

KELVA: See Wavecrest.

KEW BLAS: Lustrous or lustre decorated glass, identified by engraved (not acid etched) mark "Kew Blas." Made at Union Glass Co., Somerville, Mass. Colours: deep blue, green, rose, gold, bronze. Scarce.

LUTZ: This name is used to describe the striped glass thought to have been produced at the Boston & Sandwich Glass Co. in the mid 19th century. Nicholas Lutz, a Frenchman, worked for several American glass companies. He also produced filigree, threaded and cane glass. Most of the pieces found are similar to those made by Venetian glass makers for hundreds of years and made today by workers in Murano, Venice. Without documentation glass of this nature can only be considered "Lutz type."

MARY GREGORY: Clear and coloured glass decorated with white hand painted Kate Greenaway type figures.

MAT: A dull surface or finish on glass.

MERCURY: Glass with a silver appearance made by filling the space between two layers of clear glass with mercury or nitrate of silver.

MILLEFIORI: "a thousand flowers" A decoration made by fusing short canes of coloured glass to form a floral mosaic.

MILK GLASS: Translucent white glass with a faint blue tinge.

NAKARA: See Wavecrest.

OPALESCENT: Iridescent, like an opal, various colours that can refract light and then reflect it in a play of colours.

PEACHBLOW (MOUNT WASHINGTON): Was made only at the Mount Washington factory from 1886 - 1888. It was an unlined homogeneous glass, the same colour through the thickness of the piece.

PEACHBLOW (NEW ENGLAND): Made by Edward D. Libbey proprietor of the New England Glass Co., Cambridge, Mass., which became the Libbey Glass Co. after moving to Toledo, Ohio. New England Peachblow was patented March 2nd 1886 and made until 1888. The original name was Wild Rose. Colour is solid through thickness of glass; opaque white to deep red rose at the top. Most pieces have the acid finish, giving a lovely soft mat effect. A limited number of pieces were left with a polished surface.

PEACHBLOW (WHEELING): The original made in Wheeling, West Virginia by J.H. Hobbs, Brockunier & Co. First produced in 1883. Colour is deep yellow to crimson cased with opal or opaque milk white, acid polished finish.

POMONA: Made at the New England Glass Co. Clear glass with pale amber border at top decorated with tinted flowers and foliage on a background that is covered with fine lines or stippling.

PRESSED: Pattern glass made in a mould. Found in clear and colours.

QUEZAL: Made at the Quezal Art Glass & Decorating Co., New York City, 1901 - 1925 (a company established by two former employees of Tiffany). Iridescent with design in outer layer. Colours: mainly gold and green, some blue, rose and purple. Beautiful glass, made using techniques learned at the Tiffany works.

RUBENA CRYSTAL: Transparent, clear at base shading to red.

RUBENA VERDE: Transparent, yellow at base shading to red.

SATIN: Cased glass, mat finish with satin texture. Colours: pastels.

SLAG: Also referred to as marble glass. Opaque white glass streaked with another opaque colour such as rose, purple, yellow or blue.

SPANGLE: Multi-coloured, usually cased, with flakes of metal on a dark or pastel ground.

SPATTER: Multi-coloured, decorated with an over-all blending of melted pieces of coloured glass.

VASA MURRHINA: See spangle and spatter.

VASELINE: Resembles the blue yellow colour of petroleum jelly.

WAVECREST (KELVA & NAKARA): Made by the C.F. Monroe Co., Meriden, Conn. Used three trade names on toilet articles (dressing table sets) and many covered pieces such as biscuit barrels, frequently having metal hinges and trims. Fine enamel decoration was applied to creamy opal glass All three of these wares were made in rich, extravagant styles. Only the trademarks which they carry distinguish one from the other. The trademarks were registered in 1892. Wavecrest items appear in the T. Eaton Co. catalogue of that period.

# Art Glass

Following is a selection of marks found on nineteenth and twentieth century art glass. Marks were engraved, stamped or etched on the form or added in the shape of a label.

## ENGLAND

John Northwood, Stourbridge, England, 1836 - 1902
Mark(s): "John Northwood"

Stevens & Williams, Stourbridge, England, 1847 - present
Mark(s): "S & W" "SW"

Thomas Webb & Sons, Stourbridge England, 1837 - present
Mark(s): "Queen's Burmese/Thomas Webb & Sons/Patented"
"Webb" "W & W" "Woodhall"

## FRANCE

Argy-Rousseau, Paris, France, 1913 - 1931
Mark(s): "Argy-Rousseau"

Almaric V. Walter, Nancy, France, 1859 - 1942
Mark(s): "A. Walter"

Baccarat, Baccarat, France, 1764 - present
Mark(s): "Baccarat"

D'Argental, Munzthal, (Germany) France, 1809 - present
Mark(s): "D'Argental"

Daum Nancy, Nancy, France, 1875 - present
Mark(s): "Daum Nancy"
"Daum Nancy, France" (after 1919)
"Daum" (after 1960)

Andre Delatte, Nancy, France, 1921 —
(Mark(s): "De Latte"

# FRANCE

Emile Galle, Saint Clement, France, 1846 - 1904
(Mark(s): "E Galle a Nancy"
"Cristallerie d'E"
"Galle Nancy"
"Galle"
"Emile Galle"

Legras & Cie, St. Denis, France, 1864 - 1920
Mark(s): "Le Gras"

Mueller Freres, Croismare, France, 1895 - 1936
Mark(s): "Mueller"
"Mueller Freres"

Pantin (E.S. Monot) Pantin, France, 1851 - present
Mark(s): "De Vez"

Schneider, Epinay-sur-Seine, France, 1913 - present
(Mark(s): "Schneider"

Val St. Lambert, Val St. Lambert, France, 1802 - present
Mark(s): "Val St. Lambert"

# GERMANY

Loetz, Klostermuhle (Bohemia; Austria), Germany, 1840 - 1943
Mark(s): most pieces not marked, some are marked "Loetz, Austria" or with circled crossed arrows.

Ludwig Moser & Sohne, Karlsbad, Germany, 1857 - present
Mark(s): "Leo Moser"
"Moser"
"Moser Alexandrite"

# U. S. A.

Steuben Glass Works, Corning, New York, 1903 - present
Mark(s): etched fleur-de-lis and "Steuben" until 1932, later pieces marked "Steuben"

## RENE LALIQUE, PARIS, FRANCE

Rene Lalique (1860 - 1945) was a successful jeweller, well known for his Art Noveau designs. During the 1890's and early 1900's he experimented with glass making incorporating some of the glass in his designs for jewellry. He was commissioned by Coty and other perfume manufacturers to design bottles and packaging for their products during this period and by 1915 he was concentrating on glass design and manufacture.

Rene Lalique's main aim was to exploit the luminous properties of the glass metal to its fullest. The proportions of all-coloured glass used for his work is relatively small. A slight concession to the uniformity of the typical Lalique opalescence was made probably during the late 1920's and early 1930's, with the application of dull-blueish colour traces about the edges of the relief decoration, thus breaking the unity of the design. This later period, and through the 1930's date the cigarette boxes, ashtrays, powder boxes, scent bottles, clocks and mirrors with motifs of cupids, lovebirds, nymphs, doves and rabbits.

Characteristic Lalique glass shows a subtly frosted effect. Another distinctive and very beautiful Lalique creation is a moulded crystal glass with an interior, milky-cloud effect, reminiscent of vaseline glass, revealing a pale ochre tinge when held against the light; it is so subtly blended into the metal that it seems difficult to define how this was contrived.

Rene Lalique did not rely on multi-coloured effects of symbolic plant forms to lend expression to his work. There are no over-balanced shapes with narrow rising stems and sudden bulbous protuberances. He relied on the aesthetics of the form itself to satisfy, and on the subtle use of the glass-metal to entrap and reflect natural and artificial light, to give his material its distinctive luminescent quality. Sometimes he decorated his glass with stark enamel colours, applied after completion of the article, and this particular type of embellishment is seen on some of the early heavily sculptured pieces.

| | |
|:---:|:---:|
| R.LALIQUE<br>FRANCE | *R. Lalique France* |
| pre-1945 | pre-1945 |
| LALIQUE FRANCE | *Lalique France* |
| 1945 - 1960 | 1945 - 1960 |
| LALIQUE | *Lalique*<br>*France* |
| 1960+ | 1960+ |

## LOUIS COMFORT TIFFANY

Tiffany or Favrile* glass is noted for its unique quality, exquisite blending of vibrant colours and its true iridescence. This type of blown glass comprising both ornamental and useful objects was produced by the Tiffany factories during the 1890's until 1918. The years 1918 to 1928 are known as the Nash period at the Tiffany works. Mr. A. Douglas Nash supervised the factories during this time and changes were made in the type of glass produced, most notably the colours used. Pale colours with thin iridescence instead of the rich colours of previous years. The Tiffany name, signatures and marks continued to be used during this period.

*FAVRILE: Registered as part of the Tiffany trademark November 13, 1894. Derived from the old English 'fabrile' meaning hand made.

### OTHER TIFFANY PRODUCTS

As well as blown glass the Tiffany enterprises also made other fine decorative items in a wide variety of materials; pressed glass for tiles and jewels; glass for pictorial windows and mosaics; lamps, lamp shades and fixtures; pottery; enamels; jewelry; desk sets; candlesticks; picture frames; boxes; door knockers and paperweights etc. These pieces can also be identified by the "Tiffany" mark.

### THE A. DOUGLAS NASH CORPORATION

The Tiffany furnaces closed in 1928. The Corona, Long Island, New York works were sold to A. Douglas Nash. From December, 1928 until 1931 the A. Douglas Nash Corporation continued to make glass at the Corona works, but a condition of the sale stated that the Tiffany name could not be associated with the firm or its products. Sometimes called Tiffany-type, this glass is marked NASH or ADNA.

## Marks on Tiffany Glass/Products

*Marks are engraved, stamped or etched on the form or added as a label.*

*On glass, the name or initials were cut or etched by workmen — vary in size and style. Know the glass, signatures have been forged.*

*It has been said — "collect glass, not signatures."*

L C T & Co or L C T  
In block, script  
or monogram

Tiffany Studios  
New York

Louis C. Tiffany Furnaces Inc.  
Favrile

Louis C. Tiffany and Co., Associated Artists

Tiffany Glass Co.

Tiffany Studios

Tiffany Glass and Decorating Co.

*Louis C. Tiffany*

**TIFFANY**

**TIFFANY & Co.**

*Favrile fabrique*

Tiffany Studios  
New York

**ADNA or NASH** are the marks used by the A. Douglas Nash Corporation, 1928 to 1931.

# MARY GREGORY

GLASS DECORATOR
SANDWICH & BOSTON GLASS COMPANY
Sandwich, Mass., U.S.A.

"MARY GREGORY" GLASS

Clear and coloured glass decorated with hand painted Kate Greenaway type figures. Many forms were decorated in this manner, such as, cruets, decanters, dressing table sets, pitchers, and vases etc.

The young lady who was believed to have originated the paintings of children on this attractive glassware was a decorator in the lamp department of the Boston & Sandwich Glass Company from 1880 to 1884. Rural scenes, rather than children, were most often used as decoration. No one would be more surprised than Miss Gregory herself to find that her name had been associated with this European glassware.

The earlier peices, which date from about 1895 to the early 1900's are superior in quality and detail of decoration to later mass produced copies.

# Cut Glass Manufacturers: American

Marks are engraved, stamped or etched on the form or added as a label.

C.G. ALFORD & COMPANY
New York City. 1872 - 1918

T.B. CLARK & COMPANY
Honesdale, Pa. 1884 - 1930

ALMY & THOMAS
Corning, N.Y. 1903 - 1918

C. DORFLINGER & SONS
White Mills, Pa. 1852 - 1921

AVERBECK CUT GLASS COMPANY
New York City. 1892 - 1923

O.F. EGGINTON COMPANY
Corning, N.Y. 1899 - 1920

J.D. BERGEN COMPANY
Meriden, Conn. 1880 - 1916

H.C. FRY GLASS COMPANY
Rochester, Pa. 1901 - 1934

T.G. HAWKES & COMPANY          IRVING CUT GLASS COMPANY INC.
Corning, N.Y. 1880 - 1964      Honesdale, Pa. 1900 - 1930

J. HOARE & COMPANY             LACKAWANA CUT GLASS COMPANY
Corning, N.Y. 1853 - ?         Scranton, Pa. 1903 - 1905

HOBBS GLASS COMPANY            LAUREL CUT GLASS COMPANY
Wheeling, W.Va. 1845 - 1891    Jermyn, Pa. 1903 - 1920

HOPE GLASS WORKS               LIBBEY GLASS COMPANY
Providence, R.I. 1872 - 1951   Toledo, Ohio 1888 - 1936

HUNT GLASS COMPANY             LOTUS CUT GLASS CO.
Corning, N.Y. 1895 - ?         Barnesville, Ohio 1911 - ?

LYONS CUT GLASS COMPANY, Lyons, N.Y.  1903 - 1905

MAJESTIC CUT GLASS COMPANY
Emira, N.Y. 1900 - 1916

PITKIN & BROOKS
Chicago, Ill. 1872 - 1920

MAPLE CITY GLASS COMPANY
Hawley, Pa. 1910 - ?

QUAKER CITY CUT GLASS CO.
Philadelphia, Pa. 1902 - 1927.

MT. WASHINGTON
GLASS COMPANY
New Bedford, Mass. 1837 - 1894

SIGNET GLASS COMPANY
Address and dates not known

NEWARK CUT GLASS COMPANY
Newark, N.J. Dates — unknown.

H.P. SINCLAIRE & COMPANY
Corning, N.Y. 1904 - 1929

PAIRPOINT CORPORATION
New Bedford, Mass. 1880 - 1938

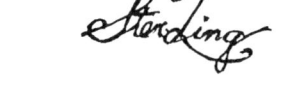

STERLING CUT GLASS COMPANY
Cincinnati, Ohio 1904 - 1950

P.X. PARCHE & SON COMPANY
Chicago, Ill. Dates — unknown.

L. STRAUS & SONS
New York City 1888 - ?

STEUBEN GLASS WORKS
Corning, N.Y. 1903 -

UNGER BROS.
Newark, N.J. 1901 - 1918

TAYLOR BROS.
Philadelphia, Pa. 1902 - 1915

CHARLES VANHEUSEN COMPANY
Albany, N.Y. 1893 - ?

TUTHILL CUT GLASS COMPANY
Middleton, N.Y. 1900 - 1923

WRIGHT RICH CUT GLASS COMPANY
Anderson, Indiana, 1904 - 1915

# Cut Glass Manufacturers: Canadian

Marks are engraved, stamped or etched on the form or added as a label.

HENRY BIRKS & SONS
Montreal, Quebec
1894 - 1907
Glasscutting factory bought by
George Phillips & Company, 1907.

CLAPPERTON & SONS LIMITED
GUNDY - CLAPPERTON COMPANY
Toronto & Deseronto
1905 - 1931

Gundy-Clapperton mark with retailer's name.

GOWANS & KENT COMPANY LIMITED
Toronto, Ontario
Ca. 1905

## RODEN BROS. LIMITED
Toronto, Ontario
Ca. 1891 - Ca. 1922

PORTE & MARKLE

Roden Bros. Limited mark with retailer's name.

Belleville Cut Glass Co., Belleville, Ontario. (1912)
Not marked.

The Excelsior Glass Company, Montreal, Quebec. (1880 - 1883)
Mark not known.

Lakefield Cut Glass Company, Lakefield, Ontario. (1915)
Some pieces marked with a small Union Jack.

Ottawa Cut Glass Company, Ottawa, Ontario. (1913)
Mark not known.

George Phillips & Co. Ltd., Montreal, Quebec. (1907)
Mark not known.

The St. Lawrence Glass Company, Montreal, Quebec. (1867 - 1875)
Mark not known.

The Wallaceburg Cut Glass Company, Wallaceburg, Ontario.
(1913 - 1930) Not marked.

 Unidentified mark. Possibly a Canadian company.

# Canadian Factories

## CANADIAN CONTAINER MANUFACTURERS AND THEIR MARKS

From about 1840 onwards glass containers for household and commercial use were manufactured in Canada. Prior to that time items of this type were imported into Canada from Europe and the United States.

Methods of manufacture gradually improved during the late 19th century and with the new technology the factories of Canada were able to satifsy the growing demand for large and small glass containers. During this period the industry was in a state of flux and by the end of the century seven factories had been absorbed by the blossoming Diamond Glass Company Limited which later became the Diamond Flint Glass Company Limited and in 1913 the Dominion Glass Company Limited. The output of the several plants of this large company, now known as Domglas Inc., still includes large quantities of bottles and jars for commercial and domestic use.

Canadian glass works, their dates of operation and the types of containers produced follows:

### NOVA SCOTIA

THE HUMPHREYS GLASS COMPANY, Trenton-New Glasgow (1890 - 1917) Bottles and fruit jars.

THE LAMONT GLASS COMPANY, Trenton-New Glasgow (1890 - 1902) Bottles and fruit jars.

## NEW BRUNSWICK

THE NEW BRUNSWICK CRYSTAL GLASS COMPANY, Saint John (1874 - 1878) The exact nature of the products of this factory is unknown at this time, however, it is believed that bottles and fruit jars were two of the items made there.

THE HUMPHREYS GLASS COMPANY, Moncton (1917 - 1920) Gerald Stevens in "Canadian Glass" states production appears to be the same as that of the Nova Scotia plant.

## QUEBEC

FOSTER BROTHERS, St. Johns (1854 - 1860) Advertised that they made a variety of containers including bottles and jars. To date the only type of bottle identified as a product of this factory is a bottle embossed "Foster Brothers St. Johns C.E."

OTTAWA GLASS WORKS, Como (1848 - 1857) became the BRITISH AMERICAN GLASS WORKS, Como (1857 - 1865) Exploration of this site has revealed that case gins and druggists' bottles were made there. It is also reported that soda water bottles were a product of these factories.

THE CANADA GLASS WORKS, Hudson (1867 - 1871) Advertised that they made several types of food and medicine bottles as well as fruit jars.

THE ST. LAWRENCE GLASS COMPANY, Montreal (1867 - 1873) Bottles.

THE (EARLY) DOMINION GLASS COMPANY, Montreal (1886 - 1898) Fruit jars.

THE ST. JOHNS GLASS COMPANY, St. Johns (1875 - 1878) was purchased by William Yuille and became THE EXCELSIOR GLASS COMPANY (1879 - 1880) Examples of products from these firms have not been identified, but it is reported that they made mould blown containers.

## QUEBEC, Continued

In 1880 THE EXCELSIOR GLASS COMPANY moved to Montreal and operated under that name until 1883. The following series of factory names reflect the changes of ownership and reorganization that took place over three decades.

North American Glass Company Limited  (1883 - 1890)
Diamond Glass Company Limited  (1890 - 1902)
Diamond Flint Glass Company Limited  (1903 - 1913)
Dominion Glass Company Limited  (1913 - 1925)

Containers in a variety of types and forms were made over the years at the Delormier Avenue site of these factories: bottles, candy jars, fruit jars and packers.

CONSUMERS GLASS COMPANY LIMITED, Montreal (1913 - Present) bottles and fruit jars.

Consumers Glass Company Limited manufactures containers in Canada with plants at —
Candiac and Ville Ste. Pierre, Quebec; Milton and Toronto, Ontario; and Lavington, British Columbia.

## ONTARIO

MALLORYTOWN GLASS WORKS, Mallorytown (1839 - 1840)
A whiskey flask and bottle are illustrated by Gerald Stevens in "Early Canadian Glass" as products of this factory.

THE CALEDONIA GLASS WORKS, Caledonia (1844-ca. 1848)
Produced bottles and bottled the natural mineral waters on the site of the springs near Prescott. To date no examples have been identified.

THE HAMILTON GLASS WORKS, Hamilton (1865 - 1898)
Re-opened 1906. Bottles and fruit jars.

THE BURLINGTON GLASS WORKS, Hamilton (1874 - 1897)
It is believed that many types of containers were made at this factory and it is known that ink and mucilage bottles were produced there as well as fruit jars.

## ONTARIO, Continued

THE NAPANEE GLASS WORKS, Napanee (1881 - 1883) Shards of druggists' bottles have been found on the factory site.

THE ERIE GLASS WORKS, Port Colborne (1893 - 1898) Bottles and fruit jars.

THE TORONTO GLASS COMPANY, Toronto (1893 - 1920) Bottles and fruit jars.

THE SYDENHAM GLASS COMPANY, Wallaceburg (1894 - 1913) Bottles and fruit jars.

THE FOSTER GLASS WORKS, Port Colborne (1895 - 1899) Believed to have produced fruit jars, but no examples have been identified to date.

THE BEAVER FLINT GLASS COMPANY, Toronto (1897 - 1948) This factory advertised that they sold containers and it is now believed that they were distributors only and not container manufacturers. Medicinals with the mark "B F G Co." on the base usually have a small "D" in a diamond mark as well indicating that the Dominion Glass Company manufactured some bottles for this firm.

THE ONTARIO GLASS WORKS, Kingsville (1899 - 1902) The "Ferrol" cod liver oil bottle and "Beaver" fruit jars are attributed to this factory.

## MANITOBA

THE MANITOBA GLASS MANUFACTURING COMPANY, Beausejour (1904 - 1913) Bottles and fruit jars.

MID-WEST GLASS COMPANY, Winnipeg (1929 - 1937) Bottles, fruit jars and packers.

## ALBERTA

THE DOMINION GLASS COMPANY, Redcliff (1913 - present) Bottles and fruit jars.

## BRITISH COLUMBIA

THE CRYSTAL GLASS COMPANY, Sapperton (now New Westminster) (1907 - 1908) Bottles and fruit jars.

THE VICTORIA GLASS & BOTTLE COMPANY, Victoria (1913 - 1916) Little is known about this company which was in business for only about three years, therefore, their production, if any, would have been rather small. John Barclay in "The Canadian Fruit Jar Report" mentions a report in which it states the factory would make all the various sizes of bottles and jars for firms in Victoria and Vancouver, as well as the Hudson Bay Company. No examples of this firm's products have been identified at this time.

# THE DEVELOPMENT AND STRUCTURE OF THE DOMINION GLASS COMPANY LIMITED

The DIAMOND GLASS COMPANY LIMITED was formed in 1890 and acquired control of the following glass factories in Canada throughout the period of its incorporation which ended in 1903.

1890 - The Burlington Glass Works, Hamilton, Ontario
North American Glass Works, Montreal, Quebec
Nova Scotia Glass Company, Trenton-New Glasgow, N.S.
1893 - The Hamilton Glass Works, Hamilton, Ontario
1897 - The Toronto Glass Company, Toronto, Ontario
1898 - The (Early) Dominion Glass Company, Montreal, Que.
The Lamont Glass Company, Trenton-New Glasgow, N.S.

The DIAMOND GLASS COMPANY LIMITED was reorganized in 1903 and the name was changed to the DIAMOND FLINT GLASS COMPANY LIMITED and during the period 1903 to 1913 gained control of two other independent glass companies.

1907 - The Manitoba Glass Manufacturing Company, Beausejour, Manitoba
1908 - The Sydenham Glass Company, Wallaceburg, Ontario.

In 1906 the Hamilton Glass Works factory was re-opened and a new factory the Canadian Glass Manufacturing Company Limited was built in 1907 at Pte. St. Charles, Quebec.

Reorganization took place again in 1913 when the company became the DOMINION GLASS COMPANY LIMITED and expansion continued with the acquisition of the Jefferson Glass Company, Toronto, Ontario. Also in 1913 the company opened a factory at Redcliff, Alberta.

The company, now known as Domglas Inc., manufactures glass containers in Canada with plants at —
Moncton and Scoudouc, New Brunswick; Montreal, Quebec; Mississauga, Ontario; Redcliff, Alberta; and Burnaby, British Columbia.

Containers are also currently being produced at the Libbey-St. Clair Inc. factory, Wallaceburg, Ontario. Glass items have been manufactured at this site since 1894. Libbey-St Clair Inc. is jointly owned by Domglas Inc. of Canada and the Libbey Division of Owens-Illinois, U.S.A.

# TRADE MARKS ON GLASS — CANADIAN

Marks used by Canadian glass factories are illustrated below. Occasionally wholesalers had their trade mark embossed on containers. Although they sometimes designed their own containers, they did not actually make them. Due to the many changes of ownership and amalgamations that took place in the late 1800's and early in the 20th century it is not always possible to date a container by the manufacturer's mark.

**BEAVER FLINT GLASS COMPANY**

B F G Co.

NOTE:
Containers marked "B F G Co" were probably made by the Dominion Glass Company and its predecessors.

**BURLINGTON GLASS WORKS**

BGW

1875 - 1877

BURLINGTON

1875 - 1897

BG Co

1877 - 1897

**CONSUMERS GLASS COMPANY LIMITED**

1917 - 1961         1961

**Possibly the DIAMOND GLASS COMPANY LIMITED Or the (EARLY) DOMINION GLASS COMPANY**

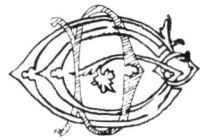

D G Co

NOTE:
A shard from a fruit jar embossed "D G Co" in a maple leaf was found at the Burlington Glass Works site. It seems likely that jars marked in this way were made at Burlington during the period of the Diamond Glass Company's ownership.

## (EARLY) DOMINION GLASS COMPANY

DOMINION

1886 - 1898

## DOMINION GLASS COMPANY LIMITED

1913 -

## ERIE GLASS WORKS

1893 - 1898

ERIE

## EXCELSIOR GLASS COMPANY LIMITED

E G Co

1879 - 1883

1879 - 1883

EXCELSIOR

1879 - 1883

EXCELSIOR IMPROVED

1879 - 1883

NOTE:
This type of mark is found on fruit jar lids which are also embossed with the company name.

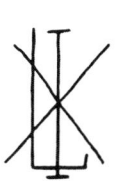

NOTE:
This type of mark is found on fruit jar lids which are also embossed with the company name.
A baby feeder ("Excelsior Feeder") is also embossed with this mark.

## HAMILTON GLASS WORKS

# HAMILTON
1865 - 1872

1865 - 1895

## HAMILTON GLASS WORKS
1865 - 1872

NOTE:
This mark is found on the base of some "Greek Key Safety Valve" fruit jars.

# RUTHERFORD & Co.
1872 - 1893

NOTE:
Used on fruit jars during George Rutherford's ownership of the Hamilton Glass Works.

   **HGW**

Ca. 1893 - 1898
&  1906 -

## LAMONT GLASS COMPANY

   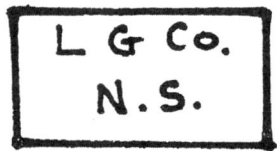

1890 - 1899

## MANITOBA GLASS MANUFACTURING CO.

# B

## MIDWEST GLASS COMPANY

## RICHARDS GLASS COMPANY

# RIGO

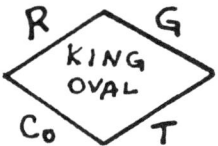

NOTE:
This company designed several types of prescription bottles and baby feeders. Although their trade mark often appears on bottles, the Richards Glass Company was a wholesaler and not a manufacturer.

## ST. LAWRENCE GLASS COMPANY

# S$^T$L

## TORONTO GLASS COMPANY

# T.G.C$^o$

## TRADE MARKS ON GLASS – VARIOUS

**A**

Adams & Co.
Pittsburg, Pa.
1861 - 1891

**A**

Arkansas Glass Container Corpn.
Jonesboro, Ark.
A. B. M.
1958 onwards.

Akro-Agate
Akron, Ohio
1911

John Agnew & Son
Pittsburg, Pa
1854 - 1866

American Art Products Corpn.
New York, N. Y.
before 1950

Anchor Glass Co.
Mount Pleasant, Pa.
1907

Anchor Hocking Glass Corp.
Lancaster, Ohio
current

ATHOSGLASS

Duryea & Potter
New York, N. Y.
1901

**ATLAS**

Hazel-Atlas Glass Co.
Wheeling, W. Va.
1902 - 1964

Armstrong Cork Co.
Lancaster, Pa.
current

**AURENE**

Steuben Glass Works
Steuben, Ohio
1904

Assigned to
Corning Glass Works
Corning, N.Y in 1924

Macbeth-Evans Glass Co.
Pittsburg, Pa.
before 1900

La Compagnie Des
Cristalleries De Baccarat
Meurthe, France
1888

Frederick W. Buning
New York, N.Y.
1893

Bartlett-Collins Co.
Sapulpa, Okla.
current

Blenco Glass Co.
Milton, W. Va.
after 1913

Geo. Borgfeldt & Co.
New York, N. Y.
1913

Ball Brothers Co.,
Muncie, Indiana
1894

## BEAVER

Illinois Pacific
Glass Co.
San Francisco, Cal.
1910

## BEAUMIROIR

Charles T. DeForest
New York, N.Y.
1884

**BLUE RIBBON**

Buckley-Newhall Co.
New York, N. Y.
1910

Baltimore
Bargain House

Baltimore Bargain House
Baltimore, Maryland
1890

Bibi & Co.
Brooklyn, N. Y.
after 1913

Best Light Co.
Canton, Ohio
1895

**BLUE RIBBON**

Standard Glass Co.
Marion, Indiana

Pilkington Bros., Ltd.
St. Helens, England
1877 and later by
Pilkington Glass Mfg. Co.
Toronto, Canada

Bryce Bros., Co.
Mt. Pleasant, Pa.
1948

BURGLAR'S HORROR

Clarke's Pyramid &
Fairy Light Co., Ltd.
London, England
1884

Pittman-Drietzer & Co.
New York, N. Y.
mid-1900's

Cambridge Glass Co., Ohio
1927 — later
Imperial Glass Co., Ohio

**CONCORD GLASS**
*"handcrafted"*

Concord Glass Mfg., Co.
New York, N. Y.
after 1935

Canton Glass Co.
Hartford City, Md.

Chatanooga Glass Co.
Chatanooga, Tenn.
1927

NOVIL  NULTRA

RESISTAL  ULTRA

1914

1880

1940

1909

**NONEX**
**1909**

1904

Corning Glass Works, Corning, N.Y.

## CENTENNIAL

First trademark to be registered in the United States for for the marking of tablewares

T. G. Cook & Co.
Philadelphia, Pa.
1873

## COHANSEY

Cohansey Glass Mfg. Co.
Bridgeton, N. J.
1870

Corona Cut Glass Co.
Toledo, Ohio
1906

Steam Gauge & Lantern Co.
Syracuse, N. Y.
1891

Diamond Glass Co.
Royersford, Pa.

Duncan & Miller Glass Co.
Washington, Pa.
after 1913

## Century

Century Inkstand Co.
New York, N. Y.
1893

T. B. Clark & Co.
Seelyville, Pa.
1898

## CRICKLITE

Clarke's Pyramid &
Fairy Light Co., Ltd.
London, England
1894

Daudt Glass & Crockery Co.
Toledo, Ohio
1909

## DEGEA

Deutsche Gasgluhlicht
Berlin, Germany
1902

Dunbar Glass Corp.
Dunbar, W. Va.
after 1913

## ChanJade

Chandler Specialty Mfg. Co.
Boston, Mass
1905

Wilbur F. Litch
Philadelphia, Pa.
1890

## COMMUNITY

Oneida Community Ltd.
Oneida, N. Y.
1914

## CRYSTO

McPike Drug Co.
Kansas City, Missouri
1904

## COLONIAL

C. Dorflinger & Sons
White Mills, Pa.
1892

C. R. De Goey
Providence, R. I.
after 1913

Emerald Glass Co
Los Angeles, Calif.
after 1913

## LORRAINE

C. Dorflinger & Sons
White Mills, Pa.
1894

Thomas Drysdale & Co.
New York, N. Y.
1886

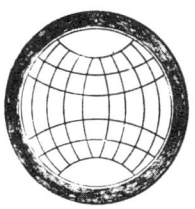

La Bastie Glass Co.
Ottawa, Illinois
first used 1876

Edmunds & Jones Mfg., Co.
Detroit, Mich.
1904

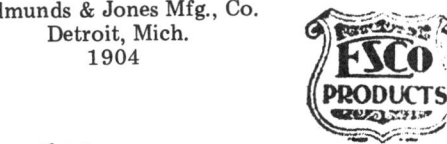

Empire State Glass Co.
New York, N. Y.
after 1913

Fairmount Glass Works
Indianapolis, Ind.
current

O. F. Eggington Co.
Corning, N. Y.
1899

## FAIRY.

Price's Patent Candle Co.
London, England
1884

Federal Glass Co.
Columbus, Ohio
after 1913

Fenton Art Glass Co.
Williamstown, W. Va.
after 1913

Foster-Forbes Glass Co.
Marion, Ind.
current

Protective "Freflo"
Stopple Co.
r, Delaware.
1914

Glenshaw Glass Co.
Glenshaw, Pa.
current

Glass Containers Inc.
Los Angeles, Cal.
current

# ACORN

Fostoria Glass Specialty Co.
Fostoria, Ohio
1908

# FOSTORIA

Fostoria Glass Co.
Moundsvill, W. Va.
1891

Fostoria Glass Co.
Moundsville, W. Va.
current

Fostoria Glass Co.
Moundsville, W. Va.
1909

Fostoria Glass Specialty Co.
Fostoria, Ohio
1910

 **NOBLAC**

Fostoria Glass Specialty Co.
Fostoria, Ohio
1904

**NOREC**

Fostoria Glass Specialty Co.
Fostoria, Ohio
1905

Fostoria Glass Specialty Co.
Fostoria, Ohio
1911

Fostoria Glass Co.
Moundsville, W. Va.
after 1913

McKee Glass Co.
Jeanette, Pa.
after 1914

United States Glass Co.
Tiffin, Ohio
after 1914

**GENERAL**

General Automobile Supply Co.
New York, N. Y.
1905

# Gral

Gruder, Blank & Co.
Berlin, Germany
1903

# Graetzin

Ehrich & Graetz
Berlin, Germany
1900

Richard Douglas & Co.
New York, N. Y.
1874

Silver City Glass Co., Inc.
Meriden, Conn.
after 1913

Eagle Dec. & Cut Glass Works
Brooklyn, N. Y.
after 1913

Current
Gulfport Glass Corpn.
Gulfport, Miss.

# GLOBE

William J. Tweed
Milville, N. J.
1904

Ebenezer Cut Glass Co., Inc.
Buffalo, N. Y.
after 1913

Grozart Glass Co.
Corona, L. I., N. Y.
after 1913

Haley Pressware Div.
Knox Glass Assocs., Inc.
Knox, Pa.
after 1913

Houze Glass Corpn.
Point Marion, Pa.
current

## GILLINDER
### 1883

# FRANKLIN
### 1860

1874
Above marks of
Gillinder & Sons
Philadelphia, Pa.

Gillinder Bros., Inc.
Erie & Liberty Sts.
Port Jervis, N. Y.
after 1913

Owens-Illinois Glass Co.
Toledo, Ohio
1914

Hazel-Atlas Glass Division
Continental Can Co.
Wheeling, W. Va.

# HALLMARK

United Jewelers Inc.
New York, N. Y.
1914

E. Gerard, Dufraisseix & Morel
Limoges, France
1882

## GLENSHAW

Glenshaw Glass Co.
Glenshaw, Pa.
1904

# GRAVIC

Three marks above of
T. G. Hawkes & Co.
Corning, N. Y.

1900

# OUR DARLING
### 1899

Two marks above of
W. H. Hamilton Co.
Pittsburg, Pa.

1907

1900

1900

**MICRA**
1911

1905

1932

**NEBULITE**
1911

1908

1908

Three marks of
Gillinder & Sons Inc.
Philadelphia, Pa.

1936

The above marks
shown with dates
are of
A. H. Heisey & Co.
Newark, Ohio

Susquehanna Glass Co.
Columbia, Pa.
after 1913

1958

IM PE
RI AL
1913

1913

1939

1914

1911

Six marks of
Imperial Glass Co.
Bellaire, Ohio

Macbeth-Evans Glass Co.
Pittsburg, Pa.
1892

William M. Decker
Kingston, N. Y.
1893

Hunt Glass Works Inc.
Corning, N. Y.
after 1913

# IDEAL

Hod. C. Dunfee
Charleston, W. Va.
1910

# Japana

M. V. Garnsey
Spring Lake &
Grand Haven, Mich.
1906

John E. Kemple Glass Works
E. Palestine, Ohio

Justrite Mfg., Co.
Chicago, Illinois
1911

J. Hoare & Co.
Corning, N. Y.
1895

Illinois Glass Co.
Alton, Illinois
1915

Iroquois Glass Ltd.
Candiac, P. Q.
current

Jeanette Glass Co.
Jeanette, Pa.
current

Hope Glass Works
E. Providence, R. I.

Indiana Glass Co.
Dunkirk, Ind.
current

Imperial Glass Corp.
Bellaire, Ohio
current

Gebr. Putzler Glass Works
Penzig, Germany
1901

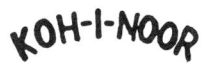

Richard Murr
San Francisco, Calif.
1905

Kimble Glass Products
Toledo, Ohio
current

Andrew Koch
New York, N. Y.
1875

Macbeth-Evans Glass Co.
Pittsburg, Pa.
1880

Liberty Glass Co.
Sapulpa, Okla.
current

Lornita Glass Corp.
Point Marion, Pa.

after 1913

Kerr Glass Mfg., Corp.
Sand Springs, Okla.
1903

Kerr Glass Mfg. Corp.
Sand Springs, Okla.
1904

Koehler & Hinrichs
St. Paul, Minnesota
1911

E. De La Chapelle
&
A. M. Paturle
Brooklyn, N. Y.
1876

## LGW

Laurens Glass Works
Laurens, S. C.
current

Lotus Glass Co.
Barnesville, Ohio
1911

Knox Glass Inc.
Knox, Pa.
current

Kruth China Co.
St. Louis, Mo.

after 1913

Lamb Glass Co.
Mt. Vernon, Ohio
current

Libbey Glass Division
Owens-Illinois
Toledo, Ohio
current

## LUSTRE

R. E. Tongue & Bros.
Philadelphia, Pa.
1894

1895

1896

1901

1901

1933

1933

Six marks of
Libby Glass Co.
now a division of
Owens-Illinois Glass Co.
Toledo, Ohio

Owens-Illinois Glass Co.
Toledo, Ohio
current

1910

## LEOTRIC

John William Gayner
Salem, N. J.
1903

Two Jefferson marks

Jefferson Glass Co.
Follansbee, W. Va.
1913

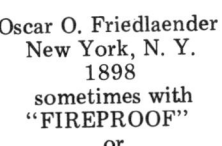

Oscar O. Friedlaender
New York, N. Y.
1898
sometimes with
"FIREPROOF"
or
"INDIFFERENT"

## LIGHTNING

Henry W. Putnam
New York, N. Y.
1882

**MANHATTAN OVAL**

Whitall, Tatum & Co.
New York, N. Y.

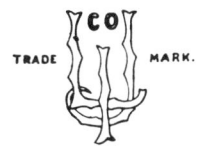

Albert Legrand
Manchester, N. H.
1898

The McBride Glass Co.
Salem, W. Va.
1913

S. Maw, Son & Sons
London, England
1871

T. C. Wheaton Co.
Milville, N. J.
1903

Metro Glass
Jersey City, N. J.
current

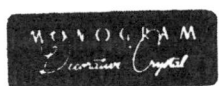

Monogram Glass Co., Inc.
Evanston, Ill.
after 1913

Mountaineer Glass Co.
Weston, W. Va.

MARIANI-LIQUEUR
1882

COCA MARIANI

Mariani & Co.
New York, N. Y.
1905

MILLER

Edward Miller & Co.
Meriden, Conn.
1893

MOONLIGHT.

Moonlight Patent Lamp Co.
Liverpool, England
1894

Marion Flint Glass Co.
Marion, Ind.
1894

MARION

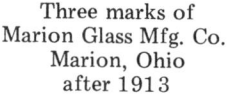

Three marks of
Marion Glass Mfg. Co.
Marion, Ohio
after 1913

MOUNT
VERNON

Cook & Bernheimer Co.
New York, N. Y.
1890

Henry Martin
Pittsburg, Pa.
1883

Merritt Glass Co.
Morganstown, W. Va.
after 1913

Metro Glass & China Dec. Co.
Brooklyn, N. Y.
after 1913

MEDALLION

Three marks by
M. S. Burr & Co.
Boston, Mass.
1874

National Glass Mfg. Co.
Buffalo, N. Y.
after 1913

Moritz Kirchberger
New York, N. Y.
1898

Moritz Kirchberger
New York, N. Y.
1903

Morganstown Glassware Guild
Morganstown, W. Va.
current

Welsbach Co.
Gloucester City, N. J.
1910

**NEARCUT**

Cambridge Glass Co.
Cambridge, Ohio
1904

Passow & Sons
Chicago, Illinois
1914

Obear-Nester Glass Co.
St. Louis, Missouri
1895

Obear-Nester Glass Co.
St. Louis, Missouri
1895

Quicksilver Mining Co.
New Almaden, Calif.
1864

1896
Rex

Obear-Nester Glass Co.
St. Louis, Missouri
1899

1900
VICTOR

Edward Kavalier
Neu Sazawa, Austria
1910

Stanley S. Cline
Philadelphia, Pa.
1896

**NULITE**

National Stamping &
Electric Works
Chicago, Illinois
1908

NIGHT DRIVERS FRIEND

Roberts & Mathews
Ansonia, Ohio
1905

Northwestern Glass Co.
Seattle, Wash.
current

137

Oil City Glass Co.
Oil City, Pa.

Current

# O-U-KID

Robert A. Vancleave
Philadelphia, Pa.
1909

Pennsylvania Glass Products Co.
Pittsburg, Pa.

Austin D. Palmer
Coshocton, Ohio
1892

Pilgrim Glass Corp.
Huntington, W. Va.

Geo. Borgfeldt & Co.
New York, N. Y.
1912

# OLD SOL

Hawthorne Mfg., Co.
Bridgeport, Conn.
1910

# OVINGTON'S

Ovington Bros., Co.
New York, N. Y.
1895

Pierce Glass Co.
Pt. Alleghany, Pa.
current

Philadelphia Vacuum
Specialty Co.
Philadelphia, Pa.
1911

# PRANA

Aerators Ltd.
London, England

Centadrink Filters Co.
New York, N. Y.
1913

Warren Fruit Jar Co.
Fairfield, Iowa

Pacific Coast Glass Works
San Francisco, Calif.
1913

Otis A. Mygatt
New York, N. Y.
1901

Phoenix Glass Co.
Monaca, Pa.
1881

# PRESCUT

McKee-Jeanette
Glass Works
Jeanette, Pa.
1903

Corning Glass Works
Corning, N. Y.

# POLYCASE

Gleason-Tiebout Glass Co.
New York, N. Y.
1910

Royal Glass Co.
Centralia, Ill.
1910

Franz A. Mehlem
Bonn, Germany
1890

Schloss Crockery Co.
San Francisco, Calif.
1910

1897

C. F. Rumpp & Sons Inc.
Philadelphia, Pa.
1892

United States Glass Co.
Pittsburg, Pa.
1911

H. Perilstein
Philadelphia, Pa.
1908

Justin Tharaud
New York, N. Y.
after 1913

1904
Three marks of
Schott & Gen
Jena, Germany

Reid Bros.
San Francisco, Calif.
1909

L. Rose & Co., Ltd.
London, England
1874

F. Schmidt & Co.
Stamford, Conn.
after 1913

Seneca Glass Co.
Morganstown, W. Va.
after 1913

1905

139

# SIGNET

Chicago Heights Bottle Co.
Chicago Heights, Ill.
1913

Sloan Glass Co.
Cumberland, Md.
after 1913

L. Straus & Sons
New York, N. Y.
1894

Taylor, Smith & Taylor Co.
East Liverpool, Ohio
after 1913

Alart & McGuire
New York, N. Y.
1908

St. Gobain
Paris, France
1895

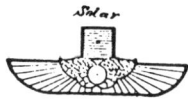

Solar Prism Co.
Cleveland, Ohio
1899

STUART CRYSTAL

Stuart Glass Works
Stourbridge, England
current

Tiffin Art Glass Corp.
Tiffin, Ohio
after 1913

Thatcher Glass Mfg. Co
New York, N. Y.

# SILEX

Silex Co.
Malden, Mass.
1913

Silver City Glass Co., Inc.
Meriden, Conn.
after 1913

# SUDAN

General Electric Co.
Schenectady, N. Y.
1913

Syl-Fau Art Glass Co.
S. Hanover, Mass.
after 1913

# TIP TOP

Charles Boldt Glass Co.
Cincinnati, Ohio
1904

Thomas Wightman
Pittsburg, Pa.
1894

Livermore & Knight Co.
Providence, R. I.
1907

Edward A. Power & Co.
Pittsburgh, Pa.
1897

United Grocers Co.
Toledo, Ohio
1913

Washington Co.
Washington, Pa.
after 1913

Wheaton Glass Co.
Millville, N. J.
current

C. E. Wheelock & Co.
Peoria, Illinois
1898

# SUN

Two marks of
Sun Vapor
Street Light Co.
Canton, Ohio
1877

Lighting Studios Co.
New York, N. Y.
1913

# VERKO

Florence Talbot Westbrook
San Francisco, Calif.
1912

Two marks of
Westmoreland Specialty Co.
Grapeville, Pa.
1910

## SUN-FLASH

Alexander Hemsley
Philadelphia, Pa.
1892

Two marks of
Universal Glass Products Co.
Parkersburg, W. Va.
current

early

Viking Glass Co.
New Martinsville, W. Va.
current

Erskine B. Van Houten
White Plains, N. Y.

## WHICHWAY

J. W. Tobin
New York, N. Y.
1909

# TRADE MARKS ON GLASS — MISCELLANEOUS

**THE BEST**

Gotham Co.
New York, N. Y.
1891

**AIR-O-LITE**

Hydro Carbon Co.
Wichita, Kansas
1911

Bottlers Protective Assn.
Baltimore, Maryland
1888

**SOCONY**

Standard Oil Co.
New York, N. Y.
1908

1914

1910

Two marks of
Smalley, Kivlan & Onthank
Boston, Mass.

L. A. Becker Co.
Jersey City, N. J.
1908

Belle Vernon
Mapes Dairy Co.
Cleveland, Ohio
1914

**GLOBE**

Hemingray Glass Co.
Covington, Ky.
1886

Fr. Steuben & Co.
Erfurt, Germany
1892

Macbeth-Evans Glass Co.
Pittsburg, Pa.
1895

Weiss & Biheller Ltd.
London, England
1906

Klepa Arts
Hollywood, Calif.

**CALORIS**

**VACO**

Two marks of
John G. Lyman
1907

Dithridge & Co.
Pittsburg, Pa.
1896

1884

1887

1890

1896

1897

1900

1901

1901

1907

**O K**
1898

**CORONET**
1900

**ROCK**
1901

**LUCKY CROSS**
1908

**PARIAN**
1911

1908

UNICORN
1911

**GRANITE**
1890

**VICTOR TOP**
1898

The above marks
shown with dates
are of
Gill Brothers Co.
Steubenville, Ohio

**ACMELITE**
1911

**GLORIA**
1912

# *Ceramics China Porcelain and Pottery*

### NOTES ON MARKS

Marks shown here are not necessarily the same size as those found on ceramics. Marks were of different sizes according to the item on which they were used. Cups and saucers often have smaller marks than those on dinner plates or soup tureens.

Since there are more than 4000 china marks attributed to Britain alone it is obvious that a handbook can contain only a sampling from each of several countries. (See list of reference books for further sources of information).

## TYPES OF MARKS FOUND ON CERAMICS

Applied Moulded Mark

Impressed mark and artist's incised monogram.

Painted mark.

Printed mark.

APPLIED MOULDED MARKS. Impressed marks in relief. Formed apart from the piece and put in place prior to firing.

INCISED MARKS. Marks are scratched into the soft clay before the initial firing.

IMPRESSED MARKS. A metal die was used to imprint names or initials into the ware before firing.

PAINTED MARKS. Marks were applied either under or over the glaze at the time of decorating the ware.

PRINTED MARKS. Came into general use about 1800. Previously printed marks were used only on porcelain decorated with blue under the glaze. Printed marks were applied to the ware by transfer printing prior to or after glazing. During the 20th century a rubber stamp or stencil was used by some potters to apply their printed marks.

# Dating - Clues

Information regarding the age of an item can be acquired from the mark found on ceramic pieces. The following list is useful, it provides a general time period that certain information began to appear in the marks of European and North American manufacturers.

| BEGINNING ABOUT – | WORDS/PHRASES ETC. MARKED ON CERAMICS – |
|---|---|
| 1810 | Pattern name first marked on china. |
| 1813 | "Ironstone" |
| 1820 | "Brevete" French: patented |
| 1842 to 1883 | Lozenge shaped British Registry Mark used. |
| 1850 | "Royal" as part of many English marks, such as Royal Worcester. |
| 1861 | "Limited" or "Ltd" |
| 1862 | "Trademark" on English made pieces. |
| 1875 | "Trademark" on American made pieces. |
| 1876 | "Copyright Reserved" on English made pieces. |
| 1880 | "Hand Painted" First appeared in mark on hand decorated china. |
| 1884 | "Registered" "Reg" or "Rd" folowed by a number – revised British Registry Mark. |
| 1887 | "Made in ........" By law, in England, imported goods had to be marked with country or origin. |
| 1890's | "Warranted" Used with factory/company name. |
| 1891 | Country of origin. Items imported to the U.S.A. after 1891 were marked with the country of origin, e.g. "England " or 'Germany" to conform with the McKinley Tariff Act of 1891. |

| BEGINNING ABOUT – | WORDS/PHRASES ETC. MARKED ON CERAMICS – |
|---|---|
| 1891 to 1921 | "Nippon" Country of origin name (Japan) or as part of company name. |
| 1892 | "Copyright" registered with the U.S. Patent Office. |
| 1900 | "Alumnite" |
| 1900 | "Bone China" or "English Bone China" Although developed about 1800, the words were not part of the mark on bone china until the twentieth century. |
| 1900 | "Depose" French: registered. |
| 1900 | "Gesetzlich Geschutze" Or "Gest Gesch" German: patened or registered. |
| 1900 | "Patented" |
| 1900 | "U.S. Patent" Patented in the United States. Found on goods made in America or abroad. |
| 1901 | "Semi-vitreaous" or "S.V." |
| 1902 | "Patent Applied For" |
| 1903 to 1945 | "Underglaze" |
| 1914 | © Registered with the U.S. Copyright Office. |
| 1920's | "Warranted 22 Karat/carat gold" |
| 1923 | "Cooking Ware" on ceramic ware suitable for use in an oven. |
| 1927 | "Designed expressly for...." "Made expressly for...." or "Made exclusively for...." Name of merchant/customer included in mark along with manufacturer's name. |
| 1930's | "22 karat/carat" |
| 1930's | "Union Label" or "Union Made" |
| 1932 | "Reg. U.S. Patent Off." |
| 1933 | "Oven-proof" or "Oven Tested" |
| 1938 to 1952 | "Refrigerator Ware" |
| 1940 | "Incorporated" |
| 1940 | "Patent Pending" |
| 1944 | Detergent Proof" |

| BEGINNING ABOUT – | WORDS/PHRASES ETC. MARKED ON CERAMICS – |
|---|---|
| 1945 to 1949 | "U.S. Zone" or "U.S. Zone, Germany" Made in the American occupied zone of Germany following World War Two. |
| 1945 to 1952 | "Made in Occupied Japan" Period of American occupation after World War Two. |
| 1949 to 1990 | "East Germany" |
| 1949 to 1990 | "West Germany" |
| 1949 | ® registered with the U.S. Patent and Trademark Office. |
| 1955 | "Dishwasher Proof" |
| 1960 | "Fast Colour" or "Permanent Colours" |
| 1960's | "Craze Proof" Under normal conditions fine lines or cracks will not develop in glaze. |
| 1960's | "Freezer - Oven - Table" |
| 1970 | "Microwave Safe" |
| 1978 | "Oven-to-Table" |

# Glossary Ceramics

AGATE WARE: Earthenware made to look like agate stone.

APPLIED DECORATION: Decoration modelled separately from the body then attached.

BACKSTAMP: Another term for "mark."

BASALT: Black stoneware used to make decorative pieces; vases, plaques, figures, etc. Many fine pieces were made by Wedgwood.

BISQUE/BISCUIT: Pottery or porcelain that has been fired but not glazed. Became fashionable during the late 1700's. Bisque pieces are found undecorated in their natural "biscuit" shade or decorated in pastel colours.

BODY: Ceramic term, e.g. "pottery body" - "porcelain body" - the mixture of clay and other materials used to make a ceramic article.

BLUE & WHITE: White porcelain or pottery body decorated in cobalt blue under the glaze. This form of decoration originated in China at the beginning of the 15th century.

BONE CHINA: Patented in 1748 by Thomas Fry of Bow and by Barr at Worcester. Made by Josiah Spode, Stoke-on-Trent in the late 1700's. Bone china became the standard English body during the 1800's. Translucent, pure white, made with the addition of ash from calcined (burned) bones.

CERAMIC: Pottery, porcelain. From the Greek word Keramos meaning pottery or potter's earth.

CHINESE EXPORT: Porcelain made in China for the European market during the 18th and 19th centuries.

CRACKLE/CRAZING: A network of fine lines. In porcelain the crazing of the glaze was often intentional for decorative purposes. In pottery crazing, a flaw, may have taken place after manufacture due to unequal contraction of glaze or body.

CREAMWARE: Cream coloured, chiefly for the table, first made at Staffordshire, England about 1740. Perfected by Josiah Wedgwood, later made by other English potters. Wedgwood's form of creamware was sometimes called Queen's Ware. Decorating generally consisted of beading, feather-edge, shell edge or octagon shaped borders.

CROCKERY: Earthenware or stoneware, utilitarian.

DELFT: Tin-glazed ware made in Holland at Delft, decorated in blue, although other colours were sometimes used. Similar ware was made in England.

EARTHENWARE: Vessels, dishes and decorative pieces of baked clayware that is not changed into a glasslike substance by fusion due to heat, and therefore, is porous and lacks the finish and translucency of porcelain or china. Glazed and unglazed.

ENAMEL PAINTING: Colouring material made from a mixture of metallic oxides and a flux. Hand painted enamel decoration is applied over the glaze, fired to fix it upon the ware and can be distinguished by its slight relief.

FACTORY NUMBER: Found on the base of a piece, usually near the factory mark, indicates factory's reference number for pattern or date etc.

FAIENCE: Tin-glazed earthenware made in France.

FIRING: To bake in a potter's kiln. The process of turning clay into ceramic by baking in a kiln. Time and temperature vary depending on the nature of the work.

GAUDY DUTCH: English porcelain and earthenware made to resemble Imari ware, simply decorated with flowers and bright splashes of colour. Originally made for those with modest incomes, and did not prove popular. Large quantities were "dumped" on the American market during the early 1800's.

GAUDY IRONSTONE: Ca. 1850's. Heavier than Gaudy Dutch, similarly decorated in bright colours.

GAUDY WELSH: Made during the mid 1800's. Decorated in blue/purple, gold, green and red in the Imari style.

GLAZE: A glasslike substance, applied as a thin coating to most porcelain and pottery making it impervious to liquids.

HARD-PASTE: First made by the Chinese late in the 17th century. Two essential ingredients of hard-paste porcelain are kaolin (china clay) and petuntse (china stone) both products of feldspar rock. Hard-paste porcelain is fired at temperatures of about 1450 degrees centigrade. The Chinese standard test for porcelain is that it ring when struck; for the Europeans translucency is important.

IMARI WARE: First made in Japan, exported to Europe and North America, got its name from the port Imari from where it was shipped. Gaudily decorated in red, blue and orange floral patterns with green foliage. Copied by English, Chinese and European factories.

IMPRESSED: Mark or decoration pressed into clay using a metal die.

INCISED: Mark or decoration scratched into clay using a pointed instrument.

IRONSTONE: A hard heavy ceramic pattented in 1813 at Staffordshire, England by Charles J. Mason.

JASPER: A hard stoneware made, and perfected, by Wedgwood since about 1775. Slightly translucent, coloured throughout - blue; green; black; pink; lilac or yellow. Wedgwood's blue jasper ware decorated in white relief is probably the best known and most often copied. "Jasper Dip" is different from jasper ware, it is dipped and coloured only on the surface.

KILN: A large oven or furnace used to fire ceramics.

LIMOGES: A porcelain making centre in France. Large deposits of kaolin were found in the area, hard and soft-paste porcelain have been made at Limoges since about 1771. By 1850, because of mass production methods, Limoges became one of the largest porcelain producing centres in Europe.

LITHOPHANE: A decorative transparency of translucent porcelain. An illustration becomes visible when viewed by transmitted light. Made for candle and lamp shades, to hang in windows and sometimes found in the base of steins or mugs.

LUSTRE: A thin coating of metal oxides. Iridescent, used to decorate the surface of pottery and sometimes porcelain. Large quantities of lustre ware were made in England from about 1800 to 1850. The metals used were copper, platinum and gold, copper being the most common.

MAIOLICA (Majolica): Italian tin-glazed earthenware with painted decoration consisting of blue, green, yellow, purple and orange. Made during the 15th to 18th centuries.

MAJOLICA: Pottery decorated in relief beneath a coloured glaze. Introduced by Minton in the 1850's, originally tin-glazed. Made at various factories in England.

MARK: Maker's mark or trade-mark found on the base of many ceramic pieces. Much information can be acquired from a mark, such as, factory name, place of manufacture, date of manufacture, pattern name, artist's name, etc., etc.

NANKING WARE: Blue and white porcelain made in China specifically for export to the U.S. and Europe. Popular during the middle and late 1800's.

PARIAN: So-called because of its resemblance to the white marble quarried on the Greek island of Paros. White unglazed hard-paste porcelain, smooth like marble. Parian ware includes busts, figures, groups, statues and doll's heads.

PATE-SUR-PATE (Clay-on-Clay): A decorative technique. Layers of white or tinted clay are applied to the pottery or porcelain body and tooled to give a cameo effect.

PORTNEUF: Crockery, bowls, jugs, mugs etc. for the kitchen. Pieces are sponge decorated with foliage, animal and bird designs. Made at potteries in the U.K. and shipped in large quantities to Canada during the late 1800's and early 1900's.

POTTERY: See earthenware.

PUZZLE JUG: Pottery drinking jug, pierced at the neck. In order to drink from such a jug the drinker must locate a hidded tube, block all other apertures and thus drain the jug by sucking. Popular during the 17th and 18th centuries.

QUEEN'S WARE: See creamware.

RED WARE: Red stoneware, made in North America and England.

RELIEF: Carved or moulded decoration, projects from the surface.

ROCKINGHAM: Made in England and North America. Pottery made at Bennington, Vermont is called Rockingham ware because the glaze, a rich mottled brown, is a copy of the glaze that was used at the Rockingham pottery in Swinton, England.

SALT GLAZE: Glaze for stoneware produced by throwing salt into the kiln at a certain temperature. Hard, transparent glaze, often with a pitted surface.

SEMI-PORCELAIN: A fine bodied china, white, very hard. Semi-porcelain tableware was made at the George Grainger & Co. works, Worcester, England.

SLIP: Liquid potter's clay or paste used to decorate pottery or used to cover the whole body of an earthenware vessel.

SLIPWARE: Pottery decorated or coated with slip.

SOFT-PASTE: The formulae for soft-paste porcelains vary, it is fired at a lower temperature than hard-paste porcelain, about 1100 degrees centigrade.

SPATTERWARE/SPONGEWARE: Pottery decorated by daubing colour on using a sponge. Popular during the last half of the 19th century.

STAFFORDSHIRE: A generic term to describe pottery made at factories in the district of Staffordshire, England.

STONEWARE: Heavy pottery, fused into a hard vitrified mass, opaque, non-porous.

TERRA-COTTA: Red, unglazed, porous earthenware.

TIN GLAZE: Lead glaze used in pottery, made opaque by the addition of oxide of tin.

TOBY JUG: A pottery jug made in the form of a person wearing a three cornered hat. First made in Staffordshire, England during the late 1760's. A toby often portrays a traditional English character - the parson, the snuff taker, the sailor or a personality from Dickens and frequently well known individuals.

TRANSFER PRINTING: A method of decorating china, introduced about 1755 at Staffordshire, England. Transfer printing made it possible for the same pattern to be reproduced with little handwork. A copper plate with an engraved impression was inked then a print was made on a thin piece of paper which was then transferred to the surface of the piece of china being decorated, the design was fixed during the firing process.

VITREOUS: Non-porous, glasslike.

# Ceramics

England; Europe; Japan; etc.

## ARKINSTALL & SONS (LTD.)

Arkinstall & Sons (Ltd.), Stoke-on-Trent, Staffordshire, England, 1904 - 1924. Taken over by Robinson & Leadbeater, A.J. Robinson & Sons and by Caulden Ltd.

A & S

1904 - 1912

ARCADIAN

1904 - 1924

ARCADIAN CHINA

1904 - 1924

Arcadian China

1904 - 1920

1904 - 1924

1904 - 1924

# G.L. ASHWORTH & BROS. (LTD.)

Established 1862 at Hanley, Staffordshire, England. Manufacturers of earthenware and ironstone etc. Made Mason's Patent Ironstone, used the Mason's mark.

| ASHWORTH | G.L.A. & BROS. | A. BROS. |
|---|---|---|
| 1862 - 80 | 1862 - 90 | 1862 - 90 |

1862 - 1890

Ca. 1862 used Mason's mark.

1862+ "Ashworths" added to mark. "England" added after 1891

1862+ Variations occur

1880+ Variations occur

1880+ "England" added 1891 "Made in England" — 20th century

1932+ Variations occur. Pattern names or styles may be included.

1957+    1957+

# IRISH BELLEEK

Belleek Pottery, David McBirney & Co., Belleek, County Fermanagh, Ireland, 1863 -

1863 - 1880

BELLEEK
CO. FERMANAGH

1863 - 1890

FERMANAGH
POTTERY

1863 - 1890

1863 - 1891

1891 - 1926

black: 1927 - 1941
green: 1946 - 1955

## AMERICAN BELLEEK

1894 - 1906
Ceramic Art Co.
Trenton, N.J.

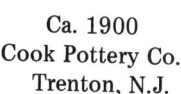
Ca. 1900
Cook Pottery Co.
Trenton, N.J.

Ca. 1895
Columbian Art Pottery Co.
Trenton, N.J.

1926 - 30
Coxon Pottery
Wooster, Ohio

AMERICAN BELLEEK Cont.

1882
Etruria Pottery (Ott & Brewer)
Trenton, N.J.

1883

1889+
Knowles, Taylor & Knowles
East Liverpool, Ohio

1906 - 1924
Lenox Inc.
Trenton, N.J.

MORGAN
BELLEEK
AZURE

ORIENT

1923 - 1934
Morgan Belleek, Canton, Ohio

1879 - 1912
Willets Mfg. Co.
Trenton, N.J.

## BING & GRONDAHL - Copenhagen, Denmark

Established 1853, manufacturers of stoneware, dinnerware and figurines. Introduced an annual Christmas plate in 1895.

| | | | |
|---|---|---|---|
| B&G  1853+ |  Danish China Works COPENHAGEN  B.&G.  1895+ | DANISH CHINA WORKS  B & G  1898+ | DANISH CHINA WORKS  B & G  1899+ |
| MADE IN DENMARK  B & G  1902+ | COPENHAGEN  B&G  1914+ | DANMARK  B&G  1915+ | DANMARK  B & G  1948+ |
| MADE IN DENMARK  1952-1958 | MADE IN DENMARK  1958+ | DENMARK  1962+ |  COPENHAGEN PORCELAIN MADE IN DENMARK  B&G  1970+ |

current

# T. & R. BOOTE LTD.

Waterloo pottery (and other addresses) at Burslem, Staffordshire England, 1842 - 1964. Manufacturers of earthenware, parian, tiles etc. In 1906 the Waterloo pottery was closed, the firm continued making tiles.

T & R B            T & R BOOTE            T B & S
1850+              Late 1800's

1890 - 1906        1890 - 1906            1890 - 1906

## CAUGHLEY — COALPORT MARKS

Caughley-Salopian Works founded by Thomas Turner, 1775. J.Rose & Co. took over and moved the works to Coalport (Colebrook Dale). Later became Coalport Porcelain Works, now part of the Wedgwood group.

1805 - 1815        1810 - 1925

1820        1820 - 1830        1830 - 1850        JOHN ROSE & CO.
COALBROOKDALE
SHROPSHIRE

1830 - 1850

Caughley - Coalport Cont.

   J. R. & CO.

1845 - 1855    1850 - 1870    1851 - 1861

      COALPORT AD 1750

1861 - 1875    1870 - 1880    1875 - 1881

1881 - 1939    1945 - 1960
"England" added from 1891

   COALBROOKDALE
           BY COALPORT
           MADE IN ENGLAND

1960+           1960+

## CAULDON

Cauldon Ltd., Shelton, Hanley, Staffordshire, England, 1905 - 1920.
Cauldon Potteries Ltd., Stoke, Staffordshire, England, 1920 - 1962.

CAULDON ENGLAND

1905 - 1920 Pattern name often included with mark.

1905 - 1920
Variations occur

1905 - 1920

1930 - 1950
Variations occur

1950 - 1962

# JOSEPH CLEMENTSON

Pheonix Works, Shelton, Hanley, Staffordshire, England, 1839 - 1864.

Clementson Bros. (Ltd.) Pheonix Works, and Bell Works, Hanley, Staffordshire, England, 1865 - 1916.

J.C.       J. CLEMENTSON
1839 - 1864      1839 - 1864

Variations occur, pattern name and/or Pheonix bird may be included.

**CLEMENTSON BROS.**

1867 - 1880      1870+      1910+
Variations occur

1901 - 1913      1913 - 1916

## COCHRANE/BRITANNIA

R. Cochrane & Co., Verreville Pottery, Glasgow, Scotland, 1846 - 1918. Earthenware, china, stoneware.

Cochrane & Fleming, Britannia Pottery, St. Rollox, Glasgow, Scotland, 1896 - 1920.

Britannia Pottery Co. Ltd., St. Rollex, Glasgow, Scotland, 1920 - 1935.

R C & Co.

1846+

R, COCHRAN & CO.

GLASGOW

1846 - 1918

C & F

1896+

C & F
G
1896+

1896 - 1920

ROYAL
IRONSTONE CHINA

COCHRAN & FLEMING
GLASGOW.    BRITAIN

1900 - 1920

FLEMING
PORCELAIN OPAQUE
GLASGOW, BRITAIN

1900 - 1920

1920 - 1935
Variations occur

HIAWATHA
Trade-name
1925+

## DAVENPORT MARKS

Factory established at Longport, Staffordshire, England in 1793, closed in 1887. Earthenware main product: porcelain manufactured from about 1820. Much Davenport ware is blue printed. Tea and dessert services in "Japan" and "India" patterns were popular lines. Landscape plaques were painted by James Rouse.

DAVENPORT

1793 - 1805

Davenport

1793 - 1810
With or without anchor

1795+

1795+

1800 - 1860

1805 - 1820

1805 - 1820

1805 - 1820

DAVENPORT
LONGPORT

1815+ With or without anchor, date marks found on earthenware from mid 1800's.

1820's

1820 - 1860 Other variations occur - with the factory name and often pattern name.

1830 - 1880

W. DAVENPORT & CO.

1830 - 1882

1840 - 1867

1842 - 1883
With British Registry Mark.

Davenport Cont.

| DAVENPORT PATENT |  |  |  DAVENPORT LONGPORT STAFFORDSHRE |
|---|---|---|---|
| 1850 - 1870 | 1860 - 1870 | 1860 - 1887 | 1870 - 1886 |

DAVENPORTS LTD.

1881 - 1887

DAVENPORTS LIMITED

1881 - 1887

## SOME OTHER FACTORIES AT LONGPORT, STAFFORDSHIRE

W. CLOWES

1783 - 1796

Phillips, Longport

1822 - 1834

A W
L
ENGLAND
(Arthur Wood)

1904 - 1928

1828 - 1830

J R
L
Rogers, J & G.

1784 - 1814

# DELFT

Various potteries have operated in and near the town of Delft in Holland since the mid 1700's. Dutch pottery marked with the name "Delft" dates from the late 1800's to the present.

Since 1879 Delft pottery has been marked with a year code impressed in the base of each piece near the factory back stamp.

DELFT YEAR CODE 1879 —

| 1879 - A  | 1880 - B  | 1881 - C     | 1882 - D     | 1883 - E  |
|-----------|-----------|--------------|--------------|-----------|
| 1884 - F  | 1885 - G  | 1886 - H     | 1887 - I     | 1888 - J  |
| 1889 - K  | 1890 - L  | 1891 - M     | 1892 - N     | 1893 - O  |
| 1894 - P  | 1895 - Q  | 1896 - R     | 1897 - S     | 1898 - T  |
| 1899 - U  | 1900 - V  | 1901 - W     | 1902 - X     | 1903 - Y  |
| 1904 - Z  | 1905 - AA | 1906 - AB    | 1907 - AC    | 1908 - AD |
| 1909 - AE | 1910 - AF | 1911 - AG    | 1912 - AH    | 1913 - AI |
| 1914 - AJ | 1915 - AK | 1916 - AL    | 1917 - AM    | 1918 - AN |
| 1919 - AO | 1920 - AP | 1921 - AQ    | 1922 - AR    | 1923 - AS |
| 1924 - AT | 1925 - AU | 1926 - AV    | 1927 - AW    | 1928 - AX |
| 1929 - AY | 1930 - AZ | 1931 - BA    | 1932 - BB    | 1933 - BC |
| 1934 - BD | 1935 - BE | 1936 - BF    | 1937 - BG    | 1938 - BH |
| 1939 - BI | 1940 - BJ | 1941 - BK    | 1942 - BL    | 1943 - BM |
| 1944 - BN | 1945 - BO | 1946 - BP/BQ | 1947 - BR    | 1948 - BS |
| 1949 - BT | 1950 - BU | 1951 - BV    | 1952 - BW    | 1953 - BX |
| 1954 - BY | 1955 - BZ | 1956 - CA    | 1957 - CB    | 1958 - CC |
| 1959 - CD | 1960 - CE | 1961 - CF    | 1962 - CG    | 1963 - CH |
| 1964 - CI | 1965 - CJ | 1966 - CK    | 1967 - CL    | 1968 - CM |
| 1969 - CN | 1970 - CO | 1971 - CP/CQ | 1972 - CR    | 1973 - CS |
| 1974 - CT | 1975 - CU | 1976 - CV    | 1977 - CW    | 1978 - CX |
| 1979 - CY | 1980 - CZ | 1981 - DA    | 1982 - DB    | 1983 - DC |

and so on —

## DERBY MARKS

Porcelain was made at Derby, England from about 1745 under various owners and managers. The works closed in 1845, re-established Ca. 1876 as Derby Crown Porcelain Company Ltd.
NOTE: Marks are rare on early Derby pieces.

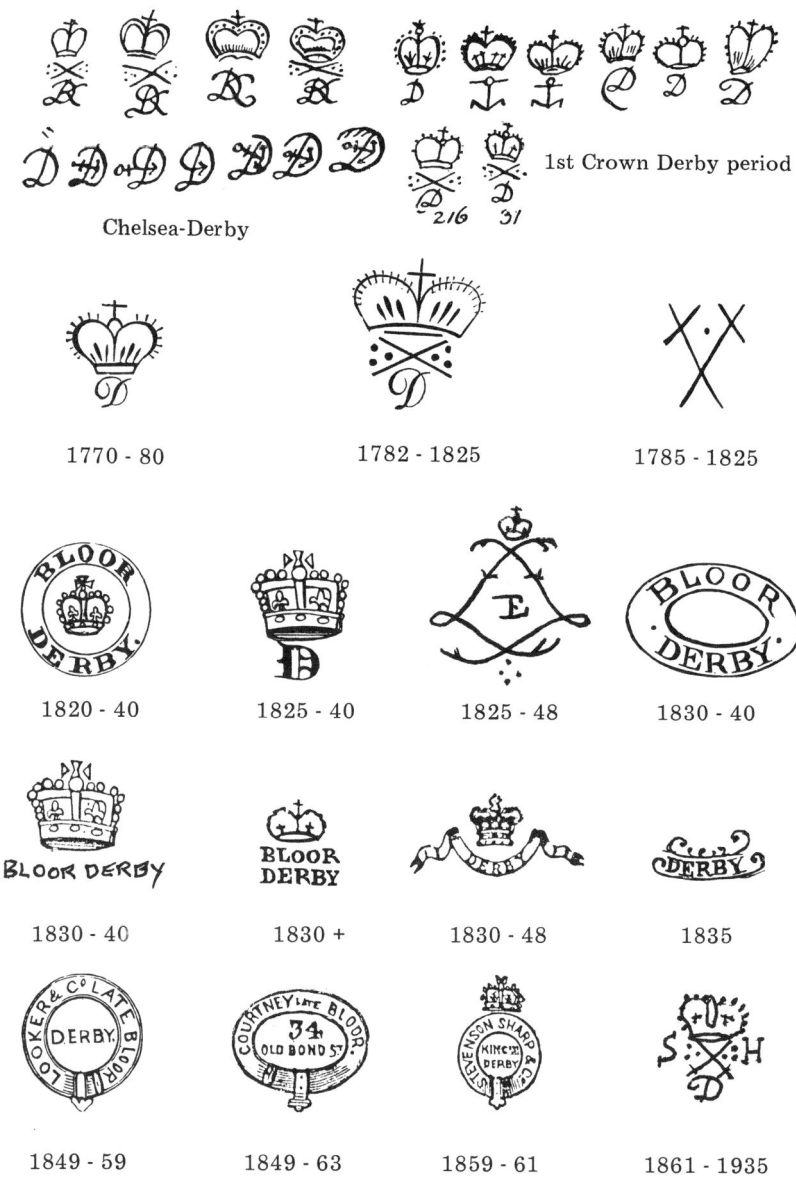

# DERBY CROWN PORCELAIN COMPANY LTD.
# ROYAL CROWN DERBY PORCELAIN CO. LTD.

1878 - 1900  Dates used in the form of numerals with this mark — e.g. 4.98 indicates April 1898.

1878 - 1890
With year cypher below the mark.

1890 +
With year cypher below the mark.
The word "England" used with this mark until 1921.
"Made in England" used with this mark from 1921.
The words "Bone China" occured after World War II.

**DERBY YEAR CYPHERS**

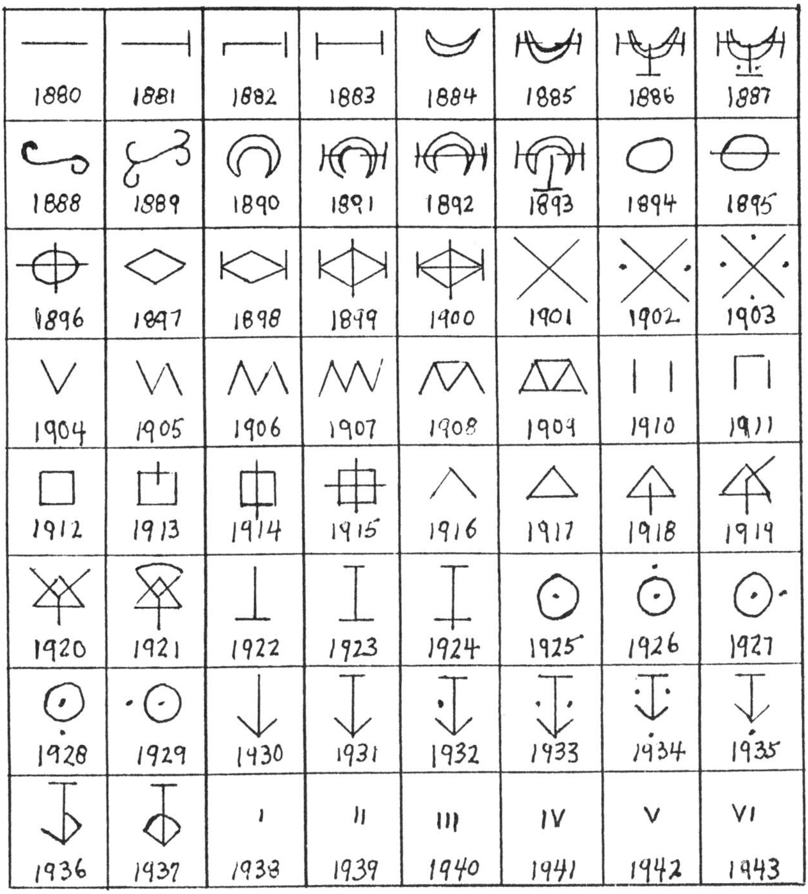

| 1880 | 1881 | 1882 | 1883 | 1884 | 1885 | 1886 | 1887 |
|---|---|---|---|---|---|---|---|
| 1888 | 1889 | 1890 | 1891 | 1892 | 1893 | 1894 | 1895 |
| 1896 | 1897 | 1898 | 1899 | 1900 | 1901 | 1902 | 1903 |
| 1904 | 1905 | 1906 | 1907 | 1908 | 1909 | 1910 | 1911 |
| 1912 | 1913 | 1914 | 1915 | 1916 | 1917 | 1918 | 1919 |
| 1920 | 1921 | 1922 | 1923 | 1924 | 1925 | 1926 | 1927 |
| 1928 | 1929 | 1930 | 1931 | 1932 | 1933 | 1934 | 1935 |
| 1936 | 1937 | 1938 | 1939 | 1940 | 1941 | 1942 | 1943 |

# DRESDEN

The "Dresden" mark is found on many pieces of porcelain in the Meissen style manufactured since the 1800's. For centuries potteries and porcelain decorators have been established in and near Dresden, Germany. A selection of the many known marks are illustrated.

## DECORATOR MARKS: DRESDEN, GERMANY

Hamman, Ca. 1866          Richard Klemm 1869 - 1916

Donath, 1872+    Used by several    Lamm 1887+
                 decorators —
                 1883 - 1893

Wolfsohn, Late 1800's.
Wolfsohn copied the Augustus Rex mark (left) until an injunction ordered her to cease in 1883.

Meyers & Son, Late 1800's.

Hirsch, 20th century.

## MANUFACTURERS – "DRESDEN"

A selection of marks — (See also, Meissen).

1903+     1905+
Carl Thieme Saxonian Porcelain
Factory, Postchappel, Soxony,
Germany.

1951 - present
Sandizell Porcelain Factory,
Sandizell, Bavaria, Germany.

1956+
Dresden Earthenware Work,
Dresden, Saxony, Germany.

Ironstone and hotel ware marked "Dresden" was made at East Liverpool, Ohio, U.S.A. by The Potter's Co-operative Co. (1882 - 1925).

Ca. 1892            Ca. 1896            Ca. 1905

## FORD

T. & C. Ford, Hanley, Staffordshire, England, 1854 - 1871.
Thomas Ford, Hanley, Staffordshire, England, 1871 - 1874.
Charles Ford, Hanley, Staffordshire, England, 1874 - 1904.

1854 - 1871

T. F

1871 - 1874

1874 - 1904     1900 - 1904     1900 - 1904

# FURNIVALS

Jacob & Thomas Furnival, Miles Bank, Shelton, Hanley, Staffordshire, England, 1843. Earthenware.

Thomas Furnival & Co., Miles Bank, Shelton, Hanley, Staffordshire, England, 1844 - 1846. Earthenware.

Jacob Furnival & Co., Cobridge, Staffordshire, England, 1845 - 1870.

Thomas Furnival & Sons, Elder Road, Cobridge, Staffordshire, England, 1871 - 1890. Earthenware.

Furnivals (Ltd.), Elder Road, Cobridge, Staffordshire, England, 1890 - 1964+. Earthenware.

|  |  |  |
|---|---|---|
| STONE CHINA J&TF | T.F. & CO. | J. F. & CO. |
| Ca. 1843 | 1844 - 1846 | 1845 - 1870 |

1871 - 1890    1871 - 1890    1871 - 1890    1871 - 1890    1878+

| | FURNIVALS ENGLAND | | FURNIVALS LTD. COBRIDGE ENGLAND | |
|---|---|---|---|---|
| 1881 - 1890 | 1890 - 1895 | 1890 - 1910 | 1895 - 1913 | 1905 - 1913 |

1913+

## GOEBEL

W. Goebel Porcelain Factory, Rodenthal, Bavaria, (West) Germany. Established 1876, made porcelain and earthenware etc. In 1934 introduced figurines based on the drawings of Sister Hummel.

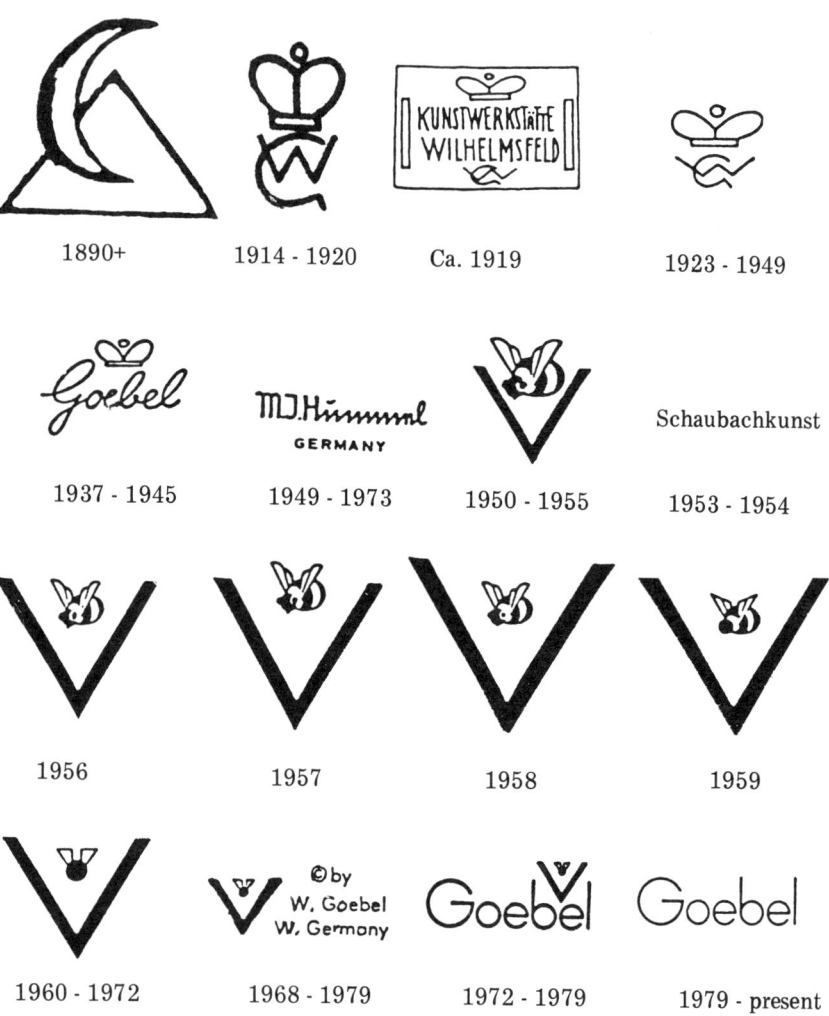

## WILLIAM HENRY GOSS (LTD.)

Falcon Pottery, Stoke-on-Trent, Staffordshire, England. Established 1858. Manufacturers of porcelain, parian and earthenware. In 1883 began making souvenir items representing attractions in tourist areas of England. Taken over by Caulden Potteries Ltd. 1934.

| W H G | W H GOSS | W H GOSS COPYRIGHT |
|---|---|---|
| 1862+ | 1862+ | 1862+ |

1862 - 1930

1891 - 1940

## GOUDA ART POTTERY

Made at several pottery workshops in the area around Gouda, Holland. Gouda pottery was decorated in the Art Nouveau style from the 1880's to the early 1980's. Pieces are marked with factory names, such as, Regina, Zenith, Zuid-Holland, Plazuid Koninklyk, Schoonhoven, and Arnhemsche etc. Frequently the pattern name and artist's initials are included in the mark. A selection of marks —

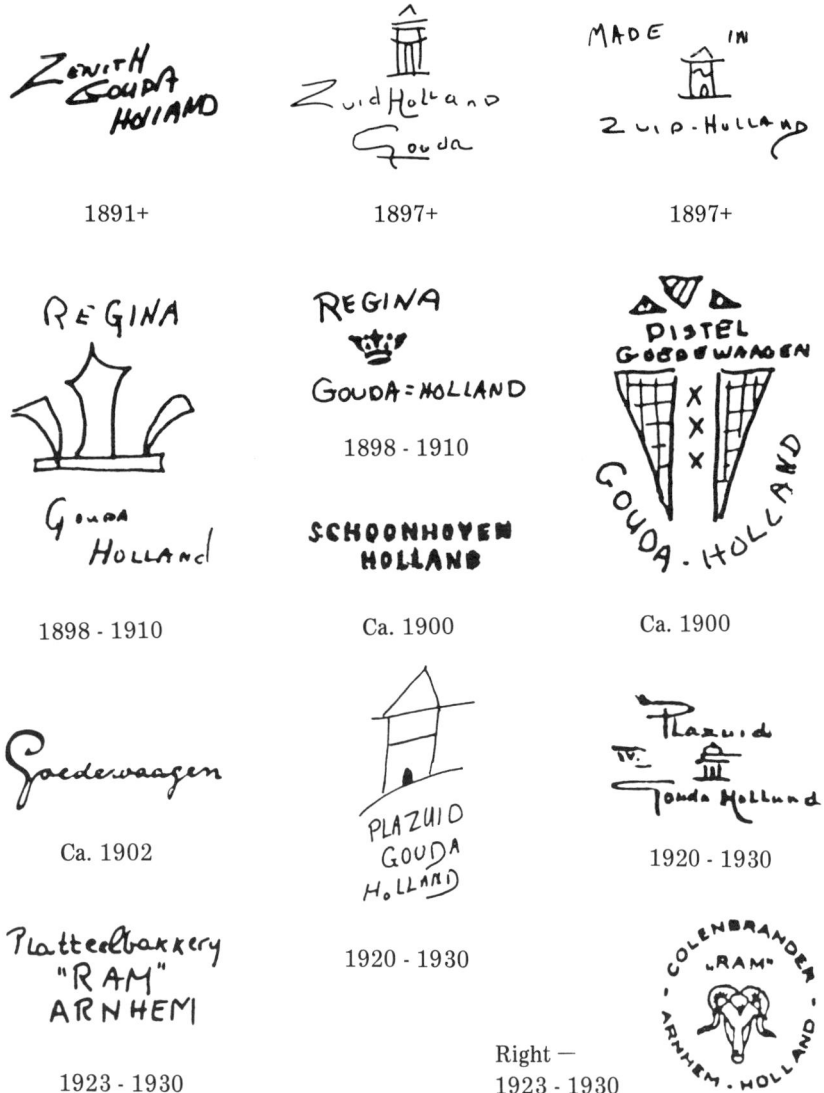

## GEORGE GRAINGER & CO.

George Grainger (& Co.), Worcester, England, 1839 - 1902. Porcelains, parian, semi-porcelain.

GEO GRAINGER
CHINA WORKS
WORCESTER
1839 - 1860. "& Co." added from Ca. 1850.

*George Grainger*
*Royal China Works*
*Worcester.*

G G & CO
S P

S P
G G W

1848+ "Semi-Porcelain" if full on some pieces.

GRAINGER
WORCESTER
S P
1848 - 1855. "Semi-Porcelain" in full on some pieces.

G W
1850 -1860. Pattern name or number may be included.

1850 - 1875

CHEMICAL
PORCELAIN
GRAINGER & CO
MANUFACTURERS
WORCESTER
1850 - 1870

G & CO W
1850 - 1889

GRAINGER & Co
WORCESTER.
1860 - 1880

G&C°
W
1870 - 1889

In 1889 George Grainger & Co. was taken over by the Worcester Royal Porcelain Co.

"England" and year letter added from 1891.

| | | |
|---|---|---|
| 1891 A | 1895 E | 1899 I |
| 1892 B | 1896 F | 1900 J |
| 1893 C | 1897 G | 1901 K |
| 1894 D | 1898 H | 1902 L |

1889 - 1902

# GRIMWADES

Grimwade Bros., Winton Potters, Hanley & Stoke, Staffordshire, England, 1886 - 1900. China, earthenware, majolica.

Grimwades Ltd., Winton, Upper Hanley and Elgin Potteries, Stoke, Staffordshire, 1900 - present. Earthenware, majolica etc.

| 1886 - 1890 | 1900+ | 1906+ | 1906+ | 1906+ |
|---|---|---|---|---|

| 1911+ | 1930+ | 1930+ | 1930+ | 1930+ |
|---|---|---|---|---|

| 1930+ | 1934 - 1939 | 1934 - 1950 | 1934 - 1950 |
|---|---|---|---|

1951+

## HOLLINGSHEAD & KIRKHAM (LTD.)

Unicorn Pottery, (Burslem 1870 - 1876), Tunstal, (1876 - 1956), Staffordshire, England. Earthenware. Factory purchased by Johnson Bros., 1956.

H. & K.

1870 - 1900

H. & K.
TUNSTALL

1870 - 1900

H. & K.
LATE WEDGWOOD

1890+

1900 - 1924

1924 - 1956

1933 - 1942

1954 - 1956

# JOHNSON BROS.

Johnson Bros. (Hanley) Ltd. Hanley and Tunstall, Staffordshire, England. Established 1883. Earthenware, ironstone etc.

1883 - 1913        1900+        1913+

1913+              1955+

## A. B. JONES & SONS LTD.

A.B. Jones & Sons (Ltd.), Grafton Works, Longton, Staffordshire, England, 1900 -

A. B. J. & SONS          A. B J. & S.          A. B. JONES & SONS
                          1900+

1900 - 1913

1913+          1920+          1930+          1935+

1949+          1950+          1957+          1961+

183

## LIMOGES

Haviland china has been manufactured continuously since the 1840's at Limoges, France. The Haviland family from New York City revolutionized the porcelain industry in France by introducing mass production techniques. Decorated in the English style for the American market this attractive china has wide appeal and is noted for its translucency, hardness and delicate patterns.

Following is a selection from the large number of 19th and 20th century marks —

HAVILAND BROTHERS & COMPANY; HAVILAND & COMPANY —

| HAVILAND DEPOSE | HAVILAND & C° | Haviland & C. Limoges | H & C° |
|---|---|---|---|
| 1855 - 65 | 1876 | 1876 - 1930 | 1879+ |

| (LAND & Co LIMOGES) | (VILAND LIMOGES) | HAVILAND & C° LIMOGES | HAVILAND FRANCE |
|---|---|---|---|
| 1879 - 1889 | 1886+ | 1889 - 1905+ | 1889 - 1905 |

| PORCELAINE HAVILAND | PORCELAINE HAVILAND FRANCE | Haviland France |
|---|---|---|
| 1889 - 1926+ | 1889 - 1941 | 1893 - 1930, 1941 - 1962 |

THEODORE HAVILAND COMPANY —

| ㅂ | MONT-MERY FRANCE | Théo Haviland Limoges FRANCE | Porcelaine Theo. Haviland Limoges FRANCE |
|---|---|---|---|
| 1892 | 1892+ | 1893+ | 1893+ |

## THEODORE HAVILAND COMPANY, Continued —

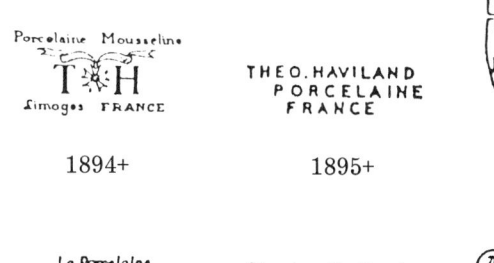

| | | | |
|---|---|---|---|
| 1894+ | 1895+ | 1920+ | 1920 -36 |
| 1925+ | 1925+ | 1937 - present | |

## CHARLES FIELD HAVILAND —

| Pre 1868 | 1868 - 82 | 1882 - 91 | 1891 - 97 |
|---|---|---|---|

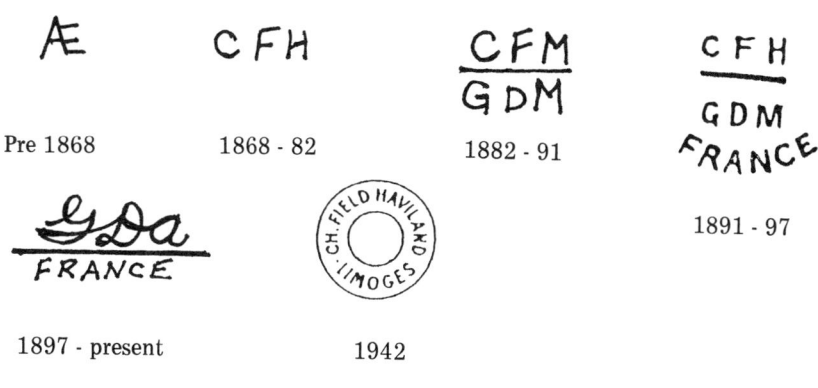

1897 - present    1942

## JOHANN HAVILAND —

| 1907 - present | 1910 - 1924 | 1912 - 1936 | 1972 |
|---|---|---|---|

ROBERT HAVILAND & C. PARLON — ROBERT HAVILAND & LeTANNEUR —

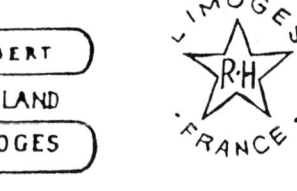

1924        1937 - 1948            1929+

FRANK HAVILAND —    JEAN HAVILAND —

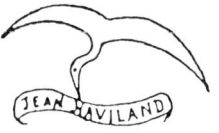

1910 - 1924      1957+        1957+

HAVILAND SA —

| HAVILAND & C°<br>LIMOGES | HAVILAND<br>FRANCE | Haviland's<br>Chantilly | HAVILAND<br>CHINA |
|---|---|---|---|
| 1941+ | 1941+ | 1948 - 1953 | 1958 - present |

| HAVILAND<br>ALUMINITE<br>FRUGIER<br>UNOCCISTIMMEL | Haviland<br>France<br>ESTABLISHED 1842 | Haviland<br>France<br>Limoges |
|---|---|---|
| 1964+ | current | current |

AMERICAN LIMOGES CHINA CO. INC., Sebring, Ohio.

1900 - 1955

# Nineteenth Century Majolica

by THE LATE GEORGE NORVAL JOHNSTON

Majolica, as we most often use the word, is now English, and should be pronounced as it is spelled. This refers to the soft bodied pottery decorated with lead glazes which have been stained with coloring oxides.

This pottery is usually molded into intricate floral shapes, or has vegetation or garden creatures incrusted on it. Such things as flowers, vines, frogs, snakes, or fish, if not an integral part of the mold design, are then moulded separately or fashioned by hand and applied to the article. The beautiful glazes which are painted on, vary in tint with the numerous factories producing the ware. Many of the pieces will have a pleasing pink lining on hollow ware, such as jugs and bowls; and quite often the backs of plates will have intriguing splashes of color on them, giving a tortise-shell effect. Some of the ware is called "sanded majolica". This will have, on portions of the surfaces, an application of frit (frit in this case being ground up pottery) so that when fired, certain areas will be very rough and pebbly.

The name majolica was first used for a nineteenth century product by Minton's in 1850. This English firm put out some things at that time with very fine painting on them, which did to some degree resemble the old Italian maiolica. It was not long after this however, that the name majolica was being used on pottery decorated with semi-translucent glazes. In England, among the most renowned makers of this Victorian pottery were Wedgwood, Moor & Co., Brownfield & Co., and George Jones. The same name was also used for this ware on the continent. In the United States it was made by many firms; and Griffin Smith & Hill, of Phoenixville, Pennsylvania, marked their product "Etruscan Majolica" from about 1878 to the early 1890's. It has been made in Canada at various times and in a number of places such as St. Johns, Quebec, the Brantford Pottery, the Newton Brook Pottery of Toronto, and by the artist potter Jarko Zavi of Brighton, Ontario.

The seventeenth and eighteenth century counterpart of this ware would be Palissy type faience, Whieldon ware, variegated ware, or tortoise-shell; although these effects were achieved through a slightly different process. The real Majolica, written with a capital M, or now more often being spelled "maiolica", and given this Spanish pronunciation, is a tin enameled pottery from Italy. This Italian majolica, or maiolica if you wish, is altogether different from the nineteenth century majolica which we are discussing. It has a fine white surface, due to a tin glaze, which was decorated with hand painting.

The idea of adding oxide of tin to a transparent glaze, so as to achieve a white opaque glaze, dates back to ancient Assyria. It was used extensively in the Near East, then through the Moors, was taken to Spain. It was sometime in the fourteenth century that the Italians adopted the technique. Because their ships picked up this Spanish cargo at the island of Majorca, the ware they later made to resemble it, was called majolica. However, when this same ware began to be made in Holland it was so associated with the town of Delft that it went by that name. Then the English too adopted the name delft for their product; although the process was being used in England before it was known in Holland. Now, when we wish to make a distinction between the Dutch and the English ware, we write the English delft with a small d. It has been reasoned that this tin glaze process was possibly taken to France by an Italian workman from Faenza, for the ware there became known as faience.

To amass a collection of majolica, early faience, or delftware now however, is quite an achievement. For the most part, these are left for the museums or for the collectors to whom price means very little. But these older pieces of maiolica, delft, or faience, with their tin glaze and beautiful painting, have nothing in common with our nineteenth century majolica — except perhaps for the work of Bernard Palissy; whose faience was made in the second half of the sixteenth century at Saintes, France.

The majolica of the nineteenth century — it is still being made today — is a favorite among collectors because well executed and nicely colored pieces are truly beautiful. It looks well in any rustic setting, and is ideal for breakfast, informal lunch, or as a kitchen decoration. It is not difficult to build up a collection; for it can be found in most antique shops, and as yet only a few patterns are expensive. The American "sheil and seaweed" and "Culiflower" are two designs which demand high prices; but most patterns are relatively inexpensive, and nevertheless gratifying to collect. Another reason for its fascinating appeal to the collector is the fact there is much to be learned about this ware. There are known marks that have yet to be ascribed, and known factories whose pieces are as yet unidentified. Consequently, the owner of a bright piece of majolica has not only a feast for the eye, but usually a mystery to be pursued. This, then, can be truly great fun.

There are such patterns in plates and serving pieces to choose from as Begonia leaf, Lily, Blackberry, Thorn, Pansy, Geraneum, Oak, Cosmos, Wild Rose, Corn, Strawberry, Fern, Sunflower, Dolphin, Swan, Lion or Bird. Cups and saucers are especially hard to come by, for they were not made in all the patterns. However, you can find them in Shell and Seaweed,' Tea Plant, Maple Leaf, Bamboo, Lettuce Leaf, Butterfly, and Fan, among others.

Besides dinner and tea-ware, there are such things to be had as match holders, ash trays, tobacco boxes, cuspidors, vases and flowerpots, wall plaques, garden seats, and all manner of figures and figural jugs.

A lot has been written about the old maiolica; books are filled with pictures of these beautiful pieces. But little has been published about Victorian majolica as a ware distinct from other contemporary pottery. Therefore it is up to those who collect this ware, to find out all they can and to pass on their findings to others, so that we may better understand and appreciate this interesting — if somewhat garish — but always decorative ware.

# MALING

Maling's Ouseburn Pottery, Newcastle, England, 1817 - 1859. Earthenware.

C.T. Maling, A & B Ford Potteries, Newcastle-Upon-Tyne, England, 1859 - 1890. Earthenware.

C.T. Maling & Sons (Ltd.), A & B Ford Potteries, Newcastle-Upon-Tyne, England. 1890 - 1963. Earthenware.

| M | MALING | C.T. MALING | C.T.M. |
|---|---|---|---|
| 1817 - 1830 | 1817 - 1890 | 1859+ | 1859 - 1890 |

| 1875 - 1908 | 1890+ | 1908+ |
|---|---|---|

| 1924+ | 1949 - 1963 |
|---|---|

# MASON'S
## MASON'S IRONSTONE

George Miles Mason and Charles James Mason made Patent Ironstone at Lane Delph, Staffordshire England 1813 - 1829. The firm became Charles James Mason & Co., Patent Ironstone Manufactory 1829 - 1845. From 1845 - 1848 it was designated Charles James Mason - Fenton Works Delph Lane Staffordshire and Longton 1851 - 1854. Continued by Francis Morley (& Co.) Hanley Staffordshire, Ca. 1848 and subsequently by G. L. Ashworth & Bros. Ltd. Hanley, Staffordshire, Ca. 1862

G.M. & C.J. MASON     G. & C. J. M.

Before 1829

MASON'S PATENT IRONSTONE CHINA

1813 - 1825

PATENT IRONSTONE CHINA

1813 - 1825

1813 - 1825

1820+

FENTON STONE WORKS

1825+

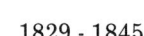

FENTON STONE WORKS

1829 - 1845

C. J. M. & Co. GRANITE CHINA

1829 - 1845

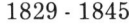

1829 - 1845

1829 - 1845

MASON'S IMPROVED IRONSTONE CHINA

1840+

1845+

## MEAKIN MARKS

There are a great variety of Meakin marks since there were several firms with that name. A selection of marks follows —

Alfred Meakin (Ltd.), Royal Albert, Victoria and Highgate Potteries, Tunstall, Staffordshire, England. Commenced 1875. "Ltd." added 1897 - 1930. Firm name changed to Alfred Meakin (Tunstall) Ltd. 1913.

Charles Meakin Burslem 1870 - 1882 and Eastwood Potteries, Hanley, Staffordshire, 1883 - 1889.

Henry Meakin, Abbey Pottery, Cobridge, Staffordshire, 1873 - 1876.

J. & G. Meakin (Ltd.), Eagle Pottery and Eastwood Works, Hanley, Staffordshire, 1851 —. Sold the Eastwood Pottery 1958, modernized and enlarged the Eagle Works.

ALFRED MEAKIN (LTD.) —

1875 - 1897

1891+

1891+

1897+

1907+

1914+

1914+

Ca. 1920

1930+

1937+

1937+

1937+

ALFRED MEAKIN ENGLAND

Left — 1947+ Slight variations occur.

Right — 1947+ Slight variations occur.

ALFRED MEAKIN ENGLAND

# MEAKIN MARKS Cont.

### CHARLES MEAKIN —

1870 - 1882     1883 - 1889

### HENRY MEAKIN —

IRONSTONE CHINA
H. MEAKIN

1873 - 1876

### J. & G. MEAKIN (LTD.) —

Ca. 1890     Ca. 1890     1890+     1907+

1912+ Many variations of Sol & Sunface mark.     1912+     1939+

"ROMANTIC ENGLAND"

1947+ Included in the mark. Found on series of scenic patterns.

1946+     1946+             1953+

J.& G.
MEAKIN
ENGLAND

1955+     1958+     1962+

## MEIGH MARKS

Job Meigh, Old Hall Pottery, Hanley, Staffordshire, England, 1805 - 1834. Became Job Meigh & Son 1812.

Charles Meigh took over 1835 - 1849, became Charles Meigh, Son & Pankhurst, 1850 - 1851 and Charles Meigh & Son 1851 - 1861.

The company name was changed to Old Hall Earthenware Co. in 1861 to 1886. The firm became the Old Hall Porcelain Works Ltd. in 1886 until 1902.

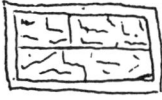 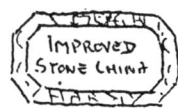 

1805 - 1861
Used by J. Meigh and C. Meigh firms

| MEIGH | OLD HALL | J.M.S. | | J.M. & S. |
|---|---|---|---|---|
| 1805 - 34 | 1805+ | 1812 - 1834 | 1815 - 1825 | 1815 - 1825 |

| | CHARLES MEIGH | C.M. | |
|---|---|---|---|
| 1835 - 1847. Pattern name often included. | 1835 - 1849 | 1835 - 1849 | 1835 - 1849. Pattern name often included. |

| C.M.S.P.&S. | | |
|---|---|---|
| 1850 - 1851 | 1851 - 1861 | 1851 - 1861 |

**MEIGH MARKS Cont.**

| CHINA | M & S | C. MEIGH & SON | MEIGH'S | OPAQUE PORCELAIN |

1851 - 1861

O.H.E.C.  O.H.E.C. (L)    IMPERIAL PARISIAN GRANITE (EAGLE CREST) OLD HALL E'WARE CO. (LIMD)

1861 - 1886

INDIAN STONE CHINA    OPAQUE PORCELAIN        ENGLAND

1861 - 1886        1884+        1891 - 1902

## MEISSEN

The Royal Porcelain Manufactory was founded in 1710 at Meissen, near Dresden, Saxony, Germany. It was the first hard paste factory in Europe, until the 1760's the manufactory had no equal and was known for its superior figures, brilliant painted decoration and moulded ornamentation.

Large quantities of porcelain was exported to North America during the nineteenth century.

The crossed swords mark introduced Ca. 1725 has been copied by many manufacturers and many variations occur. For example — Derby, Bristol, Coalport, Worcester and Sampson, England; Samson Petit and Bloch, France, Dornheim, Koch & Fischer, Germany.

NOTE: The name "Dresden" is the English term used for nineteenth century Meissen porcelain. There were several potteries and porcelain decorating shops in the Dresden area.

A Selection of Meissen (Dresden) marks —

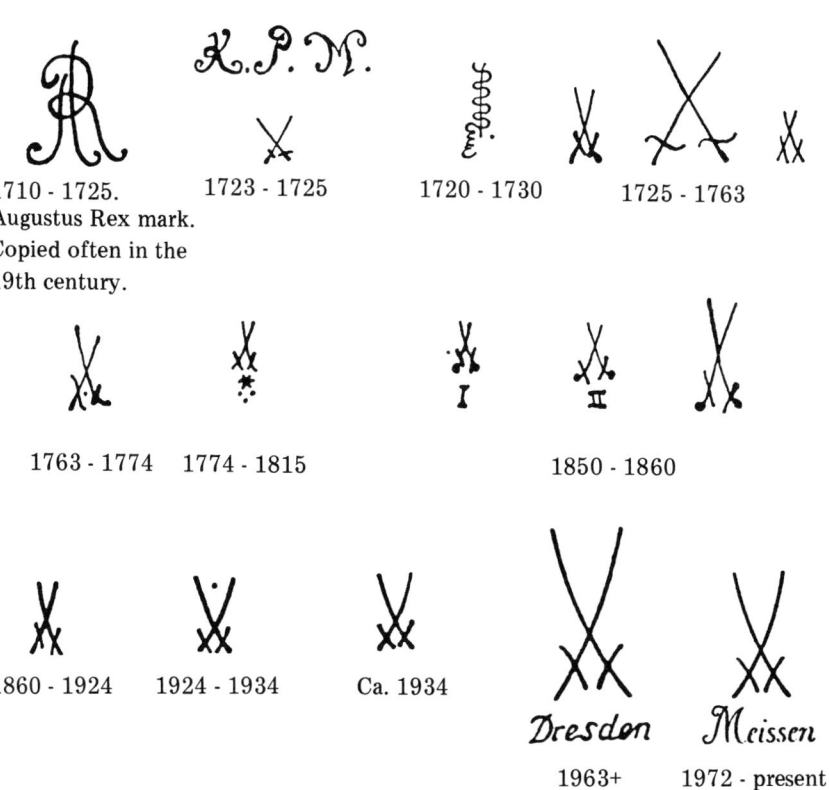

# MINTON

Established 1793, Stoke-on-Trent, Staffordshire, England. Used various trade names — Minton; Mintons; Mintons Ltd.; Thomas Minton & Son; Minton & Hollins; Minton, Hollins & Co.; Minton & Boyle; Minton & Co.

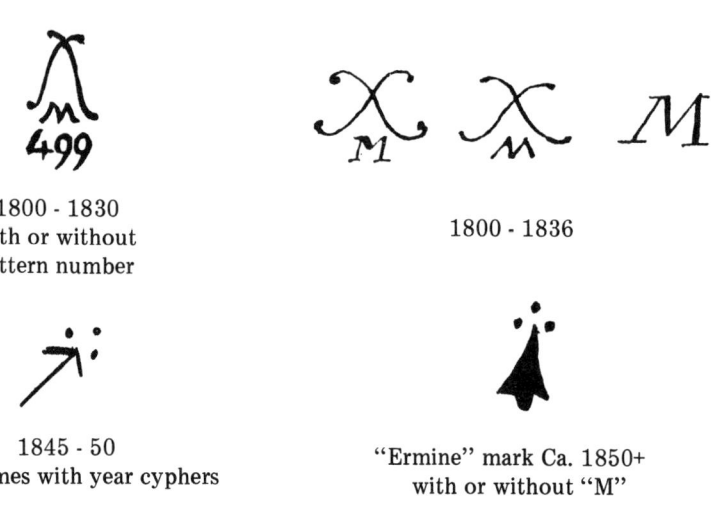

1800 - 1830
with or without pattern number

1800 - 1836

1845 - 50
sometimes with year cyphers

"Ermine" mark Ca. 1850+
with or without "M"

M (Minton) 1822 - 16. Many other examples are known.

M & B (Minton & Boyle) 1836 - 41

MINTON Cont.

M & H (Minton & Hollins)
1845 - 68

M & Co. (Minton & Co.) Ca. 1841 - 73

Ca. 1851  Rare    1860's    MINTON

                            1862 - 1871
                            with year cyphers

/8
MINTON
72

1863 - 1872   1868 - 1880    1871 - 1875    1872
              with year of
              manufacture

MINTONS

1873

**MINTON Cont.**

| | |
|---|---|
| 1873+ | |
| 1891 | England below mark |
| 1901 | On some pieces crown deleted |
| 1902 - 1911 | Made in England added to mark |

Specialty marks such as this usually include date

**MINTONS ENGLAND**

1890 - 1910

**MINTONS**

1900 - 1908

1912 - 1950

**SOLAR MINTON ENGLAND**

1918+
Uranium Glaze

**MINTON**

1951+

MINTON YEAR CYPHERS  Used with month letter, ⚹·✕ I =June, 1845

| Jan | (J) | Feb | (F) | Mar | (M) | Apr | (A) | May | (E) | Jun | (I) |
| Jul | (H) | Aug | (Y) | Sep | (S) | Oct | (O) | Nov | (N) | Dec | (D) |

| 1842 | 1843 | 1844 | 1845 | 1846 | 1847 | 1848 | 1849 |
|---|---|---|---|---|---|---|---|
| 1850 | 1851 | 1852 | 1853 | 1854 | 1855 | 1856 | 1857 |
| 1858 | 1859 | 1860 | 1861 | 1862 | 1863 | 1864 | 1865 |
| 1866 | 1867 | 1868 | 1869 | 1870 | 1871 | 1872 | 1873 |
| 1874 | 1875 | 1876 | 1877 | 1878 | 1879 | 1880 | 1881 |
| 1882 | 1883 | 1884 | 1885 | 1886 | 1887 | 1888 | 1889 |
| 1890 | 1891 | 1892 | 1893 | 1894 | 1895 | 1896 | 1897 |
| 1898 | 1899 | 1900 | 1901 | 1902 | 1903 | 1904 | 1905 |
| 1906 | 1907 | 1908 | 1909 | 1910 | 1911 | 1912 | 1913 |
| 1914 | 1915 | 1916 | 1917 | 1918 | 1919 | 1920 | 1921 |
| 1922 | 1923 | 1924 | 1925 | 1926 | 1927 | 1928 | 1929 |
| 1930 | 1931 | 1932 | 1933 | 1934 | 1935 | 1936 | 1937 |
| 1938 | 1939 | 1940 | 1941 | 1942 | | | |

In 1943 a new dating system was instituted, a single digit followed by two digits, e.g. 6—63 — 6 being an employee number and 63 the year of production.

## MOORCROFT

William Moorcroft was manager of the art pottery department of James MacIntyre & Co., Burslem, England from 1898 until 1913 when he began his own pottery, W. Moorcroft (Ltd.), Burslem. The signature mark, registered as a trademark by William Moorcroft in 1919, was also used by him on articles he decorated while at the MacIntyre works. When William Moorcroft died in 1945 the pottery was taken over by his son, Walter.

**MOORCROFT**

Signature used with other marks:  Transfer printed or impressed.
Transfer printed   1898 - 1935   With "Burslem"   1913 - 1921
Impressed   1930 - 1949   With "Made in England"   Ca. 1921+

Paper label, 1930 - 1949

1945+

# MYOTT

Myott, Son & Company took over the Alexander Pottery (1888 - 1898) already at Stoke, Staffordshire, England. Moved to Cobridge 1902 - 1946 then to Hanley in 1947.

Alexander Pottery, 1888 - 1898
George T. Mountford, Proprietor.

1898 - 1902   1900+   1907+   1930+

1930+   1936+   1959+   1961+

1961+

# NIPPON

The McKinley Tariff Act of 1891 specified that items imported into the United States be marked with the name of country of origin.

NIPPON is the Japanese word for Japan, it was used as the country of origin name from Ca. 1891 to Ca. 1921 when regulations in the U.S. required that the word Japan be used to specify country of origin.

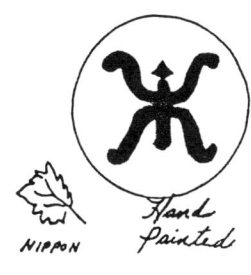

  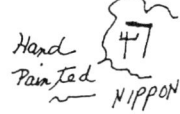

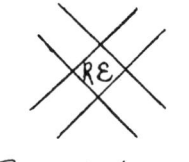

BABY BUD NIPPON

NIPPON
D

MADE IN
NIPPON

NIPPON

NIPPON 84

NIPPON 144

221
NIPPON

L.W & Co.
NIPPON

NORITAKE
NIPPON

NORITAKE
NIPPON

Studio
Handpainted
Nippon

Royal Sometuke
NIPPON

Hand Painted
NIPPON

ROYAL SOMETUKE
Nippon

Hand Painted
Nippon

HAND PAINTED
NIPPON

Hand Painted
NIPPON

Handpainted
NIPPON

## QUIMPER (Say "Kam-Pair")
### By Susan and Al Bagdade

Quimper pottery derives its name from a town of the same name in Brittany, in the northwest corner of France, where the potteries were located. Jean Baptiste Bousquet settled in Quimper in 1685 and produced functional faience wares. His son Pierre succeeded him in 1708. In 1731, Pierre Bellevaux, Pierre's son-in-law was included in the business.

Pierre Clement Caussy joined the factory in 1739, took over the direction of the faiencerie and expanded the works. Through marriage Antoine de la Hubaudiere took over the Caussy factory in 1782 and it became known as the Grande Maison de HB.

Francois Eloury opened a rival factory in 1776 and in 1778 Guillaume Dumaine opened a third. By 1780 there were three rival faience factories operating in Quimper.

The Eloury factory passed to Charles Porquier and later to Adolphe Porquier. In 1782 the master artist Alfred Beau joined the factory.

In 1884 Jules Henriot took over the Dumaine factory and later purchased the Porquier factory in 1904. Noted artists Meheut, Sevellec, Maillard and Nicot worked at the Henriot concern.

The HB factory introduced the Odetta line of stoneware in the 1920's.

The Henriot factory merged with the Grande Maison HB in 1968 with each retaining its individual characteristics and marks. The factory was closed in the early 1980's, but has been taken over by an American couple and is still producing pottery today.

### GRANDE MAISON HB

|  |  |  |
|---|---|---|
| Pierre Caussy late 18th century | de la Hubaudiere early 19th century | de la Hubaudiere late 19th century |

de la Hubaudiere 1882 - 1883

de la Hubaudiere late 19th century to 1910

### ELOURY-PORQUIER-BEAU

| P | A | B |
|---|---|---|
| Eloury-Porquier 1843 | Adolphe Porquier 1880's - 1890's | Porquier-Beau 1898 |

QUIMPER Cont.

## JULES HENRIOT FACTORY

Jules Henriot
1904

HeNRιoT Quimper

Faiencerie Henriot
after 1922

Many early pieces were unmarked. The following guidelines will help identify these unmarked examples as Quimper.
1. Body is often thick. Plates may appear wobbly, and large pieces asymmetrical.
2. Pinkish red clay used on early pieces and often shows through the glaze.
3. Prior to World War 1, pieces were fired in wood burning ovens. Pits and streaky glaze are common on these pieces.
4. Unglazed rest spots or scars are often found on the bottoms of pieces fired in the wood burning ovens.
5. Florals and exotic birds were common subjects. After 1860, peasant figures dominated.
6. Due to the nature of the glaze, rim wear is common and often indicates age.

Additional notes on marks:
1. Many pieces were made on consignment for department stores and carry the store mark, i.e. "MACY."
2. Numbers and letters in conjunction with Quimper marks are usually pattern or style numbers.
3. Souvenir pieces were potted for various resorts and were marked as such.
4. Many pieces were re-issued. Museum quality reproductions were often marked in brown.
5. The word "France" added to the mark after 1891.
6. Peasant pieces with the mark $PB_X$ are not from Quimper, but from Malicorne, near Paris, and were an attempt to capitalize on the popularity of the Quimper peasant theme.

### BIBLIOGRAPHY

BAGDADE, Susan and Al. "Peasant Pottery: The Pride of Quimper," Hobbies Magazine, March, 1982.
BAGDADE, Susan and Al. "The Pottery of Quimper," Antique Trader Price Guide, Winter, 1981.
BONDHUS, Sandra. "Quimper Pottery: A French Folk Art Faience." 1981.
BONDHUS, Sandra. "Quimper Pottery," Joel Sater's Antiques and Auction News, January 4, 1980.
BONDHUS, Sandra. "Quimper Pottery," Spinning Wheel. December, 1979.
MALI, Millicent. "Quimper Faience," Airon, Inc. 1979.
MOGUIS, Robert F. "How To Date Quimper Ware," Antiques Journal. Dubuque, Iowa, March, 1973.
TABURET, Marjatta. "La Faience de Quimper," Editions Jos, Le Doare-Chateaulin (Finistere), 1975.

## R.S. PRUSSIA, R.S. GERMANY, R.S. POLAND & R.S. TILLOWITZ

Made by the Schlegelmilch family during the late 19th century and early 20th century. A wide variety of this popular china was made, such as tableware and decorative pieces.

Erdman Schlegelmilch
Suhl, Thuringia, Soxony-Prussia, Germany
1861 - Ca. 1938

R.S. Prussia, R.S. Germany, R.S. Poland & R.S. Tillowitz Cont.

Reinhold Schlegelmilch
Tillowitz, Silesia, Prussia, Germany (German-Poland)
1869 - Ca. 1938.

1891+  Ca. 1898 - 1908

1904+

1919 - 1921  1932 - 1938

Oscar Schlegelmilch,
Langewiessen, Thuringia, Germany
1892 - Ca. 1972

1892+  1896+  1900+

1904+  1950+

# RIDGWAY

Ridgway, Sparks & Ridgway, Bedford Works, Shelton, Hanley, Staffordshire, England, 1873 - 1879.

Ridgways, Bedford Works, Shelton, Hanley, Staffordshire, England, 1879 - 1920.

Ridgways (Bedford Works) Ltd., Bedford Works, Shelton, Hanley, Staffordshire, England, 1920 - 1952.

Ridgway & Adderley Ltd., 1952 - 1955.

Ridgway Potteries Ltd., 1955 -

Companies that formed the Ridgway Group — Booths, Tunstal; Colcloughs, Longton; North Staffordshire Pottery, Cobridge; Portland Pottery, Cobridge and Adderley Floral China Works, Longton.

A selection of marks —

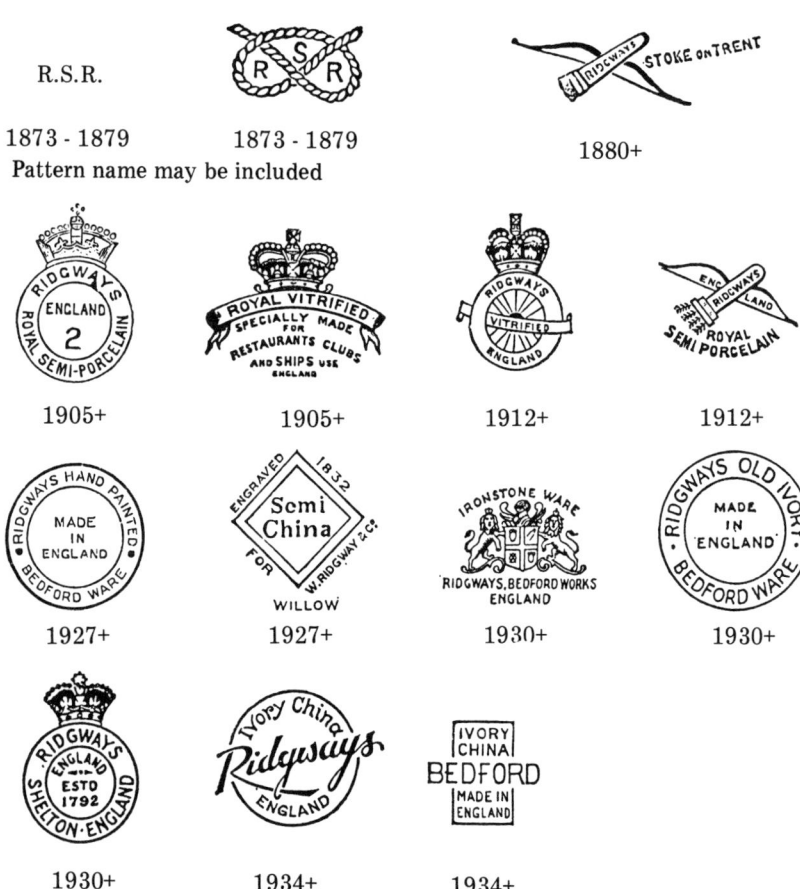

RIDGWAY Cont.

1950+

1950+

1962+

1962+

213

## ROBINSON & LEADBEATER (LTD.)

Robinson & Leadbeater (Ltd.), Stoke, Staffordshire, England, 1864 - 1924. Parian, etc.

1855+

1905 - 1924
Variations occur

# ROSENTHAL & CO.

Rosenthal & Co., Selb and Kronach, Bavaria (Germany). Established 1879. Decorators and manufacturers of fine porcelain, tableware, figurines and Christmas plates etc.

1891 - 1907    1901 - 1956    Ca. 1900    Ca. 1900

1917 - 1952    Selb, Bavaria 1907 - 1933    1922+
               Selb, Germany 1934 - 1956

1935 - 1956    1937+    1953 - present

Current

## ROYAL BAYREUTH

Established 1794. Continues today as Tettau Porcelain Factory. Noted for floral, scenic and portrait china, and fruit and vegetable forms, as well as figural and souvenir articles.

Many versions of the mark are known, slight variations occur.

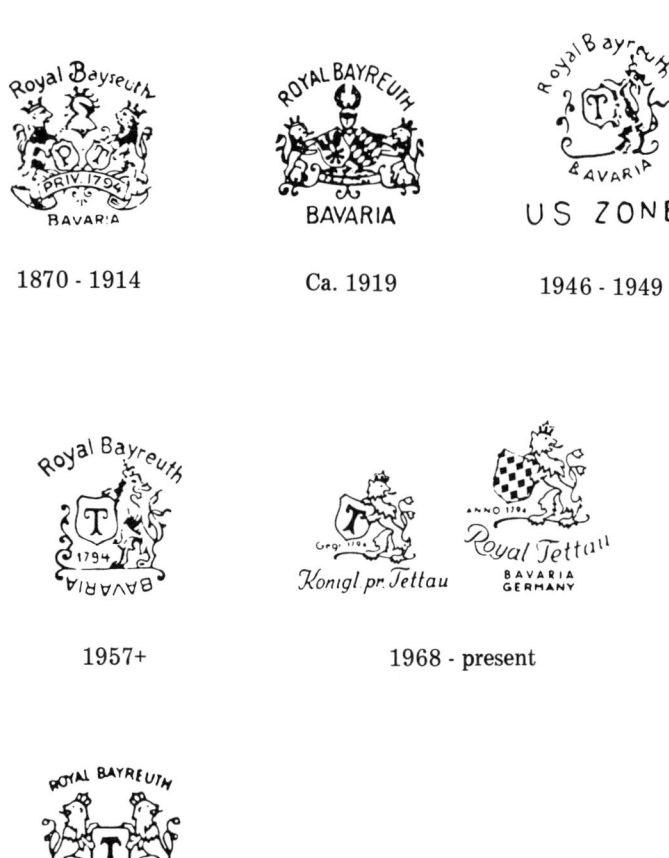

1870 - 1914    Ca. 1919    1946 - 1949

1957+    1968 - present

1972+

## ROYAL COPENHAGEN PORCELAIN MANUFACTORY
### Copenhagen & Fredericksberg, Denmark

Established in the 1770's. Supported and owned by the Danish Royal family until it went into private ownership in 1868. Produced tableware, figurines and decorative items etc. Christmas plates were introduced in 1908.

# Royal Doulton

## DATE MARKS AND OTHER MARKS FOUND ON SOME DOULTON PIECES

Often, numbers and/or initials are found along with the manufacturer's mark. Examples of methods used by Doulton —

A-Mark. A factory control mark. Used by Doulton, Ca. 1939 - Ca. 1955. Found along with the back-stamp on some character jugs, series ware and tableware.

HN Prefix. Found on figurines, first used in 1913. Henry Nixon was the artist in charge of painting Royal Doulton figurines, his initials, H N, prefix the number assigned to each figure.

M Prefix. Miniature. 1932 - 1949.

Between 1902 and 1914 a lower case letter in a shield is found marked on some pieces: c for 1902, d for 1903, e for 1904 and so on to the letter o for 1914.

Between 1913 and 1930 Doulton used a date-number method to specify when a mould was made. 21 - 11 - 13 would indicate that a mould was made on the 21st day of November, 1913. Only two numbers, for instance, 11 - 13 indicates month and year — November 1913.

After 1927 another way Doulton dated some of their products was by adding a two digit number to the right of the mark. To ascertain the year of manufacture, add the number, for example, 16 to the year 1927 to arrive at the year of production, 1943.

# DOULTON & WATTS, DOULTON & CO.
## ROYAL DOULTON
Lambeth, London, England (1827 - 1956)
Burslem, Staffordshire, England (1882 - present)

Ca. 1827 - 1858

DOULTON
LAMBETH

1858 - Ca. 1910
England added
from 1891

1869 - 1877
Often year of
production in
centre

Ca. 1873 - Ca. 1914

Ca. 1873 - Ca. 1914
Occasionally with year
of production in centre.

1877 - 1880

1877 - 1880

1879 - 1900

1880 - 1902
England added from
1891. Occasionally with
year of production.

1881 - 1910
Also without word
"Crown"

1881 - 1912
England added
from 1891

DOULTON

1882+

**DOULTON Cont.**

1882 - 1902
England added from 1891

DOULTON
& SLATER'S
PATENT

DSP

1882 - 1914

1886 - 1914
(Doulton & Slater's Patent)

1887 - 1902
With variations in wording.

DOULTON
LAMBETH
ENGLAND

ROYAL
DOULTON
FLAMBE

**ROYAL
DOULTON
KALON**

1888 - 1898

1891 - 1956

Ca. 1900 —

Ca. 1900 —

1902 - Ca. 1930

1902 - 1956

1912 - 1956

1918 - 1932
Rare

ENGLISH
TRANSLUCENT
CHINA

1920 - 1936

1922 - 1956

1930+

1960+

## ROYAL DOULTON – ARTISTS

Artists who worked at Doulton & Co. signed their work with initials or a monogram. The following is a list of artists and their years of employment at Doulton.

Margaret Aitken –
Ca. 1881 - Ca. 1882

Elizabeth Aitkins –
Ca. 1876 - Ca. 1883

Eliza S. Banks –
Ca. 1876 - Ca. 1884

Arthur B. Barlow –
Ca. 1871 - Ca. 1878

Florence E. Barlow –
Ca. 1873 - Ca. 1909

Hannah B. Barlow –
Ca. 1871 - Ca. 1913

Lucy A. Barlow –
Ca. 1882 - Ca. 1884

Harry Barnard –
Ca. 1880 - Ca. 1890

John Broad –
Ca. 1873 - Ca. 1919

Frank A. Butler –
Ca. 1872 - Ca. 1911

Mary Butterton –
Ca. 1875 - Ca. 1890

Mary Capes – C
Ca. 1876 - Ca. 1883

Miss F.M. Collins –
Ca. 1875 - Ca. 1880

Minna L. Crawley – C
Ca. 1876 - Ca. 1883

Louisa J. Davis –
Ca. 1873 - Ca. 1895

W. Edward Dunn –
Ca. 1882 - Ca. 1895

Emily J. Edwards –
Ca. 1872 - Ca. 1876

Louisa E. Edwards –
Ca. 1873 - Ca. 1890

Herbert Ellis –
Ca. 1879 - Ca. 1928

John Eyre –
Ca. 1884 - Ca. 1890

Elizabeth Fisher –
Ca. 1873 - Ca. 1888

Arthur Leslie Herradine –
Ca. 1902 - Ca. 1914

Miss Agnete Hoy –
Ca. 1952 - Ca. 1957

Vera Huggins –
Ca. 1923 - Ca. 1950

Francis E. Lee –
Ca. 1875 - Ca. 1890

Florence Lewis –
Ca. 1875 - Ca. 1897

Florence Linnell –
Ca. 1880 - Ca. 1885

Edith D. Lupton –
Ca. 1875 - Ca. 1889

Mark V. Marshall –
Ca. 1876 - Ca. 1912

John H. McLennan –
Ca. 1880 - Ca. 1910

# ROYAL DOULTON – ARTISTS Cont.

Isabella Miller –
Ca. 1880 - Ca. 1884

Mary Mitchell –
Ca. 1874 - Ca. 1887

William Parker –
Ca. 1879 - Ca. 1892

Arthur E. Pearce –
Ca. 1873 - Ca. 1920

Francis C. Pope –
Ca. 1880 - Ca. 1923

Florence C. Roberts –
Ca. 1879 - Ca. 1930

Edith Rogers –
Ca. 1881 - Ca. 1884

Kate Rogers –
Ca. 1880 - Ca. 1892

Martha M. Rogers –
Ca. 1881 - Ca. 1884

William Rowe –
Ca. 1883 - Ca. 1939

Eliza A. Sayers –
Ca. 1877 - Ca. 1881

Harry Simeon –
Ca. 1894 - Ca. 1936

Eliza Simmance –
Ca. 1873 - Ca. 1928

Elizabeth M. Small –
Ca. 1881 - Ca. 1884

Emily E. Stormer –
Ca. 1877 - Ca. 1892

Katie Sturgeon –
Ca. 1880 - Ca. 1883

George Hugo Tabor –
Ca. 1878 - Ca. 1890

Margaret E. Thompson –
Ca. 1900

George Tinworth –
Ca. 1866 - Ca. 1913

Linnie Watt –
Ca. 1880 - Ca. 1886

Bessie J. Youatt –
Ca. 1873 - Ca. 1890

# ROYAL DUX

The Dux Porcelain Manufactory was founded in 1860 by E. Eichler, at Dux in Bohemia, Austria (after 1918 Duchcov, Czechoslovakia). The Dux Porcelain Company specialized in making statues, busts, figurines and decorative vases.

      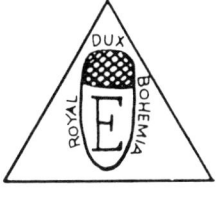   

1860+           Ca. 1860 - 1900        Ca. 1900 - 1918        pre-1918

## SAMPSON HANCOCK (& SONS)

Sampson Hancock (& Sons), Bridge Works, Stoke, Staffordshire, England. 1858 - 1937. (At Tunstall 1858 - 1870) Earthenware.

| S. HANCOCK | S.H. | S. H. & SONS | S. H. & S. |
|---|---|---|---|
| 1858+ | 1858 - 1891 | 1891 - 1935 | |

Name of pattern may be included with mark.

1900 - 1906      1900 - 1906      1906 - 1912      1906 - 1912

1906 - 1912      1912 - 1937

## SEVRES MANUFACTORY, FRANCE

Factory at Vincennes 1745 until 1756 when it was moved to Sevres. In 1876 the factory moved to St. Cloud. The products of Sevres are noted for their artistic painting and decoration.

A selection of marks —

Soft Paste       Hard Paste
1753 - 1793      1753 - 1793

*R.F*            M.Imp^le
*Sèvres*         de Sevres.

1793 - 1804      1804 - 1814      1810 - 1814

Date letters were used with the "crossed L" mark from 1753 until 1793. The letters in either upper or lower case were either inside or beside the "crossed L" mark.

| | | | | |
|---|---|---|---|---|
| 1753 - A | 1754 - B | 1755 - C | 1756 - D | 1757 - E |
| 1758 - F | 1759 - G | 1760 - H | 1761 - I | 1762 - J |
| 1763 - K | 1764 - L | 1765 - M | 1766 - N | 1767 - O |
| 1768 - P | 1769 - Q | 1770 - R | 1771 - S | 1772 - T |
| 1773 - U | 1774 - V | 1775 - X | 1776 - Y | 1777 - Z |
| 1778 - AA | 1779 - BB | 1780 - CC | 1781 - DD | 1782 - EE |
| 1783 - FF | 1784 - GG | 1785 - HH | 1786 - II | 1787 - JJ |
| 1788 - KK | 1789 - LL | 1790 - MM | 1791 - NN | 1792 - OO |
| 1793 - PP | | | | |

For six years it appears no date code was used and in 1801 Sevres began using another method to refer to the year.

| | | | |
|---|---|---|---|
| 1801 - T9 | 1802 - X | 1803 - II | 1804 - ÷ |
| 1805 - ‖ | 1806 - ∽ | 1807 - 7 | 1808 - 8 |
| 1809 - 9 | 1810 - 10 | 1811 - oz | 1812 - dz |
| 1813 - tz | 1814 - qz | 1815 - qn | 1816 - sz |
| 1817 - ds | | | |

SEVRES Cont.

After 1817 Sevres indicated the year of manufacture in their mark by using the last two digits of the year.

1814 - 1824                         1824 - 1830

1830        1834        1843 - 1845            1845 - 1848

                                                                     T.
1848 - 1852                          Hard Paste    Soft Paste
                                       1852 - 1870
                                  T refers to Soft Paste

1854 - 70        1871 - 1946                      1900+

1902 - 1941      1928 - 1940       1941+

## J. SPODE, W. COPELAND, T. GARRETT

Josiah Spode, Stoke-on-Trent, Staffordshire, England, 1784 - 1833. Manufacturers of earthenware, porcelain and bone china etc. William Copeland became a partner about 1813 and Thomas Garrett joined the firm in 1833. In 1833 the company name was changed to Copeland & Garrett and in 1847 to W.T. Copeland & Son. (Continued as part of Royal Worcester Spode Ltd.)

A selection of 19th and 20th century marks —

|  |  |  |  |
|---|---|---|---|
| SPODE |  | SPODE'S NEW STONE |  *SPODE Felspar Porcelain* |
| 1805+ | Black 1805 - 1815<br>Blue 1815 - 1830 | 1805 - 1820 | Ca. 1810 |

1805 - 1833

1815 - 1827
Variations occur

| N. S. | C. & G. | COPELAND & GARRETT |  |  |
|---|---|---|---|---|
| 1820 - 1840 |  | 1833 - 1847 | 1833 - 1847 | |

1833 - 1847

|  | COPELAND | COPELAND, LATE SPODE |
|---|---|---|
| 1847 - 1851 | 1847 - 1867 | 1847 - 1867 |

Spode/Copeland/Garrett Cont.

COPELAND
1850 - 1867

Copeland Late Spode
1850 - 1890

Copeland
Stone China
1850 - 1890

COPELAND
1851 - 1885

1867 - 1890

1875 - 1890

SPODE
COPELANDS CHINA
ENGLAND
1891+

1891+

COPELAND
SPODE
ENGLAND
After 1891 and early 20th century

COPELAND
SPODE
ENGLAND
New Stone

1894 - 1910

Ca. 1900

1930's & 1950's

SPODE
BONE CHINA
ENGLAND
1950+

*Spode*
*Imp*$^{l}_{..}$
ENGLAND

Spode
FORTUNA
England.
1950's

*Spode*
BONE CHINA
ENGLAND
1960+

1962+
"x" omitted after 1962

228

# WADE

Wade & Co., Union Pottery, Burslem, Staffordshire, England, 1887 - 1927.

George Wade & Son Ltd., Manchester Pottery, Burslem, Staffordshire, England, 1922 -

Wade Heath & Co., (Ltd.) Royal Victoria Pottery, Burslem, Staffordshire, England, 1927 -

Wade (Ulster) Ltd., Portadown, Co. Armagh, Northern Ireland, 1953 -

## WADE & CO.

W. & CO.
B.

WADE'S

1887 - 1927

1887 - 1927

## G. WADE & SON

1936+

1936+

1947+

## WADE HEATH & CO.

1927+

ORCADIA WARE
BRITISH MADE

1934+

1934+

1936+

Flaxman Ware
Hand Made Pottery
BY WADEHEATH
ENGLAND.

1936+

1939+ With or without "Flaxman"

Wade Heath & Co., Cont.

1953+     1953+     1957+

## WADE ULSTER

1953+     1953+
Variations occur     1954+

1955+

230

# WEDGWOOD

Josiah Wedgwood (& Sons Ltd.), Burslem, Etruria and Barlaston, Staffordshire, England. Records of potters, Wedgwood, date back to the early 1600's. Josiah Wedgwood's is the great name in Staffordshire pottery, and is famous for its wide variety of products, such as bone china, jasper, majolica etc., etc. The firm Wedgwood continues today and through acquisitions and mergers many well known potters have joined the Wedgwood group.

A selection of marks.

| wedgwood | WEDCWOOD | WEDGWOOD | WEDGWOOD & BENTLEY |
|---|---|---|---|
| 1759 - 1769 | 1759+ From 1860 with date code (see table) From 1891 "ENGLAND" "MADE IN ENGLAND" occurs in the 20th century. | | 1768 - 1780 |

| W. & B. | (Wedgwood & Bentley Etruria circular mark) | Wedgwood | WEDGWOOD |
|---|---|---|---|
| Ca. 1775 | 1769 - 1780 Variations occur | 1780 - 1798 | 1812 - 1822 |

| WEDGWOOD ETRURIA | PEARL | P | |
|---|---|---|---|
| 1840 - 1845 | 1840 - 1868 | 1868+ | |

WEDGWOOD

Standard Mark. Occurs with date mark. "ENGLAND" added from 1891. "MADE IN ENGLAND" added Ca. 1910.

*E Lessore*

Artist signature.
Emile Lessore
Ca. 1858 - 1876

Wedgwood Cont.

WEDGWOOD

1878+ "ENGLAND"
added 1891

WEDGWOOD
ETRURIA. ENGLAND

1891 - 1900

WEDGWOOD

1900+ With "ENGLAND"
or "MADE IN ENGLAND"

WEDGWOOD
BONE CHINA
MADE IN ENGLAND

1920+

N W
or
NORMAN WILSON

1927 - 1962 With
standard mark.

WEDGWOOD

1929 - present

1940+

WEDGWOOD
BONE CHINA
MADE IN ENGLAND

Post WWII

ENGRAVED BY
WEDGWOOD
STUDIO

1952+

1962+ Pattern name or
number may be included.

## WEDGWOOD DATE CODE 1860 - 1906

A set of three capital letters was used by Wedgwood as a date mark — the first the month of manufacture, the second the potter and the last letter indicates the year. This system is somewhat confusing because in 1886 Wedgwood began to repeat the letters used from 1860 until 1885. From 1891 onwards the word "England" should be included in the mark.

### YEAR MARKS 1860 - 1906

| | | | | |
|---|---|---|---|---|
| 1860 - O | 1861 - P | 1862 - Q | 1863 - R | 1864 - S |
| 1865 - T | 1866 - U | 1867 - V | 1868 - W | 1869 - X |
| 1870 - Y | 1871 - Z | 1872 - A | 1873 - B | 1874 - C |
| 1875 - D | 1876 - E | 1877 - F | 1878 - G | 1879 - H |
| 1880 - I | 1881 - J | 1882 - K | 1883 - L | 1884 - M |
| 1885 - N | 1886 - O | 1887 - P | 1888 - Q | 1889 - R |
| 1890 - S | 1891 - T | 1892 - U | 1893 - V | 1894 - W |
| 1895 - X | 1896 - Y | 1897 - Z | 1898 - A | 1899 - B |
| 1900 - C | 1901 - D | 1902 - E | 1903 - F | 1904 - G |
| 1905 - H | 1906 - I | | | |

### MONTH MARKS 1860 - 1864

| | | | | |
|---|---|---|---|---|
| Jan - J | Feb - F | mar - M | Apr - A | May - Y |
| Jun - T | Jul - V | Aug - W | Sep - S | Oct - O |
| Nov - N | Dec - D | | | |

### MONTH MARKS 1864 - 1906

| | | | | |
|---|---|---|---|---|
| Jan - J | Feb - F | Mar - R | Apr - A | May - M |
| Jun - T | Jul - L | Aug - W | Sep - S | Oct - O |
| Nov - N | Dec - D | | | |

## WEDGWOOD DATE CODE 1907 -

In 1907 Wedgwood changed the month code from a letter to the number 3 or 4, but continued using letters of the alphabet to indicate the year.

### YEAR MARKS 1907 - 1929

| | | | | |
|---|---|---|---|---|
| 1907 - J | 1908 - K | 1909 - L | 1910 - M | 1911 - N |
| 1912 - O | 1913 - P | 1914 - Q | 1915 - R | 1916 - S |
| 1917 - T | 1918 - U | 1919 - V | 1920 - W | 1921 - X |
| 1922 - Y | 1923 - Z | 1924 - A | 1925 - B | 1926 - C |
| 1927 - D | 1928 - E | 1929 - F | | |

Wedgwood's date mark code changed again beginning in 1930. For the month of manufacture, a number from 1 to 12 is used, the potter is identified by a letter and the year by two digits, for example, 43 indicates the year, 1943.

# WEDGWOOD & CO. (LTD.)

Unicorn and Pinnox Works, Tunstall, Staffordshire, England, 1860 - Earthenware, stoneware etc. NOTE: Not to be confused with Josiah Wedgwood & Sons Ltd.

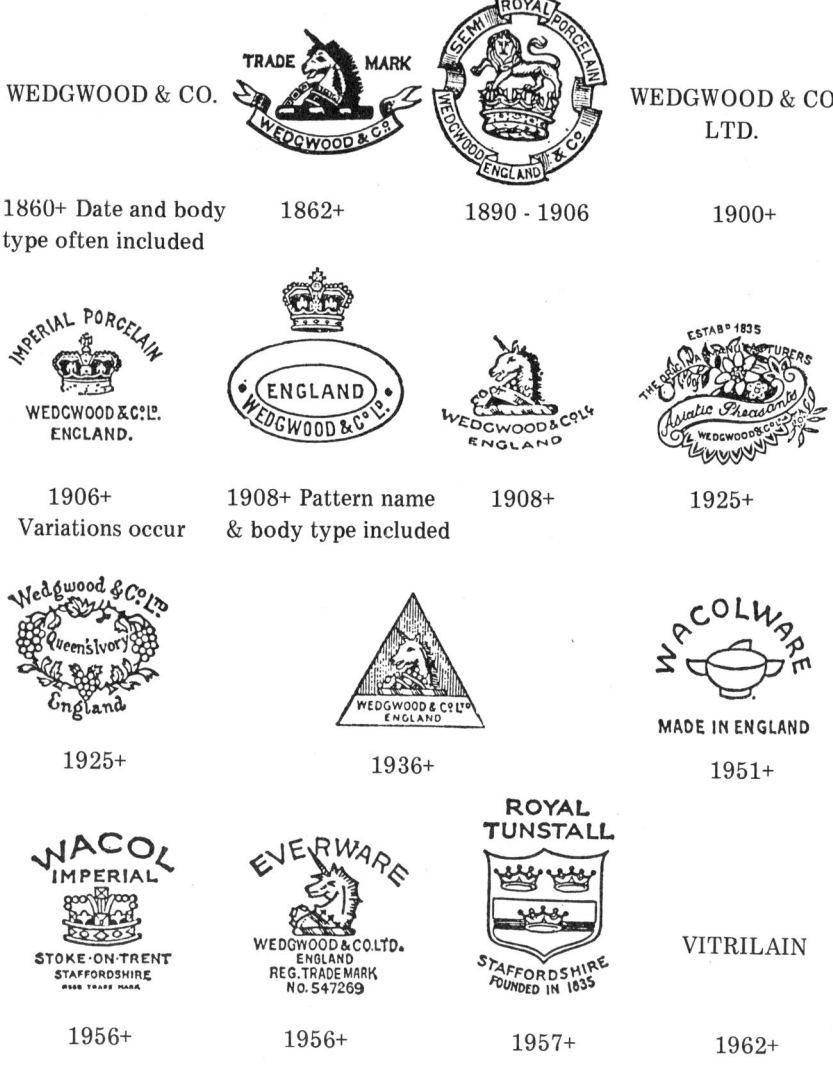

| WEDGWOOD & CO. | | | WEDGWOOD & CO. LTD. |
|---|---|---|---|
| 1860+ Date and body type often included | 1862+ | 1890 - 1906 | 1900+ |

| 1906+ Variations occur | 1908+ Pattern name & body type included | 1908+ | 1925+ |
|---|---|---|---|

| 1925+ | 1936+ | | 1951+ |
|---|---|---|---|

| 1956+ | 1956+ | 1957+ | VITRILAIN 1962+ |
|---|---|---|---|

Some other companies that used a "Wedgwood" or "Wedgewood" mark — Ferrybridge Pottery (1792 - ), Hollingshead & Kirkham (1870 - 1956), Podmore, Walker & Co. (1834 - ), William Smith & Co. (1825 - 1855), Ralph Wedgwood & Co. (1766 - 1837) and John Wedge Wood (1841 - 1860).

# WILEMAN & CO., & SHELLEY POTTERIES LTD.

Wileman & Co., Foley Potteries, Foley China Works, Fenton, Longton, England, 1892 - 1925. Earthenware and china.

Shelley Potteries Ltd., Foley, Longton, Staffordshire, England, 1925 - China.

| THE FOLEY CHINA ENGLAND | Trade Mark Late Foley SHELLEY ENGLAND. | CHINA SHELLEY ENGLAND |
|---|---|---|
| 1892+ | 1911+ | 1923+ |

| Shelley ENGLAND | FINE BONE CHINA Shelley ENGLAND | CHINA SHELLEY ENGLAND |
|---|---|---|
| 1925 - 1940 | 1925 - 1940 | 1945+ |

# ARTHUR J. WILKINSON (LTD.)

Royal Staffordshire Pottery, Burslem, Staffordshire, England, 1885 - Earthenware.

1891+      Ca. 1896      Ca. 1907
Variations occur

Ca. 1910      1930+      1930+

1930+      1947+

## WILTSHAW & ROBINSON (LTD.)

Wiltshaw & Robinson (Ltd.), Carlton Works, Stoke, Staffordshire, England, 1890 - 1957. China, earthenware.

Carlton Ware Ltd., Carlton Works, Stoke, Staffordshire, England, 1958 - Earthenware.

1890+

1894+

1906+ Mark continued by Carlton Ware Ltd.

Ca. 1914

1925 - 1957

1925+ Mark continued by Carlton Ware Ltd.

1958+

## WORCESTER MARKS

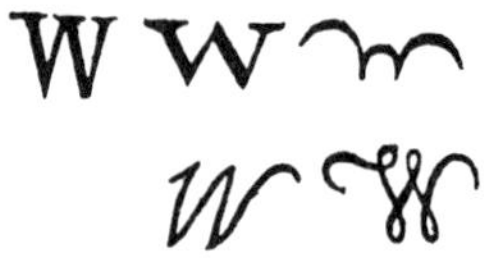

W W ᵐ
𝒲 𝒲
1755 - 1770

### THE ROYAL WORCESTER FACTORY TREE

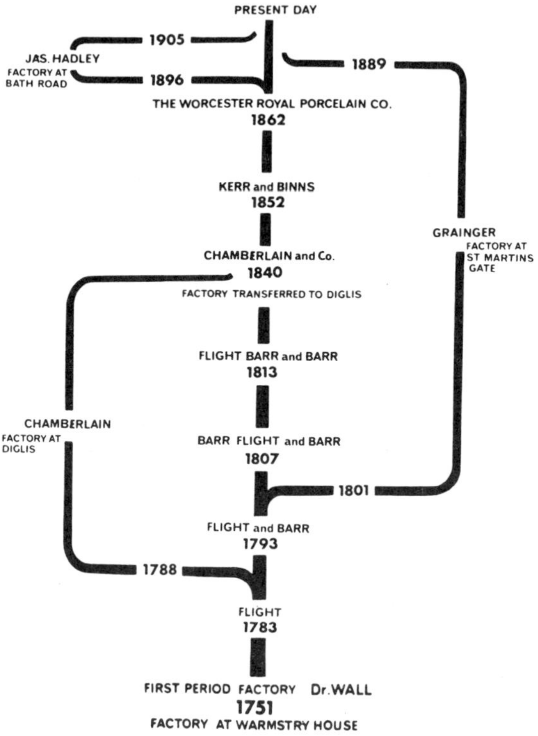

PRESENT DAY
JAS. HADLEY — 1905 —
FACTORY AT BATH ROAD — 1896 — — 1889 —
THE WORCESTER ROYAL PORCELAIN CO.
1862

KERR and BINNS
1852

GRAINGER
FACTORY AT
ST MARTINS GATE

CHAMBERLAIN and Co.
1840
FACTORY TRANSFERRED TO DIGLIS

C
*Flight*       *Flight* 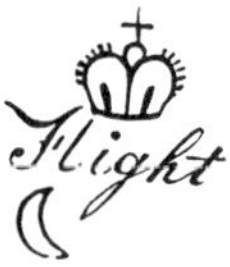
1783 - 1788    1788 - 1792

FLIGHT BARR and BARR
1813

ℬ  or  **B** incised
1792 - 1807

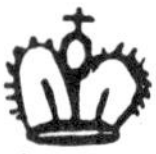

CHAMBERLAIN
FACTORY AT DIGLIS

BARR FLIGHT and BARR
1807
— 1801 —

*Flight & Barr*
1792 - 1807

FLIGHT and BARR
1793

— 1788 —

*Barr Flight & Barr*
1807 - 1813

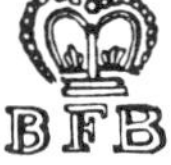

FLIGHT
1783

FIRST PERIOD FACTORY  Dr. WALL
1751
FACTORY AT WARMSTRY HOUSE

BFB
1807 - 1813

*Flight Barr & Barr*
1813 - 1840

### CHAMBERLAINS
1847 - 1850

*Chamberlain & Co., Worcester.*
After 1840

1850 - 1852

1854 - 1862

*George Grainger.
Royal China Works
Worcester*
1846

1852 - 1862

1870 - 1890

## WORCESTER MARKS — Cont.

ROYAL PORCELAIN WORKS WORCESTER
1865 - 1880

1897 - 1900

1900 - 1902

1902 - 1905

LEFT — 1862 - 1875 - numbers or a letter below the mark indicate year.
i.e.    73 for 1873    A for 1867
See Key Below —
RIGHT — 1876 - 1891 - letter below the mark indicates year. i.e. a for 1890.

### KEY TO SYSTEM OF DATING BY LETTERS

| | | | | | | |
|---|---|---|---|---|---|---|
| 1867 A | 1871 E | 1875 K | 1879 P | 1883 U | 1887 Y |
| 1868 B | 1872 G | 1876 L | 1880 R | 1884 V | 1888 Z |
| 1869 C | 1873 H | 1877 M | 1881 S | 1885 W | 1889 O |
| 1870 D | 1874 I | 1878 N | 1882 T | 1886 X | 1890 a |

LEFT — 1891 - Note: addition of words "Royal Worcester England" round the mark. and from 1892 onwards the following system was used to indicate year.

1892 — one dot between "Royal" and crown.
1893 — two dots - one either side of crown.
1894 — three dots, this method, adding a dot each year, continued until 1915 when 24 dots were used to indicate year. These dots are found on either side of the crown and also below the mark.
1916 — star - below the mark.
1917 — star and one dot - below the mark.
1918 — star and two dots - below the mark. Marking with the star and adding a dot to indicate year continued until 1927 when eleven dots had been added.
1928 — small square.
1929 — small diamond.
1930 — ÷
1931 — two interlinked circles.
1932 — three interlinked circles.
1933 — three interlinked circles - one dot.
1934 — three interlinked circles - two dots. Marking with three interlinked circles and adding a dot each year continued until 1948 when 16 dots had been added.
1949 — "V" under mark.
1950 — "W" under mark.
1951 — "W" with one dot, again a dot was added for each year until 1956.
1957 — "W" or "R" under mark, with a dot added for each following year until 1963.
1964 — "W" and 14 dots.

# CANADIAN POTTERS

*John Kulp Grimsby*

G BEECH/MAKER/ BRANTFORD/1863

*Cap Rouge Pottery*

W.E. WELDING
BRANTFORD. ONT

**BRANTFORD CANADA**

G. LAZIER
PICTON. C.W.

*Glass Bros & London*

# CANADIAN POTTERS

Among the many types of stoneware pottery made in Canada were utilitarian ware such as crocks, jugs, butter churns and flower pots etc., as well as household and hotel-ware including tableware, tea pots, vases and decorative ornaments.

Canadian-made pottery items that are marked with a potter's or pottery name were usually marked using one of the following methods.

INCISED — mark scratched into the clay using a pointed instrument.
IMPRESSED — a metal die was used to imprint names or initials into the clay.
PRINTED — marked using a stencil or rubber stamp.
MOULDED — when the maker's mark was part of the mould used in casting or pressing of pottery. It is usually found on the base.

NOTE: Place names and/or initials such as Berlin; C.E.; C.W. on pottery/stoneware gives an indication of when a piece was made, but can only be used as a general guide because often the "old name" continued in use after a new place name was assigned.

L.C.   LOWER CANADA (1792 - 1840) Part of what is now known as Quebec.
U.C.   UPPER CANADA (1792 - 1840) Part of what is now known as Ontario.
C.E.   CANADA EAST (1840 - 1867) Part of what is now known as Quebec.
C.W.   CANADA WEST (1840 - 1867) Part of what is now known as Ontario.
N.W.T. NORTH WEST TERRITORIES. Prior to joining Confederation in 1905 Alberta and Saskatchewan were part of the North West Territories.

Acadia Pottery — See: James Prescott & Sons

Jacob H. Ahrens, Paris, Ont. (1860 - 1883)
marks:  — J.H. AHRENS / PARIS, C.W.
        — J.H. AHRENS

Albion Pottery, Bolton, Ont. (1898 - 1904)
mark:   — ALBION POTTERY / C. SAUNDERS / BOLTON, ONT.

Francis Bailey, Cartwright Twp., Durham Co., Ont. (1855 - 1862)
mark:   — F. BAILEY

Orrin L. Ballard, St. Johns, Que. (1858)
Orrin L. Ballard, Cornwall, Ont. (1864 - 1869)
marks:  — ORRIN L. BALLARD / ST. JOHNS, C.E.
        — BALLARD / CORNWALL, C.W.

George Beech, Brantford, Ont. (1851 - 1869)
marks:  — G. BEECH / MAKER / BRANTFORD / 1863
        — MADE BY G. BEECH / APRIL 1862 / BRANTFORD / CANADA WEST
        — G. BEECH

Belleville Pottery Co., Belleville, Ont. (1901 - ca. 1914)
marks:  — BELLEVILLE POTTERY CO / SUCCESSORS TO / HART BROS. & LAZIER / BELLEVILLE, ONT.
        — B P & CO / BELLEVILLE / ONT. —in a heart shape

Belleville Stoneware Co., Belleville, Ont. (1870 - 1879)
mark:   — BELLEVILLE / STONEWARE / COMPANY

Bertrand & Lavoie, Iberville, Que. (ca. 1888 - 1890)
mark:   — MFG / BY / BERTRAND & LAVOIE / IBERVILLE, P.Q.

Adam Bierenstihl, Bridgeport, Ont. (1867 - 1900)
mark:   — BIERENSTIHL

Jacob Bock, Waterloo Co., Ont. (1820's)
marks:  — WATERLOO UPPER CANADA / SEPTEMBER 17, 1825 / JACOB BOCK POTTER
        — WATERLOO / THE 4 JAN / 1825

Boehler & Weber — See: Huron Pottery

Joseph Boehler, New Hamburg, Ont. (1874 - 1894)
mark:   — JOSEPH BOEHLER / NEW HAMBURG

BRANTFORD POTTERY

Justus Morton was the first to establish a stoneware pottery in Brantford, Ontario in 1849. Although several ownership/partnership changes occurred and two fires destroyed the factory, temporarily interrupting production, pottery was made at the Brantford site under several proprietorships from 1849 until 1907. "Brantford" pottery is the term often used when referring to the various products of the following firms.
Morton & Co. (1849 - 1856); Morton & Bennet (1856); James Woodyatt & Co. (1857 - 1859); Morton Goold & Co. (1859 - 1867); Welding & Belding (1867 - 1872); Belding (1872); Welding (1873 - 1894); Brantford Stoneware Manufacturing Company (1894 - 1907).

Brantford Stoneware Manufacturing Company, Brantford, Ont. (1894 - 1907)
marks:   — B S MFG. CO. LTD. / BRANTFORD
— BRANTFORD STONEWARE MFG. CO. / BRANTFORD, ONT.
— BRANTFORD / STONEWARE
— BRANTFORD / CANADA
— See also: F.P. Goold

John, Joseph & William O. Brown, Toronto and Bowmanville, Ont. (1860's - 1870's)
marks:   — BROWN with initials J & J or J & W O

Thomas Brown, Strathroy, Ont. (1881 - 1899)
mark:   — T. BROWN / STRATHROY

Brownscombe & Goodfellow, Peterborough, Ont. (1880 - 1881)
mark:   — BROWNSCOMBE & GOODFELLOW / PETERBORO, ONT.

Samuel Brownscombe, Owen Sound, Ont. (1882 - 1907)
mark:   — S. BROWNSCOMBE

William Brownscombe, Peterborough, Ont. (Estab. 1852)
mark:   — W. BROWNSCOMBE / PETERBOROUGH

Burns & Campbell, Toronto, Ont. (1879 - 1881)
mark:   — BURNS & CAMPBELL / TORONTO

David Burns, Holmesville, Ont. (ca. 1860 - ca. 1900)
mark:   — D. BURNS / MAKER

James R. Burns, Toronto, Ont. (1881 - 1887)
marks:  — J. R. BURNS / TORONTO
        — JAMES R. BURNS / TORONTO

Samuel Burns Pottery, Markham, Ont. (1870's)
mark:   — S. BURNS POTTERY / MARKHAM, ONT.

R. Campbell & Sons, Hamilton Pottery, Hamilton, Ont. (ca. 1890 - 1928)
mark:   — CAMPBELL / CANADA

Canada Potteries Ltd., Hamilton, Ont. (1928 - 1929)
mark:   — CANADA / HAMILTON / POTTERIES

Cap Rouge Pottery Co., Cap Rouge, Quebec (Estab. 1860)
mark:   — CAP ROUGE / POTTERY — is a mark used by the Cap Rouge Pottery Co. mid 1870's to early 1880's. Other potteries in the area also marked their wares with "Cap Rouge."

Cornwall Pottery, Cornwall, Ont.
mark:   — CORNWALL / POTTERY, C.W. — a mark used by O.L. Ballard or Flack and VanArsdale.

Crown Brick and Pottery Co., New Glasgow, N.S. (Estab. 1867)
mark:   — CROWN BRICK & POTTERY WORKS, NEW GLASGOW,N.S.

John Davis & Son, Davisville, Ont. (1890 - ca. 1928)
mark:   — JOHN DAVIS & SON / DAVISVILLE, ONT.

Joseph Davis, Davisville, Ont. (1845 - 1890)
mark:   — JOSEPH / DAVIS / MAKER / SEPT 1878

Derby Pottery, Kilsyth, Ont. (1869 - 1909)
mark:   — DERBY

Nicholas Eberhardt, Toronto, Ont. (1865 - 1879)
marks:  — EBERHARDT
        — N. EBERHARDT / TORONTO, C.W.
        — N. EBERHARDT / TORONTO, ONT.
        — N. EBERHARDT

Eberhardt & Halm, Toronto, Ont. (1863 - 1865)
mark:   — EBERHARDT & HALM / TORONTO, C.W.

William Eby, Conestogo, Ont. (Estab. 1856)
marks  — EBY
       — EBY, CONESTOGO

Elmsdale Pottery, Elmsdale, N.S. (Estab. 1856)
mark:   — R. MALCOM / ELMSDALE POTTERY

Farrar, St. Johns and Iberville, Que.
marks:  — MOSES FARRAR / ST. JOHNS, L.C. (1840)
        — E.L. & M. FARRAR / ST. JOHNS, C.E. (1841 - 1850)
        — E.L. FARRAR / ST. JOHNS, C.E. (1850 - 1857)
        — E.L. & G.W. FARRAR / ST. JOHNS, C.E. (1857)
        — G.W. FARRAR / ST. JOHNS, C.E. (1857 - 1871)
        — ST. JOHNS / STONEWARE (1857 - 1871)
        — ST. JOHNS / QUEBEC (1870's)
        — FARRAR & DENEAU (mid 1870's)
        — G.H. & L.E. FARRAR / ST. JOHNS, P.Q. (1871 - 1873)
        — E.L. FARRAR / IBERVILLE, P.Q. (1880's)
        — E L F (1880's)
        — E.L. FARRAR / POTTERY WORKS / IBERVILLE (1880's)
        — POTTERIES / FARRAR / IBERVILLE (1886)
        — ST. JOHNS POTTERY (1850's or 1860's) **
        — ST. JOHNS POTTERY WORKS (1873 - 1876) **
        ** Thought to be Farrar marks

Flack & VanArsdale, Cornwall, Ont. (1869 - 1907)
mark:   — FLACK & VANARSDALE / CORNWALL, ONT.

Eban T. Gilbert, Port Ryerse, Ont. (1886 - 1900)
mark:   — EBAN T. GILBERT / PORT FYERSE

Gillespie & Mace, St. Johns, Que. (1857 - 1858)
mark:   — GILLESPIE & MACE / ST. JOHNS, C.E.

Glass Bros. & Co., London, Ont. (1888 - 1899)
marks:  — GLASS BROS / & CO / LONDON
        — GLASS BROS / LONDON, ONT.
        — G B & CO / LONDON
        — GLASS BROS CO / LONDON
        — G
        — GLASS BROS / FIREPROFF / LONDON, ONT.
        — MANUFACTURED / BY / GLASS BROS & CO / LONDON, ONT.

Franklin P. Goold, Brantford, Ont. (1859 - 1867)
marks:  — F.P. GOOLD & CO / BRANTFORD, C.W.
— F.P. GOOLD / BRANTFORD
— BRANTFORD STONEWARE WORKS

Gray & Betts, Tillsonburg, Ont. (1883 - 1886)
mark:  — GRAY & BETTS / TILLSONBURG, Ont.

Gray & Glass, Tillsonburg, Ont. (1886)
mark:  — GRAY & GLASS / TILLSONBURG

John Groh, Waterloo Co., Ont. (ca. 1863 - ca. 1873)
mark:  — JOHN GROH PR

Hamilton Potteries, Hamilton, Ont. (1930 - 1947)
marks:  — HAMILTON / POTTERIES
— HAMILTON / CANADA / POTTERIES / OVEN / PROOF

H. Handley, Picton, Ont. (1894 - 1899)
mark:  — H. HANDLEY / MANUFACTURER / PICTON / ONT.

Handley Brothers, Picton, Ont. (1891 - 1894)
mark:  — HANDLEY BROS. / PICTON

W. Hart & Co., Picton, Ont. (1849 - 1855)

W. Hart & Co., Picton, Ont. (1849 - 1855)
marks:  — W. HART & CO. / PICTON, C.W.
— See also: Samuel Skinner, Picton, Ont.

Hart Bros. & Lazier, Picton, Ont. (1879 - 1887)
Hart Bros. & Lazier, Belleville, Ont. (1879 - 1901)
marks:  — H B & L
— H B & L PICTON / C.W.
— HART BROS & LAZIER / BAY OF QUINTE WORKS / PICTON, C.W.
— HART BROS & LAZIER / PICTON, C.W.
— H B & L / BELLEVILLE, ONT.
— HART BROS & LAZIER / BELLEVILLE, ONT.
— HART'S SELF BASTING ROASTER

Samuel T. Humberstone, Newton Brook, Ont. (1872 - 1920)
marks:  — S.T. HUMBERSTONE
— S.T. HUMBERSTONE / NEWTON BROOK
— S.T. HUMBERSTONE / NEWTON BROOK / ONT.

Huron Pottery, Egmondville, Ont. Established 1852 by Valentine Boehler, who formed a partnership in 1873 with Jacob Weber.
marks:  — (1873-76) BOEHLER & WEBER / MAKERS / EGMONDVILLE
— (1876) Jacob Weber became sole owner
— (1876-97) J.B. WEBER / HURON POTTERY / EGMONDVILLE, ONTARIO
— (1897) Jacob Weber sold the business to his brother, Joseph, who rented the pottery to John Allan.
— (1900) Ferdinand Burgard took over the pottery and it became F. Burgard & Son. Closed 1910.
— Miniature souvenir jugs with painted signatures often inclued F BURGARD or EGMONDVILLE.

J. A. Kennedy, Brantford, Ont. (1889 - 1897)
mark:  — J.A. KENNEDY / BRANTFORD, ONT.

John Kulp, Grimsby, Ont. (1829 - 1868)
mark:  — JOHN KULP / GRIMSBY

George I. Lazier, Picton, Ont. (1864 - 1879)
marks: — G.I. LAZIER / PICTON, C.W.
— G.I. LAZIER
— A.J. LAZIER / PICTON, C.W.

B. Lent, Lincoln, Ont. (ca. 1836 - 1841)
marks:  — B. LENT / U.C.
— B. LENT

The London Crockery Manufacturing Company, London, Ont. (1886 - 1888)
mark:  — LONDON CROCKERY MFG. CO. / LONDON, ONT.

London Pottery Mfg. Co. London, Ont. (1905 - ca. 1939)
mark:  — LONDON POTTERY / LONDON, ONT.

J.M. Marlatt & Co., Paris, Ont. (1859 - 1868)
marks:  — J.M. MARLATT / PARIS, C.W.
— J.M. MARLATT & CO. / PARIS, C.W.

McGlade & Schuler, Paris, Ont. (1868 - 1873)
mark:  — McGLADE & SCHULER / PARIS, ONT.

Medalta Stoneware Company, Medicine Hat, Alberta (1916 - 1924)
mark:  — MEDALTA STONEWARE LTD / MEDICINE HAT, ALTA.
       — Became Medalta Potteries Limited in 1924 and continued in business at Medicine Hat until 1959.
mark:  — MEDALTA / POTTERIES LTD. / MEDICINE HAT / ALBERTA

The Medalta pottery produced many types of stoneware articles: art ware, oven ware as well as tableware and used many variations of their mark on their goods, e.g. Medalta, Medicine Hat; Medalta, Canada; also pattern names and numbers were included.

Medalta pottery with the place name Redcliff dates from 1966 when the business began again at Redcliff producing the same styles and using some of the moulds from the Medicine Hat factory.

James Mooney, Prescott, Ont. (ca. 1847 - ca. 1856)
mark:  — JAMES MOONEY / PRESCOTT

Morton & Bennett, Brantford, Ont. (1856 - 1857)
mark:  — MORTON & CO. / BRANTFORD, C.W.
       — MORTON & CO. / BRANTFORD.

Morton & Goold, Brantford, Ont. (1859)
mark:  — MORTON GOOLD & CO. /BRANTFORD, C.W.

Orangeville Pottery, Orangeville, Ont. (ca. 1865 - 1880)
mark:  — ORANGEVILLE / POTTERY

Daniel Orth, Campden, Ont. (1851 - 1903)
marks: — D. ORTH
       — CAMPDEN / D. ORTH

Owen Sound Pottery Co., Owen Sound, Ont. (1894 - 1907)
mark:  — OWEN SOUND

Charles E. Pearson, Iberville, Que. (1880)
mark:  — C E P

James Prescott & Sons, Enfield, N.S. ( ca. 1880 - ?)
marks: — HENRY PRESCOT (sic)
       — HP - monogram mark
       — ACADIA POTTERY / ENFIELD, N.S.

Prince Edward Island Pottery, Charlottetown, P.E.I. (ca. 1880 - 1895)
marks:  — P.E.I. / POTTERY
        — P E ISLAND / POTTERY

John & James Richardson, Kerwood, Ont. (1860 - 1886)
marks:  — RICHARDSONS / EGYPTIAN WARE
        — RICHARDSONS WARE

St. Johns Stone Chinaware Company, St. Johns, Que. (1873 - late 1890's)
marks:  — Two types of "Royal Arms" mark with —
        — STONE CHINAWARE CO. / ST. JOHNS, P.Q. or QUE.
        — IRONSTONE CHINA / ST. JOHNS, P.Q. or QUE.
        — also without P.Q. or QUE.

Henry Schuler, Paris, Ont. (1873 - 1884)
mark:   — H. SCHULER / PARIS, ONT.

W. Schwab, Beamsville, Ont. (1853 - 1875)
mark:   — W. SCHWAB / BEAMSVILLE

Simcoe Street Pottery, Beaverton, Ont. (1876 - 1904)
mark:   — SIMCOE STREET / POTTERY / BEAVERTON

Samuel Skinner, Picton, Ont. (1855 - 1867)
   Samuel Skinner, a one-third owner of the William Hart & Co. pottery managed the firm from 1855 - 1867. The S. Skinner & Co. mark appeared on the wares made at the Hart pottery during his management.
marks:  — S. SKINNER & CO. / PICTON, C.W.
        — S. SKINNER
        — S. SKINNER & CO. / PICTON P.O.

Star Pottery, London, Ont. (1892 - 1905)
mark:   — STAR

Tara Pottery, Tara, Ont. (1867 - 1884)
mark:   — TARA POTTERY

William Taylor, Beaverton, Ont. (1873 - 1875)
mark:   — J.W. TAYLOR / BEAVERTON

Fred B. Tillson, Tillsonburg, Ont. (1870 - ca. 1883)
mark:   — F.B. TILSON / TILLSONBURG

Tillsonburg Pottery Co., Tillsonburg, Ont. (1880's)
mark:  — TILLSONBURG / ONT / POTTERY CO.

The Toronto Pottery Company was a subsidiary of the Robertson Clay Products Co., Akron, Ohio. Pottery marked by the Toronto firm was made in the U.S.A.

Joseph Wagner, Berlin (Kitchener), Ont. (1869 - 1880)
mark:  — JOSEPH WAGNER / BERLIN POTTERY

Warner & Co., Toronto, Ontario (1856 - 1863)
mark:  — WARNER & CO. / TORONTO

J.B. Weber — See: Huron Pottery

Welding & Belding, Brantford, Ont. (1867 - 1872)
William E. Welding, Brantford, Ont. (1873 - 1894)
marks:  — WELDING & BELDING / BRANTFORD, ONT.
   — W.E. WELDING / BRANTFORD, ONT.

White & Handley, Brockville, Ont. (1884 - 1890)
mark:  — WHITE & HANDLEY / BROCKVILLE, ONT.

James Woodyatt & Co., Brantford, Ont. (1857 - 1859)
marks:  — WOODYATT & CO.
   — JAMES WOODYATT & CO. / BRANTFORD, C.W.

## ECANADA ART WARE, HAMILTON, ONT., Ca. 1926 - Ca. 1952

Well designed and colourful Canadian made art pottery in the "Jasper Ware" style with moulded decoration applied in relief to the body of the ware.

George Emery who apprenticed and trained at Wedgwood, in England, emigrated to Canada in 1912. In 1926 Emery began making his pottery at his home in Hamilton and taking it to be fired at the Canadian Porcelain Co. where he was employed until 1945 when he established his own factory, Ecanada Art Pottery. Production ceased 1952 - 53.

marks:  — ECANADA/ART/WARE/HAMILTON
— ECANADA/ART POTTERY/MADE IN CANADA/ EMERY 1296
— AUCANADA
— ECANADA
— ECANADA/ART POTTERY
— EMERY/HAMILTON/CANADA

# American Potters

### BENNINGTON, VERMONT, POTTERY

Unfortunately for the collector, Bennington potteries left unmarked a large proportion of their wares. Pieces which are marked can be dated since the various combinations of markings have been recorded and are shown here with the years during which they were in use.

The first pottery was started by Captain John Norton in 1793 and continued to be a family concern until 1894.

In 1847 a second pottery was started by Christopher Webber Fenton, a relative of the Nortons by marriage. In 1848 he was in partnership with Calvin Park and Alanson P. Lyman. Many changes of name followed and in 1870 the pottery was demolished.

# A LIST OF VARIOUS BENNINGTON POTTERY MARKS

L. Norton & Co.
Bennington, Vt.
(1823 - 1828)

L. Norton
Bennington, Vt.
(1828 - 1833)

L. Norton & Son
Bennington, Vt.
(1833 - 1840)

L. Norton & Son
East Bennington, Vt.
(1833 - 1840)

Julius Norton
Bennington, Vt.
(1841 - 1845)

Julius Norton
East Bennington, Vt.
(1841 - 1845)

J. Norton
East Bennington, Vt.
(1841 - 1845)

Norton & Fenton
Bennington, Vt.
(1845 - 1847)

Norton & Fenton
East Bennington, Vt.
(1845 - 1847)

Julius Fenton
Bennington, Vt.
(1847 - 1850)

J. Norton
Bennington, Vt.
(1847 - 1850)

J. & E. Norton
Bennington, Vt.
(1850 - 1859)

J. Norton & Co.
Bennington, Vt.
(1859 - 1861)

J. & E. Norton & Co.
Bennington, Vt.
(1859 - 1861)

E. & L. P. Norton
Bennington, Vt.
(1861 - 1881)

E. Norton
Bennington, Vt.
(1881 - 1883)

Edward Norton
Bennington, Vt.
(1883 - 1894)

Edward Norton & Co.
Bennington, Vt.
(1883 - 1894)

Edward Norton & Company
Bennington, Vt.
(1883 - 1894)

E. Norton & Co.
Bennington, Vt.
(1883 - 1894)

Edward Norton Company
Bennington, Vt.
(1886 - 1894)

Lyman, Fenton & Co.
Bennington, Vt.
(1849 - 1858)

United States Pottery Co.
Bennington, Vt.
(1852 - 1858)

A.A. Gilbert Co.
Bennington, Vt.
(1859 - 1861)

NOTE:

Many types of ceramics were made in the United States — pottery, ironstone, porcelain and semi-porcelain etc.

Because there were so many manufacturers of ceramics who made a large variety of goods, such as utilitarian crocks and jugs etc.; dinner ware and decorative pieces we can only list a few American manufacturers and their marks in this book.

BUFFALO POTTERY CO.
Buffalo, New York, U.S.A.
1901 - present

1905+

1906+

1907 - 1940's    1909 - 1925

1911 - 1925    Ca. 1930

GLADDING McBEAN & CO.
Los Angeles, California, U.S.A.
1875 - present

 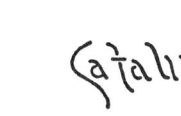

1923+           1930 - 1937

EL CAMINO
CHINA
MADE IN U S A
*California White*

Ca. 1934        1934 - 1940

1934 - 1960     1937 - 1942

   FRANCISCAN
                + + + WARE
MADE IN         MADE IN U.S.A.
U. S. A.
1938/9          1938/9

   PUEBLO
                MADE IN
                U.S.A.
                POTTERY

1939 - 1947     1940+

WILSHIRE
EL CAMINO CHINA
MADE IN U. S. A.

1942+           1947 - 1953

1963 - 1964

HALL CHINA CO.
East Liverpool, Ohio, U.S.A.
1903 - present

Hall China Co., Cont.

Ca. 1945

1903 - 1911   1903 - 1911

Ca. 1945                1950+

1916 - 1930   1930 - 1972

Ca. 1950 - Ca. 1955   1960 - present

1932 - 1963   1933 - 1976

1973 - present   1969 - 1980+

1933 - 1976   1936 - Ca. 1970

1981+

1937 - present   1939 - Ca. 1953

# HARKER POTTERY CO.
East Liverpool, Ohio, U.S.A.
1890 - 1972

## Harker Pottery Co., Cont.

Ca. 1890

1890 - 1900

Ca. 1944

1948 - 1955

1890 - 1930

Ca. 1930 - 1935

1948 - 1963

Ca. 1950

Ca. 1935

1935 - 1948

Ca. 1950

Ca. 1950

1935 - 1950

1935 - 1950

Ca. 1954 - 1965

1955 - 1960

1939 - 1947

1940 - 1948

HARKER CHINA CO.
EAST LIVERPOOL, OHIO
Ca. 1959

1960 - 1977

1960 - 1972

Ca. 1965

**HOMER LAUGHLIN CHINA CO.**
East Liverpool, Ohio, U.S.A.
1877 - present

1886+

Ca. 1900

1935 - 1955

**Homer Laughlin China Co., Cont.**

Ca. 1936

Ca. 1900

1901 - 1915

1936 - 1973

Ca. 1939

1901 - 1915

Ca. 1907

Ca. 1939

Ca. 1940

Ca. 1914

1926 - present

1940 - 1946

1940 - 1965

Ca. 1934

Ca. 1935

1941 - 1945

Ca. 1943

1935 - 1941

1935 - 1950

1946 - 1960

Ca. 1949

Homer Laughlin China Co., Cont.

Homer Laughlin China Co., Cont.

1950 - 1960

Ca. 1953

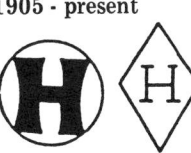
1970 - 1980

### A.E. HULL POTTERY CO.
Crooksville, Ohio, U.S.A.
1905 - present

Ca. 1953

Ca. 1955

1910 - 1935

1930's

Ca. 1955

Ca. 1957

1930's

1937 - 1944

Ca. 1960

Ca. 1960

Ca. 1950

1950's

Ca. 1965

Ca. 1965

REGAL
1952 - 1960

Tokay
U.S.A.
1958+

Ca. 1965

Ca. 1970

Coronet
U.S.A.
1960+

Imperial
U.S.A.
1960+

**EDWIN M. KNOWLES**
East Liverpool, Ohio, U.S.A.
1900 - 1963

1900 - 1948

Ca. 1905

Edwin M. Knowles, Cont.

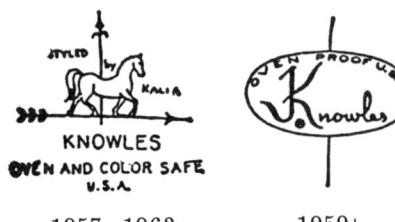
1957 - 1963   1959+

**KNOWLES, TAYLOR & KNOWLES**
East Liverpool, Ohio, U.S.A.
1870 - 1929

1910 - 1948

THE
EDWIN M. KNOWLES
1925 - 1931

STONE CHINA
K.T. & K.
1878 - 1885

1880 - 1890

1929+

1929+

1890 - 1905

1890 - 1907

1934+

1934+

1891 - 1898

1891 - 1898

Ca. 1935

1953+

1955 - 1957

Ca. 1956

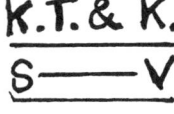
Ca. 1925

Redwing Pottery, Cont.

**LENOX INC.**
Trenton, New Jersey, U.S.A.
1906 - present

1906 - present

Temper.ware
1970+

1935+

1935+

OXFORD® BONE CHINA
MADE IN USA
current

LENOX
current

Ca 1967

LENOX
current

**ROOKWOOD POTTERY CO.**
Cincinnati, Ohio, U.S.A.
1880 - 1967

**NEWCOMB POTTERY**
New Orleans, Louisiana, U.S.A.
1896 - 1945

1895 - 1910

1896 - 1945

1880 - 1882

Rookwood Pottery
Ca. 1881

**REDWING POTTERY**
Red Wing, Minnesota, U.S.A.
1878 - 1967

1881 - 1882

ROOKWOOD
1882
1882+

1930+

RumRill
1933 - 1938

1880 - 1834

ROOKWOOD POTTERY
2075 EASTERN AVE
1891
CINCINNATI
Ca. 1883

Rookwood Pottery Co., Cont.

Roseville Pottery Co., Cont.

Ca. 1883

1914+

1914 - 1930

Rookwood began using the "RP" mark in 1886 adding a flame a year beginning in 1887 until 1900.

Beginning in 1901 the year was indicated in Roman numerals below the mark.

1915+

Roseville

Ca. 1930

ROSEVILLE POTTERY CO
Zanesville, Ohio, U.S.A.
1892 - 1954

1935 - 1954

1939 - 1953

AZUREAN

1900+  1900+

raymor
by Roseville
U.S.A.
OVEN PROOF
PAT. PEND.

1950's

Lotus

1950's

 ROZANE
RPCo

Ca. 1904  Ca. 1904

Ca. 1905  Ca. 1906

ROYAL CHINA CO.
Sebring, Ohio, U.S.A.
1933 - present

Royal China Co., Cont.

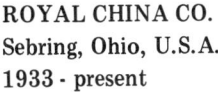

1940 - 1960

1950 - 1960

1933 - present

1934 - 1935

1951 - 1960

Ca. 1968

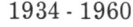

1934 - 1960

1934 - 1960

Ca. 1970

1934 - 1960

1938 - 1951

SALEM CHINA CO.
Salem, Ohio, U.S.A.
1898 - 1967

ROYAL CHINA
WARRANTED
22 KT. GOLD

Ca. 1940

Ca. 1940 - Ca. 1950

1918+

1918+

1940 - 1955

1940 - 1955

Ca. 1940

1940's

Salem China Co., Cont.

1940's

1940+

Sebring Pottery, Cont.

Ca. 1925 - 1940

Ca. 1925 - 1942

Ca. 1960

Ca. 1970

Ca. 1925 - 1943

**SEBRING POTTERY**
East Liverpool, Ohio, U.S.A.
1887 - 1948

**STANGL POTTERY**
Trenton, New Jersey, U.S.A.
Ca. 1929 - 1978

Ca. 1895

Ca. 1895

Ca. 1930

Ca. 1941

1890 - 1905

Ca. 1900

Ca. 1972

**STERLING CHINA CO.**
East Liverpool, U.S.A.
1917 - present

Ca. 1905

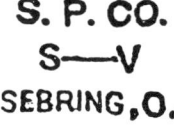
1900 - 1935

STERLING CHINA

Ca. 1920 - 1972

Ca. 1940

Ca. 1920 - 1935

S. P. CO.
S—V
SEBRING, O.

Ca. 1925

Ca. 1945 - Ca. 1955

Ca. 1946 - present

Sterling China Co., Cont.   Steubenville Pottery Co., Cont.

1947 - 1948

Ca. 1949

Ca. 1900

Ca. 1904

Ca. 1949

1951 - 1976

1904+

Ca. 1904

1951 - 1976

1951 - 1976

Ca. 1904

Ca. 1905

Ca. 1972

1920's - 1930's

1939+

**STEUBENVILLE POTTERY CO.**
Steubenville, Ohio, U.S.A.
1879 - 1960

Ca. 1879 - Ca. 1904

Ca. 1900+

Ca. 1960

Ca. 1960 - 1978

**SYRACUSE CHINA CORP.**
Syracuse, New York, U.S.A.
1871 - present

1886 - 1898

1893 - 1898

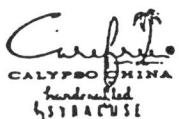
1930+

1935+

1966+

Ca. 1972

1972+

**TAYLOR, SMITH & TAYLOR**
East Liverpool, Ohio, U.S.A.
1901 - present

1901 - 1935

1908 - 1915

**Taylor, Smith & Taylor, Cont.**

Ca. 1920

Ca. 1925

Ca. 1928 - 1945

Ca. 1935

1935 - 1981

1937 - 1950

1938 - 1945

Ca. 1957

Ca. 1960

**T.S.&T.
DURABLE EDGE**

Ca. 1960

Taylor, Smith & Taylor, Cont.    Vernon Kilns, Cont.

VERNON KILNS
Vernon, California, U.S.A.
1912 - 1958

Vernon Kilns, Cont.         Weller Pottery, Cont.

Ca. 1950

Ca. 1950

1897 - 1898

1897 - 1910

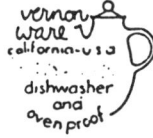
1950 - 1954

Ca. 1953/54

WELLER
1900 - 1925

SICARDO
WELLER.
1902 - 1907

Ca. 1903

Ca. 1904

1955

1955 - 1958

Ca. 1910

Ca. 1910

1920's

1956 - 1960

**WELLER POTTERY**
Zanesville, Ohio, U.S.A.
1882 - 1948

1920+

Ca. 1925

1895 - 1915

LOUWELSA
WELLER
1895 - 1918

Ca. 1928

Weller Pottery
Since 1872
1935+

# Furniture Styles and Periods

Furniture can be confusing, styles, periods and reigns of monarchs are all terms used to explain various fluctuations in taste and design. The chart on the following two pages lists furniture styles and periods, in England, France and the United States, from the 1100's to early in this century.

Characteristics of style did not change immediately at the beginning or end of a period, but were gradual. Also stylistic differences occurred with intrepretation. Furniture made in North America during colonial times did not always copy the style exactly as it was made in Europe and what was fashionable in England and on the continent may not have become popular in the colonies until a later date, i.e. Queen Anne style.

In Canada and the United States all the popular styles were made in formal (by cabinet makers) and simple forms (often called country, pioneer or cottage furniture because it was made locally).

The furniture collector is fortunate that many excellent books are available illustrating furniture styles. Also throughout North America there are many museums and pioneer villages where documented examples of furniture are on display from different eras of development.

Museums are an invaluable source of information, often displaying furniture with social histories of the area giving the nationality of those who settled there. By studying furniture in museums one can see how designs were modified to suit various needs and tastes.

| ENGLAND | FRANCE | UNITED STATES of AMERICA |
|---|---|---|
| Reign: Mary (1553 - 1558)<br>Period: Stuart | Period: Gothic (1100 - 1500)<br>Period: Early Renaissance (1550 - 1610)<br>Period: High Renaissance (1550 - 1610) | |
| Reign: Elizabeth I (1558 - 1603)<br>Period: Renaissance | Style: Provincial French (1600's - late 1800's) | |
| Reign: James I (1603 - 1625)<br>Period: Jacobean | Reign: Louis XIII (1610 - 1643) | |
| Reign: Charles I (1625 - 1649)<br>Period: Carolean | Reign: Louis XIV (1643 - 1715)<br>Style: Baroque | Period: Colonial (1620 - 1776) |
| Period: Commonwealth (1649 - 1660)<br>Cromwellian or Commonwealth | | |
| Reign: Charles II (1660 - 1685)<br>Period: Restoration | | |
| Reign: James II (1685 - 1689)<br>Period: Restoration | | |
| Reign: William & Mary (1689 - 1694)<br>Period: William & Mary | | |
| Reign: William III (1694 - 1702)<br>Period: William III or William & Mary | | Period: William & Mary (1690 - 1720) |
| Reign: Anne (1702 - 1714)<br>Period: Queen Anne | | |

| ENGLAND | | FRANCE | | UNITED STATES of AMERICA | |
|---|---|---|---|---|---|
| Reign:<br>Period: | George I (1714 - 1727)<br>George I or<br>Early Georgian | Reign:<br>Style: | Louis XV (1715 - 1774)<br>Rococo | Style:<br>Style: | Queen Anne (1720 - 1750)<br>Chippendale (1750 - 1775) |
| Reign:<br>Period: | George II (1727 - 1760)<br>Early Georgian | Reign:<br>Style: | Louis XVI (1774 - 1793)<br>Classic Revival | Style: | Shaker (1780 to middle 1800's) |
| Reign:<br>Period: | George III (1760 - 1811)<br>Late Georgian | Period:<br>Period: | Directoire (1793 - 1799)<br>Empire (1804 - 1815) | Period:<br>Style:<br>Style: | Federal (1780 - 1830)<br>Hepplewhite (1785 - 1800)<br>Duncan Phyfe (1800 - 1820) |
| Reign:<br>Period: | George III (1811 - 1820)<br>Regency | | | Period:<br>Style: | Directoire (1805 - 1815)<br>American Empire (C.1810-1840) |
| Reign:<br>Period: | George IV (1820 - 1830)<br>Regency | | (1815 - 1875)<br>Several Styles<br>i.e. Resotration<br>Gothic Revival<br>Classic Revival<br>Renaissance Revivalism | | |
| Reign:<br>Period: | William IV (1830 - 1837)<br>Late Regency or<br>William IV | | | | |
| Reign:<br>Period: | Victoria (1837 - 1901)<br>Early Victorian until 1860.<br>Late Victorian 1860 - 1901 | Style: | Art Nouveau (1875 - 1910) | Period:<br>Style:<br>Style: | Victorian (1837 - 1901)<br>Eastlake (1874 - late 1800's)<br>Mission (1890 - 1920) |
| Reign:<br>Period: | Edward (1901 - 1910)<br>Edwardian | Style: | Art Deco (1925 - 1940) | | |

# *Glossary*

ADAM BROTHERS. Robert (1728 - 1792). James (1730 - 1794). Architects and designers who were responsible for the introduction of furniture in the "classic revival" styles in England. Formal furniture with extensive use of classic motifs.

AMERICAN EMPIRE. (1815 - 1840) Not as ornate as French Empire.

ART DECO. (1925 - 1940) Simple angular design with flowing lines and usually decorated with nude figures, birds, animals or fish.

ART NOUVEAU. "New Art" (1875 - 1910) A style incorporating long, flowing, slightly curving lines inspired by natural growing forms, frequently ornamented with flowers, leaves, buds or nude figures.

ARTS & CRAFTS MOVEMENT. Began about 1875. Groups of artworkers whose aim was to re-establish the individual quality of craftsmanship. Although they were not too successful at their time, their ideas were later studied by twentieth century schools of design and influenced the design of modern furniture.

BAROQUE. After the Renaissance. Massive and complex with extravagant ornamentation and curved lines.

BIEDERMEIER. German, mid 19th century, heavy, solid, a variation of the French Empire style.

CHIPPENDALE. Thomas Chippendale (1718 - 1779). A designer who published "The Gentleman & Cabinet Makers Director" in 1754, and later editions in 1759 and 1762. His publication was the most comprehensive at that time and his designs were a guide to style in Europe and North America. The Chippendale style was adaptations, modifications, and amalgamations of late Baroque, Rococo, Louis XV, and Georgian with some Chinese and Gothic influence (with carving, veneer, fretwork, cabriole legs, claw and ball feet, also bracket feet). Chippendale made very few pieces of furniture himself, but his designs were used by furniture makers everywhere.

CLASSIC. Many styles of furniture were inspired by the ancient architecture of Greece, Italy, Northern Africa and the Mediterranean islands. Folios containing architectural details discovered during excavations at ancient sites were published and have inspired furniture designers ever since the Renaissance. Styles known as "classic revival" are Louix XVI; those of the Adam brothers; Hepplewhite; Sheraton; Directoire; Empire; Regency and Biedermeier.

COLONIAL. Furniture made in America 1620 to 1776. Many of the furniture styles popular during those years were made in America during colonial times. The settlers required furniture that was plain, simple and functional, whilst the wealthier preferred the type of furniture that followed the English tradition.

DIRECTOIRE. Less ostentatious than Louis XVI. Style of furniture that emphasized Greco-Roman form: sabre leg sofas; Grecian couches; curule legs; lyre-back chairs; and forward curving chair legs. Made after the reign of Louis XVI of France. So-called because of the type of government set up by Napolean, the Directoire 1793 - 1799, prior to France becoming an Empire in 1804. Forerunner to French Empire fashions. Popular in the United States 1805 - 1815. France aided the American fight for independence and after the war with England anti-British sentiment prompted this change of style.

DUNCAN PHYFE. Died 1854. A New York cabinet maker. Made furniture for the well-to-do in Adam, Hepplewhite, Sheraton and Directoire styles. Duncan Phyfe's work is known for the fine delicate carvings of leaf, plume and animal motifs.

EASTLAKE. Charles Lock Eastlake, a painter, architect, and art critic, maintained in his book "Hints on Household Taste, in Furniture, Upholstery, and Other Details," published in England 1869, that the time had come to return to simple styles. Furniture was made using his ideas until the late 1800's when mechanization in European and North American factories had a deteriorating effect on design. Ornate carving, fretwork and ornamentation was added to the simple designs he advocated.

EDWARDIAN. Revival of Queen Anne, Sheraton and Chippendale styles.

ELIZABETHAN. (1558 - 1603) Large furniture of severe straight outline. Gothic in style with elaborate use of Renaissance carving.

EMPIRE. A style originated by furniture designers during the first French Empire, 1804 - 1815. Based on ancient Egyptian, Greek and Roman architecture, simple rectangular structure, richly decorated with wreaths, urns, winged figures, and Napoleonic emblems. Sheraton and Duncan Phyfe made furniture in the Empire style. The Empire style of furniture made in Canada was similar to the American interpretation.

GEORGIAN. A term used for furniture made during the reigns of George I and George II. Early Georgian (1714 - 1760) furniture was a heavier version of the Queen Anne style with gilding and lavish decorations, e.e. eagles' heads; lions' heads; mythological figures and ball and claw feet. Late Georgian (1760 - 1811) Chippendale, Hepplewhite, Sheraton and Adam brothers styles were amongst those made in the late Georgian period.

GOTHIC. The style of architecture prevelant in Western Europe from the 12th to 16th century. Characteristics of furniture in the Gothic style have a similarity to the architecture, i.e. pointed arches, clustered pillars and ornate carving.

HEPPLEWHITE. Died 1786. An English cabinet maker whose furniture designs were simpler versions of the styles of Chippendale and the Adam brothers. Frequent use of oval shields and square tapering legs.

MISSION. Heavy, square furniture with psuedo mortise and tenon jointing, simple cut-outs with slat work in chairs and sofas. A style of furniture originally built by missionaries and Indians at Spanish missions in California and Mexico. This style was made popular by the Arts & Crafts Movement in America and England during the 1890's. Its popularity dwindled during the 1920's.

REGENCY. (1811 - 1830) A period in England when the country was ruled by a Regent. George III was declared permanently insane November 1810. His son, George, Prince of Wales, became Regent in 1811 and ruled England while his father was incapable. George III died in 1820, and George IV reigned until 1830. Furniture styles during this time were influenced by French fashion, such as Directoire and Empire.

RENAISSANCE. Revival of interest in art, literature and scholarship etc. that began in Italy in the 14th century and continued until the 16th century. End of the Gothic styles, beginning of "classic revival."

ROCOCO. Succeeded Baroque. Elaborately decorated with many shapes, such as, rocks, shells, scrolls, flowers, leaves and applied ornamentation of gilt bronze, gilding or inlay.

SHAKER. A rural American religious sect who believed that simplicity was a virture. Shaker furniture is well constructed, of simple and unadorned design in good proportion.

SHERATON. (1750 - 1806) English author, designer and cabinet maker. A style in the manner of Hepplewhite and Adam, he was also influenced by the Directoire style. Used carving rather than inlay, favoured reeded legs and half-round columns.

WILLIAM & MARY. Elegantly designed furniture with curved and molded stretchers, turned legs, bun feet and often decorated with marquetry. Furniture style changed during this period from large and imposing to pieces of more convenient dimensions.

# CANADIAN FURNITURE STYLES

Furniture made in Canada during colonial times and afterwards, whether in formal styles or utilitarian, was influenced by the traditions and furniture styles most popular in the homelands of the people who immigrated to Canada. Furniture was made in the major styles of the English, French and American periods and sometimes enrichments were added or simpler forms were made. Many fine pieces of Canadian-made furniture exist and are interesting examples of various interpretations of the different styles in fashion since the sixteenth century.

Some terms used to describe the various influences or periods of Canadian-made furniture are:

Anglo-American
English-Quebec
Doukhobor
French
Loyalist
Mennonite
New Brunswick
Nova Scotia

Ontario
Ontario-German
Polish
Pre-Confederation
Pre-Conquest
Pre-Loyalist
Ukrainian

Often provenance is mentioned when Canadian-made furniture is described, this type of information is most useful to one researching the historic brackground of a piece, often the place of origin will help to determine the style and tradition.

# *The British Registry Mark*

Beginning in 1842 decorative art designs were registered at the patent office in Britain. The British Registry Mark is a method for dating decorated metal, wood, glass and ceramic items.

A diamond shaped mark was used from 1842 until 1883, with the aid of several tables the date of registry is determined.

In 1884 a simpler method of marking the registry date was introduced. Design registry numbers preceded by the letters "Rd. No." were marked on a decorative piece, the year of registry is determined. by referring to one chart.

Other countries are known to have used the British Registry Mark. Japanese makers used a red painted design representing the mark. Haviland & Co. registered some of their porcelain designs and shapes in England and Limoges wares were exported by them to the United States and Canada. The mark "H & Co." or the full name are found with the registration mark. The date cypher does not indicate the exact year the wares were made as the registration protected the maker's design for three years and was renewable.

## 1842–1867

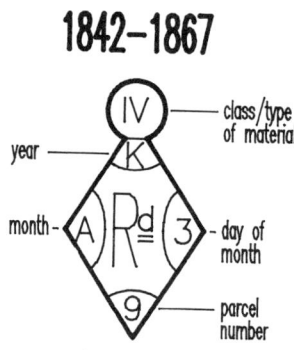

YEAR OF MANUFACTURE

| X — 1842 | E — 1855 |
|---|---|
| H — 1843 | L — 1856 |
| C — 1844 | K — 1857 |
| A — 1845 | B — 1858 |
| I — 1846 | M — 1859 |
| F — 1847 | Z — 1860 |
| U — 1848 | R — 1861 |
| S — 1849 | O — 1862 |
| V — 1850 | G — 1863 |
| P — 1851 | N — 1864 |
| D — 1852 | W — 1865 |
| Y — 1853 | Q — 1866 |
| J — 1854 | T — 1867 |

MONTH OF MANUFACTURE

| C — January | I — July |
|---|---|
| G — February | R — August |
| W — March | D — September |
| H — April | B — October |
| E — May | K — November |
| M — June | A — December |

TYPE OF MATERIAL OR CLASS

| I metal | III glass |
|---|---|
| II wood | IV ceramics |

PARCEL NUMBER: Indicates person or company who registered the design.

# 1868-1883

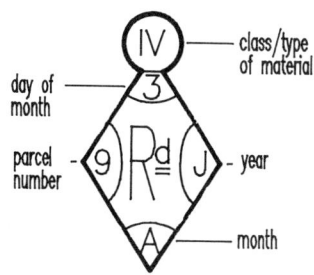

day of month — class/type of material — parcel number — year — month

### MONTH OF MANUFACTURE

| | | | |
|---|---|---|---|
| C — | January | I — | July |
| G — | February | R — | August |
| W — | March | D — | September |
| H — | April | B — | October |
| E — | May | K — | November |
| M — | June | A — | December |

### TYPE OF MATERIAL OR CLASS

| | | | |
|---|---|---|---|
| I | metal | III | glass |
| II | wood | IV | ceramics |

### YEAR OF MANUFACTURE

| | | | |
|---|---|---|---|
| X — | 1868 | V — | 1876 |
| H — | 1869 | P — | 1877 |
| C — | 1870 | D — | 1878 |
| A — | 1871 | Y — | 1879 |
| I — | 1872 | J — | 1880 |
| F — | 1873 | E — | 1881 |
| U — | 1874 | L — | 1882 |
| S — | 1875 | K — | 1883 |

PARCEL NUMBER: Indicates person or company who registered the design.
NOTE:
From March 1, to 6, 1868 the registration letter for the month was G — for the year W.

## REGISTRY NUMBERS (Rd. No.) BY YEAR

EXAMPLE:

Registry date 1902

Rd. No. 389307

R<sup>d</sup>N°38930

| Year | Rd. No. | Year | Rd. No. | Year | Rd. No. |
|---|---|---|---|---|---|
| 1884 — | 1 | 1902 — | 385180 | 1930 — | 751160 |
| 1885 — | 20000 | 1903 — | 403200 | 1931 — | 760583 |
| 1886 — | 40800 | 1904 — | 424400 | 1932 — | 769670 |
| 1887 — | 64700 | 1905 — | 447800 | 1933 — | 779292 |
| 1888 — | 91800 | 1906 — | 471860 | 1934 — | 789019 |
| 1889 — | 117800 | 1907 — | 493900 | 1935 — | 799097 |
| 1890 — | 142300 | 1908 — | 518640 | 1936 — | 808794 |
| 1891 — | 164000 | 1909 — | 535170 | 1937 — | 817293 |
| 1892 — | 186400 | Sep. 1909 — | 548919 | 1938 — | 825231 |
| 1893 — | 206100 | Oct. 1909 — | 548920 | 1939 — | 832610 |
| 1894 — | 225000 | Jan. 1911 — | 575817 | 1940 — | 837520 |
| 1895 — | 248200 | 1912 — | 594195 | 1941 — | 838590 |
| 1896 — | 268800 | 1913 — | 612431 | 1942 — | 839230 |
| 1897 — | 291400 | 1914 — | 630190 | 1943 — | 839980 |
| 1898 — | 311677 | 1915 — | 644935 | 1944 — | 841040 |
| 1899 — | 332200 | 1916 — | 653521 | 1945 — | 842670 |
| 1900 — | 351600 | 1917 — | 658988 | 1946 — | 845550 |
| 1901 — | 368186 | 1918 — | 662872 | 1947 — | 849730 |
| | | 1919 — | 666128 | 1948 — | 853260 |
| | | 1920 — | 673750 | 1949 — | 856999 |
| | | 1921 — | 680147 | 1950 — | 860854 |
| | | 1922 — | 687144 | 1951 — | 863970 |
| | | 1923 — | 694999 | 1952 — | 866280 |
| | | 1924 — | 702671 | 1953 — | 869300 |
| | | 1925 — | 710165 | 1954 — | 872531 |
| | | 1926 — | 718057 | 1955 — | 876067 |
| | | 1927 — | 726330 | 1956 — | 879282 |
| | | 1928 — | 734370 | 1957 — | 882949 |
| | | 1929 — | 742725 | 1958 — | 887079 |

| Year | Rd. No. |
|---|---|
| 1959 — | 891665 |
| 1960 — | 895000 |
| 1961 — | 899914 |
| 1962 — | 904638 |
| 1963 — | 909364 |
| 1964 — | 914356 |
| 1965 — | 919607 |
| 1966 — | 924510 |
| 1967 — | 929335 |
| 1968 — | 934515 |
| 1969 — | 939875 |
| 1970 — | 944932 |
| 1971 — | 950046 |
| 1972 — | 955342 |
| 1973 — | 960708 |
| 1974 — | 965185 |
| 1975 — | 969249 |
| 1976 — | 973838 |
| 1977 — | 978426 |
| 1978 — | 982815 |
| 1979 — | 987910 |
| 1980 — | 993012 |
| 1981 — | 998302 |

Designs Registry,
Patent Office,
Chancery Lane,
London,
WC2A 1LR
U.K.

# BRITISH MONARCHY
## ACCESSION & CORONATION DATES

|  | Crowned |
|---|---|
| William I (Ca. 1027 - 1087) | Dec. 25  1066 |
| William II (Ca. 1056 - 1100) | Dec. 26  1087 |
| Henry I (1068 - 1135) | Aug. 5   1100 |
| Stephen (Ca. 1097 - 1154) | Dec. 26  1135 |
| Henry II (1133 - 1189) | Dec. 19  1154 |
| Richard I (1157 - 1199) | Sep. 3   1189 |
|  | and Apr. 17  1194 |
| John (1167 - 1216) | May 27   1199 |
| Henry III (1207 - 1272) | Oct. 28  1216 |
| Edward I (1239 - 1307) | Aug. 19  1274 |
| Edward II (1284 - 1327) | Feb. 25  1308 |
| Edward III (1312 - 1377) | Feb. 1   1327 |
| Richard II (1367 - 1400) | Jul. 16  1377 |
| Henry IV (1366 - 1413) | Oct. 13  1399 |
| Henry V (1387 - 1422) | Apr. 9   1413 |
| Henry VI (1421 - 1471) | Nov. 6   1429 |
| Edward IV (1442 - 1483) | Jun. 28  1461 |
| Edward V (1470 - 1483) | Never crowned |
| Richard III (1452 - 1485) | Jul. 6   1483 |
| Henry VII (1457 - 1509) | Oct. 30  1485 |
| Henry VIII (1491 - 1547) | Jun. 24  1509 |
| Edward VI (1537 - 1553) | Feb. 20  1547 |
| Mary I (1516 - 1558) | Oct. 1   1553 |
| Elizabeth I (1533 - 1603) | Jan. 15  1559 |
| James I (1566 - 1625) | Jul. 25  1603 |
| Charles I (1600 - 1649) | Feb. 2   1626 |
| Charles II (1630 - 1685) | Apr. 23  1661 |

## British Monarchy Accession & Coronation Dates — Cont.

|  |  | Crowned |
|---|---|---|
| James II (1633 - 1701) |  | Apr. 23 1685 |
| William III (1650 - 1702 |  | Apr. 11 1689 |
| & Mary II (1662 - 1694) |  | Apr. 11 1689 |
| Anne (1665 - 1714) |  | Apr. 23 1702 |
| George I (1660 - 1727) |  | Oct. 20 1714 |
| George II (1689 - 1760) |  | Oct. 11 1727 |
| George III (1738 - 1820) |  | Sep. 22 1761 |
|  | Accession | Crowned |
| George IV (1762 - 1830) | Jan. 29 1820 | Jul. 19 1821 |
| William IV (1765 - 1837) | Jun. 26 1830 | Sep. 8 1831 |
| Victoria (1819 - 1901) | Jun. 20 1837 | Jun. 28 1838 |
| Edward VII (1841 - 1910) | Jan. 22 1901 | Aug. 9 1902 |
| George V (1865 - 1936) | May 6 1910 | Jun. 22 1911 |
| Edward VIII (1894 - 1972) | Jan. 20 1936 | Abdicated Dec. 11 1936 Never crowned |
| George VI (1895 - 1952) | Dec. 11 1936 | May 12 1937 |
| Elizabeth II (1926 - ) | Feb. 6 1952 | Jun. 2 1953 |

# IT'S A FAKE

We have in our collection a piece which we have dubbed "the genuine fake". It belonged to my husband's late uncle Sam who was a very serious collector and took care to authenticate his finds. This piece is seemingly a Roman medallion and possibly worth more than the original, because it was faked by men who became famous for their forgeries.

The medallion has a king on one side and a warrior on the other. There is wording round the edge and a snake forms the loop by which it hangs.

The Leicester Museum describes it thus:

> A well known class of 19th century forgery — called "Dock" forgeries or "Billy and Charleys." They were produced at the time of the excavations of a dock at Shadwell in the 1870's by two men known as Billy and Charley, who lived in Rosemary Lane on Tower Hill.

We are fond of this particular piece, it is a real "conversation piece" — it's a fun starter and stirs up so much in the imagination. You are not concerned with this type of fake, you are worried lest you buy a reproduction as really old, you wonder how to tell new glass or if that pine chest is early Canadian furniture or late barn door.

Reproductions and fakes are a business, everything that sells well has been copied from time to time. No one person can lay down hard and fast rules on how to avoid being deceived, — some of the greatest experts have been mistaken and misled, but not often. I can give you some general hints which will be useful (if followed) in avoiding costly errors of judgement.

1. **Look,** — that is, examine thoroughly in good light.

2. **Handle,** (with permission of the owner) different kinds or items have a different feel, this you can only understand by experience.

3. **Compare,** Does it have the style, shape and design, the right marks of the piece you are seeking? Is the price right for an authentic piece?

4. If you think you have a find, check the history of the piece — if you decide to buy, get a **receipt** which permits you a full refund if the piece is not what it is supposed to be, i.e. have the description, date, etc., in writing, then authenticate.

5. The above does not apply to **small** investments but even with inexpensive purchases don't buy on impulse if it will worry you that you have made a mistake.

6. Experience is a safeguard, when large sums are involved, get a **second opinion**.

7. Deal with those in the trade who have an established **reputation** for knowledge and fair trading. If you want specific items but lack real awareness of the values — let the dealer search for you — he can and will. This will save you time and money and result in your getting pieces that you are happy with.

8. For the greatest pleasure in collecting antiques, **study** your field, visit museums, old houses, pioneer villages, antique shops, read books, magazines, check modern furniture stores, department stores and gift shops also mail order cataloques for reproductions.

9. When in doubt — **find out** — remember the saying — "Caveat Emptor" if an item seems too cheap, apply it.

10. Buy what you can **afford**. Live with antiques. Good pieces have instrinic beauty, style, line and form, plus quality of craftmanship.

# Reference Books

Many thousands of marks exist on all types of goods produced by man.

It would be impossible for one book to contain all information. This list mentions some books on the subject of marks. Books that are now out of print can usually be found on the shelves of the public library.

ARONSON, Joseph. The Encyclopedia of Furniture. New York. Crown Publishers, Inc. 1965.

BARRET, Richard Carter. Bennington Pottery & Porcelain. New York. Bonanza Books. 1963.

BUXTON, Virginia Hillway. Roseville Pottery: For Love or Money. Nashville, Tn. Timbre Hill. 1977.

CHAFFERS, W. Collector's Handbook of Marks and Monograms on Pottery and Porcelain. London. William Reeves. 1968.

COLE, Ann Kilborn. Antiques: How to Identify, Buy, Sell, Refinish & Care for Them. New York. David McKay Company Inc. 1957.

COLLARD, Elizabeth. Nineteenth Century Pottery & Porcelain in Canada. Montreal. McGill University Press. 1967.

COWIE, Donald & Henshaw, Keith. Antique Collector's Dictionary. New York. Gramercy Publishing Company. 1962.

COX, Alwyn and Angela. Rockingham Pottery & Porcelain, 1745 - 1842. London. Faber & Faber. 1983.

CUNNINGHAM, Jo. Collector's Encyclopedia of American Dinnerware. Paducah, Ky. Collector Books. 1982.

CUSHION, J.P. Handbook of Pottery & Porcelain Marks. London. Faber & Faber. 1980.

——————— Pocket Book of French & Italian Ceramic Marks. London. Victoria & Albert Museum. 1965.

——————— Pocket Book of German Ceramic Marks. London. Victoria & Albert Museum. 1962.

DENKER, Ellen and Bert. The Warner Collector's Guide to North American Pottery & Porcelain. New York. Warner Books. 1982.

EAGLESTONE, Arthur A and Lockett, T.A. The Rockingham Pottery, (Revised). Rutland, Vt. Charles E. Tuttle Co. 1973.

ENGE, Delleen. Franciscan Ware. Paducah, Ky. Collector Books. 1981.

EVANS, Paul. Art Pottery of the United States. New York. Paul Scribner's Sons. 1974.

EYLES, Desmond. The Doulton Lambeth Wares. Totowa, N.J. Rowman & Littlefield. 1975.

GASTON, Mary Frank. Collector's Encyclopedia of Flow Blue China. Paducah, Ky. Collector Books. 1983.

GODDEN, Geoffrey A. Encyclopedia of British Pottery & Porcelain Marks. New York. Crown Publishers, Inc. 1964.

⸻⸻⸻⸻ Illustrated Guide to Mason's Patent Ironstone China. New York. Prager Publishers. 1971.

HUXFORD, Sharon and Bob. Collector's Encyclopedia of Fiesta. Padacah, Ky. Collector Books. 1981.

JENKINS, Dorothy H. A Fortune in the Junk Pile. New York. Crown Publishers, Inc. 1963.

KLAMKIN, Marian. Made in Occupied Japan: A Collector's Guide. New York. Crown Publishers, Inc. 1976.

KOVEL, Ralph M. and Terry H. Dictionary of Marks: Pottery and Porcelain. New York. Crown Publishers, Inc. 1953.

⸻⸻⸻⸻ The Kovels' Collector's Guide to American Art Pottery. New York. Crown Publishers, Inc. 1974.

⸻⸻⸻⸻ The Kovels' Illustrated Price Guide to Depression Glass and American Dinnerware. 3rd. Ed. New York. Crown Publishers, Inc. 1988.

⸻⸻⸻⸻ Kovels' Illustrated Price Guide to Royal Doulton. 2nd Ed. New York. Crown Publishers, Inc. 1984.

⸻⸻⸻⸻ Kovels' Know Your Collectibles. New York. Crown Publishers, Inc. 1981.

⸻⸻⸻⸻ Kovels' New Dictionary of Marks: Pottery & Porcelain, 1850 - present. New York. Crown Publishers, Inc. 1986.

LANGDON, John E. American Silversmiths in British North America. The Author.

⸻⸻⸻⸻ Canadian Silversmiths 1700 - 1900. The Author. 1966.

⸻⸻⸻⸻ Guide to Marks on Early Canadian Silver. Toronto. Ryerson Press. 1968.

LEHNER, Lois. Complete Book of American Kitchen & Dinner Wares. Des Moines, Ia. Wallace-Homestead Book Co. 1980.

⸻⸻⸻⸻ Ohio Pottery & Glass Marks & Manufacturers. Des Moines, Ia. Wallace-Homestead Book Co. 1978.

LESSARD, Michel and Marquis, Huguette. Complete Guide to French-Canadian Antiques. Agincourt, Ont. Gage Education Publishing. 1974.

MacDONALD-TAYLOR, Margaret. A Dictionary of Marks: Ceramics, Metalwork, Furniture. New York. Hawthorn Books. 1968.

MEYER, Florence E. Colorful World of Nippon. Des Moines, Ia. Wallace-Homestead Book Co. 1971.

NEWLANDS, David, L. Early Ontario Potters. Toronto. McGraw Hill Ryerson Ltd. 1979.

PAIN, Howard. Ther Heritage of Upper Canadian Furniture. Toronto. Key Porter Books. 1984.

RANDOM HOUSE. Collector's Encyclopedia, Victoriana to Art Deco. New York. Random House. 1974.

REBERT, M. Charles. American Majolica 1850 - 1900. Des Moines, Ia. Wallace-Homestead Book Co. 1981.

REVI, Albert Christian. The Spinning Wheel's Complete Book of Antiques. New York. Grosset & Dunlap. 1972.

RONTGEN, Robert E. The Book of Meissen. Exton, Pa. Schiffer Publishing, Ltd. 1984.

RYDER, Huia, G. Antique Furniture of New Brunswick Craftsmen. Toronto. Ryerson Press. 1965.

SANDON, Harry. Royal Worcester Porcelain from 1862 to the Present Day. New York. Van Nostrand Reinhold Co. 1973.

SAVAGE, George. Dictionary of Antiques. New York. Praegar Publishers.

SAVAGE, George and Newman, Harold. Illustrated Dictionary of Ceramics. New York. Van Nostrand Reinhold Co. 1974.

SHACKLETON, Philip. The Furniture of Old Ontario. Toronto. MacMillan of Canada. 1973.

SYMONDS, Richard and Jean. Medalta Stoneware & Pottery for Collectors. The Authors.

TOULOUSE, Julian H. Bottle Makers & Their Marks. New York. Thomas Nelson & Son. 1971.

TRAQUAIR, Ramsay. The Old Silver of Quebec. Toronto. Macmillan. 1973.

UNITT, Doris and Peter. Canadian Silver, Silverplate & Related Glass. Peterborough, Ont. Clock House Publications. 1970.

——————————————— Roden Bros. Limited 1917 Catalogue Reprint. Peterborough, Ont. Clock House Publications. 1974.

——————————————— Toronto Silver Plate Co. 1888 Catalogue Reprint. Peterborough, Ont. Clock House Publications. 1977.

——————————————— Treasury of Canadian Glass. Peterborough, Ont. Clock House Publications. 1969.

UNITT, Peter and Worrall, Anne. Unitt's Bottles & Values & More. Markham, Ont. Fitzhenry & Whiteside. 1990.

——————————————— Unitt's Book of Marks: Antiques & Collectables. Revised. Markham, Ont. Fitzhenry & Whiteside, 1990.

VANPATTEN, Joan F. Collector's Encyclopedia of Nippon Porcelain. Paducah, Ky. Collector Books. 1979.

WEBSTER, Donald Blake. The Book of Canadian Antiques. Toronto. McGraw-Hill Ryerson Limited. 1974.

——————————————— Brantford Pottery, Occasional Paper No. 13. Toronto. Royal Ontario Museum. 1968.

WEBSTER, Donald Blake. Early Canadian Pottery. Toronto. McClelland & Stewart. 1971.

———————————— English Canadian Furniture of The Georgian Period. Toronto. McGraw-Hill Ryerson Limited. 1979.

WHITER, Leonard. Spode. New York. Praegar Publishers. 1970.

WILLS, Geoffrey. Practical Guide to Antique Collecting. New York. Gramercy Publishing Co.

WYLER, Seymour B. The Book of Old Silver. New York. Crown Publishers, Inc. 1937.

# INDEX

| CERAMICS ........ 145 - 268 | Ceramics, Continued |

A & S ................ 156
A B J & S ............. 183
A B J & Sons .......... 183
A Bros ............... 157
A E .................. 185
A P .................. 208
A R .............. 172, 195
A W L ................ 168
Acadia Pottery ......... 249
Adderley Floral China Works . . 212
Ahrens, J. H ........... 243
Albion Pottery ......... 243
Alexander Pottery ....... 201
Aluminia .............. 217
American Limoges China Co . . 186
Anchor. ............ 163, 167,
 ........ 168, 174, 175, 261
Animal/Fish/Insect 157, 158, 159,
 161, 165, 166, 172, 175, 176,
 178, 181, 182, 191, 192, 194,
 205, 212, 214, 216, 218, 220,
 228, 229, 234, 235, 255, 260,
 265, 266
Arcadian ............. 156
Arcadian China ......... 156
Arkinstall & Sons ....... 156
Arrows ........ 212, 257, 260
Ashworth ............. 157
Ashworth, G L & Bros 157, 190
Atlas ................ 180
Aucanada ............. 252
Azurean .............. 262

B ................... 238
B F B ................ 238
B & G ................ 160
B P .................. 255
B P & Co ............. 243
B S Mfg Co Ltd ........ 244
Bailey, F ............. 243
Bakerite .............. 257
Ballard, Orrin L ........ 243

Banners .... 170, 184, 185, 191,
 .... 201, 227, 239, 256, 261,
 .... 262, 263, 267
Barr Flight Barr ......... 238
Bedford ............... 212
Beech, G ............. 243
Beehive ........ 173, 210, 217
Bennington ........ 253, 254
Belding ............... 244
Belleek ........... 158, 159
Belleville Potter Co ....... 243
Belleville Stoneware Co .... 243
Bertrand & Lavoie ....... 243
Bierenstihl, Adam ....... 243
Bing & Grondahl ......... 160
Birds . . 165, 174, 177, 183, 186,
 .... 204, 210, 225, 226, 229,
 .... 237, 255, 258, 260, 261
Bloor ................ 170
Bock, Jacob ........... 243
Boehler, Joseph ......... 244
Boehler & Weber ........ 248
Book ................. 259
Boote, T & R ........... 161
Bowl/Urn etc. .... 159, 169, 206,
 ........ 232, 234, 260, 266
Brantford ............. 244
Brantford Pottery ....... 244
Brantford Stoneware Works . . 247
Britannia Potter Co Ltd .... 166
Brown, J & J .......... 244
Brown, J & W O ........ 244
Brown, T ............. 244
Brownscombe, S ........ 244
Brownscombe, W ........ 244
Brownscombe & Goodfellow . . 244
Building/Tower/Statue ..... 160,
 173, 178, 184, 186, 189, 190,
 194, 206, 211, 224, 257, 266
Buffalo Pottery Co ........ 55
Burgard, F ............ 248
Burns, D ............. 245

Ceramics, Continued

Burns, J R . . . . . . . . . . . . . . 245
Burns, S . . . . . . . . . . . . . . . . 245
Burns & Campbell . . . . . . . . 244

C . . . . 162, 163, 226, 228, 238
C & F . . . . . . . . . . . . . . . . 166
C & F G . . . . . . . . . . . . . . . 166
C & G . . . . . . . . . . . . . . . . 227
C B D . . . . . . . . . . . . . . . . 163
C D . . . . . . . . . . . . . . . . . . 162
C E P . . . . . . . . . . . . . . . . 249
C F . . . . . . . . . . . . . . . . . . 174
C F H . . . . . . . . . . . . . . . . 185
C F M . . . . . . . . . . . . . . . . 185
C J M & Co . . . . . . . . . . . . 190
C M . . . . . . . . . . . . . . . . . 193
C M & S . . . . . . . . . . . . . . . 193
C M S P & S . . . . . . . . . . . . 193
C R A . . . . . . . . . . . . . . . . 163
C S N . . . . . . . . . . . . . . . . 163
C T M . . . . . . . . . . . . . . . . 189
C T M & Sons . . . . . . . . . . . 189
Calypso China . . . . . . . . . . . . 266
Campbell . . . . . . . . . . . . . . 245
Canada Potteries Ltd. . . . . . . 245
Canton China . . . . . . . . . . . . 265
Cap Rouge . . . . . . . . . . . . . . 245
Carefree . . . . . . . . . . . . . . . . 266
Caribe . . . . . . . . . . . . . . . 265
Carlton China . . . . . . . . . . . . 237
Carlton Ware Ltd. . . . . . . . . 237
Cartouche . . . . . . 162, 167, 173,
    179, 190, 193, 196, 197, 202,
    210, 211, 226, 227, 228, 234,
    257, 259, 260
Cataline . . . . . . . . . . . . . . . . 255
Caughley/Coalport . . . . 162, 163
Cauldon Ltd. . . . . . . . . . . . . 164
Ceramic Art Co . . . . . . . . . 158
Cetem Ware . . . . . . . . . . . . 189
Chamberlain & Co . . . . . . . 238
Circle/Oval . . 156, 157, 158, 159,
    163, 165, 166, 167, 168, 170,
    175, 180, 181, 183, 184, 185,
    191, 193, 196, 197, 200, 202,
    203, 204, 208, 212, 213, 214,
    217, 219, 220, 224, 226, 228,

Ceramics, Continued

Circle/Oval    229, 231, 255, 256,
    257, 258, 259, 260, 262, 263,
    265, 266, 267, 268
Clarice Cliff . . . . . . . . . . . 236
Classic . . . . . . . . . . . . . . . 260
Classic Heritage . . . . . . . . . 267
Clementson Bros . . . . . . . . . 165
Clementson, Joseph . . . . . . . 165
Cliff, Clarice . . . . . . . . . . . 236
Clio . . . . . . . . . . . . . . . . . 265
Clowes, W . . . . . . . . . . . . . 168
Coalbrookdale . . . . . . 162, 163
Cochrane, R & Co . . . . . . . 166
Cochrane & Fleming . . . . . 166
Colclough . . . . . . . . . . 212, 213
Columbia Chinaware . . . . . 257
Columbian Art Pottery Co . . 158
Cook Pottery Co . . . . . . . . . 158
Copeland . . . . . . . . . 227, 228
Copeland & Garrett . . . . . . . 227
Copeland Late Spode . . 227, 228
Copeland, W T & Son . . 227, 228
Cornwall Pottery . . . . . . . . . 245
Coronado Pottery . . . . . . . . 267
Coronet . . . . . . . . . . . . . . . 257
Courtney . . . . . . . . . . . . . . 170
Coxon Pottery . . . . . . . . . . 158
Craftsman . . . . . . . . . . . . . 258
Crescent . . 159, 176, 186, 264
Crescent China Co . . . . . . . . 264
Crossed Swords
    . . . . . . . 162, 170, 172, 195
Crown  157, 160, 163, 164, 165,
    168, 170, 171, 172, 173, 176,
    178, 180, 182, 183, 185, 186,
    190, 191, 192, 197, 198, 201,
    204, 205, 210, 211, 212, 213,
    215, 217, 220, 224, 225, 226,
    227, 228, 234, 235, 236, 237,
    238, 239, 257, 258, 263, 264
Crown Brick & Pottery Works  245

D . . . . . . . . . . . . . . . . 170, 172
D S P . . . . . . . . . . . . . . . . 220
Dale, C . . . . . . . . . . . . . . . 162
Davenport . . . . . . . . . 167, 168
Davis, John & Son . . . . . . . . 245

Ceramics, Continued

| | |
|---|---|
| Davis, Joseph | 245 |
| Delft | 169 |
| Derby | 170, 171 |
| Derby Crown Porcelain Company Ltd. | 170, 171 |
| Derby Pottery | 245 |
| Distel Goedenaagen | 178 |
| Don | 265 |
| Don, Edward & Co | 256 |
| Donatello | 262 |
| Donath | 172 |
| Doulton | 218 - 222 |
| Doulton & Rix's | 220 |
| Doulton & Slater's | 220 |
| Doulton & Watts | 219 |
| Dresden | 172, 173, 195 |
| Dupoma | 223 |
| Dux Porcalain Manufactory | 223 |
| | |
| E | 223, 230 |
| E L F | 246 |
| E M K | 260 |
| E S | 210 |
| Eberhardt & Halm | 246 |
| Eberhardt, Nicholas | 245 |
| Ebu, William | 246 |
| Ecanada | 252 |
| Egmondville | 248 |
| El Camino | 255 |
| Emery | 252 |
| Etruria Pottery | 159 |
| | |
| F | 255 |
| Farrar | 246 |
| Farrar & Deneau | 246 |
| Feathers | 158, 198 |
| Fenton | 190, 254 |
| Fenton's Works | 253 |
| Fermangh Pottery | 158 |
| Ferrybridge Pottery | 234 |
| Fiesta | 258 |
| Flack & Vanarsdale | 246 |
| Fleming | 166 |
| Flight | 238 |
| Flight & Barr | 238 |
| Flight Barr & Barr | 238 |
| Flower/Tree etc. | 157, 191, 192, |

Ceramics, Continued

| | |
|---|---|
| Flower/Tree | 204, 205, 211, 226, 230, 257, 264, 268 |
| Foley China | 235 |
| Ford, A B | 189 |
| Ford, Charles | 174 |
| Ford, T C | 174 |
| Ford, Thomas | 174 |
| Franciscan Ware | 255 |
| Furnival | 175 |
| | |
| G | 246 |
| G & Co | 179, 238 |
| G B | 180 |
| G B & Co | 246 |
| G Bros | 180 |
| G & C J M | 190 |
| G D A | 185 |
| G G & Co | 179 |
| G G W | 179 |
| G Mc B | 255 |
| G T M | 201 |
| G W | 179 |
| Garrett | 227 |
| Gilbert | 254 |
| Gilbert, Eban T | 246 |
| Gillespie & Mace | 246 |
| Gla Bros | 157 |
| Gladdin McBean & Co | 255 |
| Glass Bros | 246 |
| Goebel, W Porcelain Factory | 176 |
| Goedewaagen | 178 |
| Golden Wheat | 259 |
| Goold, F P | 247 |
| Goss, William Henry Ltd. | 177 |
| Gouda | 178 |
| Grafton China | 183 |
| Grainger, George & Co | 179, 238 |
| Gray & Betts | 247 |
| Grimwades | 180 |
| Groh, John | 247 |
| | |
| H | 172, 259 |
| H & Co | 184 |
| H & K | 181 |
| H B | 208 |
| H B & L | 247 |
| H L | 258, 259 |

Ceramics, Continued

| | |
|---|---|
| H P | 249 |
| H P Co | 257 |
| H R | 209 |
| Hadley's | 239 |
| Hancock & Sons | 224 |
| Hancock, Sampson & Sons | 224 |
| Hall China Co | 256 |
| Hallcraft | 256 |
| Hall's | 256 |
| Hamilton Potteries | 247 |
| Hamman | 172 |
| Handley Bros | 247 |
| Harker Pottery Co | 257 |
| Harkerware | 257 |
| Harlequin | 256 |
| Hart Bros & Lazier | 247 |
| Hart, W | 247 |
| Haviland | 184, 185, 186, 215 |
| Henriot | 209 |
| Hiawatha | 166 |
| Hirsch | 172 |
| Holkirk | 181 |
| Hollingshead & Kirkham | 181, 234 |
| Homer Laughlin China Co | 258, 259 |
| Hull, A E | 259 |
| Hull Pottery | 259 |
| Human | 166, 167, 211, 257, 259, 263, 268 |
| Humberstone, S T | 247 |
| Hummel | 176 |
| Huron Pottery | 248 |
| | |
| Imperial | 259 |
| Indian Stone China | 194 |
| Ironstone China | 250 |
| | |
| J & T F | 175 |
| J C | 165 |
| J F & Co | 175 |
| J H | 186 |
| J M S | 193 |
| J M & S | 193 |
| J R L | 168 |
| J R & Co | 168 |
| John, Ernest Creations | 256 |
| Johnson Bros | 182 |
| Jones, A B & Sons Ltd | 183 |

Ceramics, Continued

| | |
|---|---|
| K | 260 |
| K P M | 195 |
| K T & K | 260 |
| Kennedy, J A | 248 |
| Klemm, Richard | 172 |
| Knot | 212 |
| Knowles, Edwin M | 260 |
| Knowles, Taylor & Knowles | 159, 260 |
| Kokus | 264 |
| Kulp, J | 248 |
| | |
| L | 261 |
| Lamm | 172 |
| Laughlin China | 258 |
| Late Spode | 227 |
| Lazier, A J | 248 |
| Lazier, G I | 248 |
| Lenox Inc | 159, 261 |
| Lent, B | 248 |
| Lessore | 231 |
| Limoges | 184, 185, 186 |
| London Crockery Mfg Co | 248 |
| London Pottery | 248 |
| Looker & Co | 170 |
| Lotus | 262 |
| Lyman Fenton & Co | 253 |
| | |
| M | 172, 189, 196, 220 |
| M & B | 196 |
| M & Co | 197 |
| M & H | 197 |
| M & S | 194 |
| M S & Co | 201 |
| MacIntyre, James & Co | 200 |
| Magnet | 224 |
| Majestic | 258 |
| Majolica | 187, 188 |
| Malcom, R | 246 |
| Maling | 189 |
| Malvern | 213 |
| Marcrest | 259 |
| Marlatt, J M | 248 |
| Mason's | 157, 190 |
| McBirney, David & Co | 158 |
| McGlade & Schuler | 248 |

Ceramics, Continued

Meakin . . . . . . . . . . . . . 191, 192
Medalta . . . . . . . . . . . . . . . . 249
Meigh . . . . . . . . . . . . 193, 194
Meissen . . . . . . . . . . . . . . . . 195
Melba . . . . . . . . . . . . . . . . 213
Meyers & Son . . . . . . . . . . . . 172
Minton . . . . 196, 197, 198, 199
Morgan Belleek . . . . . . . . . . 159
Mooney, J . . . . . . . . . . . . . . 249
Moorcroft, W . . . . . . . . . . . . 200
Morley, Francis & Co . . . . . . 190
Morton & Bennet . . . . . . . . 244
Morton & Co . . . . . . . . 244, 249
Morton Goold & Co . . . . 244, 249
Mountford, George T . . . . . . 201
Myott Son & Co . . . . . . . . . . 201

N . . . . . . . . . . . . . . . . 173, 226
N C . . . . . . . . . . . . . . . . . . 261
N S . . . . . . . . . . . . . . . . . . 227
N W . . . . . . . . . . . . . . . . . . 232
Nasco . . . . . . . . . . . . . . . . 255
Newcomb Pottery . . . . . . . . 261
Nippon . . . . . . . . . . . . 202 - 207
Norton . . . . . . . . . . . . . . . . 254
Norton & Fenton . . . . . . . . 254
N S Pottery Co Ltd . . . . . . . . 213
North Staffordshire Pottery . . 212

O H E C . . . . . . . . . . . . . . . . 194
O P Co . . . . . . . . . . . . . . . . 266
O S . . . . . . . . . . . . . . . . . . 211
Old Curiosity Shop . . . . . . . . 263
Old Hall . . . . . . . . . . . . . . . 193
Old Hall E'Ware Co . . . . . . . . 194
Old Rose . . . . . . . . . . . . . . 260
Old Spice . . . . . . . . . . . . . . 259
Opaque Porcelain . . . . . . . . 194
Orangeville Pottery . . . . . . . . 249
Orth, D . . . . . . . . . . . . . . . 249
Ott & Brewer . . . . . . . . . . . 159
Owen Sound Pottery Co . . . . 249

P . . . . . . . . . . . . . . . . 208, 231
P B . . . . . . . . . . . . . . . . . . 208
P C . . . . . . . . . . . . . . . . . . 208
Patent Ironstone China . . . . . . 190

Ceramics, Continued

Pauleo Pottery . . . . . . . . . . 262
Pearl . . . . . . . . . . . . . . . . . 231
P E I Pottery . . . . . . . . . . . . 250
Phillips . . . . . . . . . . . . . . . 168
Plazuid . . . . . . . . . . . . . . . 178
Podmore, Walker & Co . . . . . . 234
Portland Pottery . . . . . . . . . . 212
Potter's Co-operative Co . . . . 173
Prescott, Henry . . . . . . . . . . 249
Prescott, James . . . . . . . . . . 249
Priscilla . . . . . . . . . . . . . . . 258
Pueblo Pottery . . . . . . . . . . 255

Quimper . . . . . . . . . . 208, 209

R . . . . . . . . . . . . . . . . 215, 262
R & B . . . . . . . . . . . . . . . . 238
R C . . . . . . . . . . . . . . 215, 263
R & C . . . . . . . . . . . . . . . . 215
R C & Co . . . . . . . . . . . . . . 166
R F . . . . . . . . . . . . . . 226, 227
R H . . . . . . . . . . . . . . . . . . 186
R K . . . . . . . . . . . . . . . . . . 172
R & L . . . . . . . . . . . . . . . . 214
R P . . . . . . . . . . . . . . . . . . 262
R P Co . . . . . . . . . . . . . . . . 262
R S . . . . . . . . . . . . . . 210, 211
R S R . . . . . . . . . . . . . . . . 212
R V . . . . . . . . . . . . . . . . . . 262
Ram . . . . . . . . . . . . . . . . . 178
Redwing Pottery . . . . . . . . . 262
Regal . . . . . . . . . . . . . . . . 259
Regina . . . . . . . . . . . . . . . 178
Richardsons . . . . . . . . . . . . 250
Ridgway . . . . . . . . . . 212, 213
Riviera . . . . . . . . . . . . . . . 265
Robinson & Leadbeater Ltd . . 214
Rogers, J & G . . . . . . . . . . . 168
Roma . . . . . . . . . . . . . . . . 260
Romantic England . . . . . . . . 192
Rookwood Pottery . . . . 261, 262
Rosenthal & Co . . . . . . . . . . 215
Roseville Pottery Co . . . . . . 262
Roxon China . . . . . . . . . . . 267
Royal . . . . . . . . . . . . . . . . 263
Royal Bayreuth . . . . . . . . . . 216
Royal Cauldon . . . . . . . . . . 164

Ceramics, Continued

| | |
|---|---|
| Royal China Co | 263 |
| Royal China Works | 179 |
| Royal Copenhagen Porcelain Manufactory | 217 |
| Royal Coronaware | 224 |
| Royal Crown Derby Porcelain Co Ltd | 170, 171 |
| Royal Doulton | 218-222 |
| Royal Dux | 223 |
| Royal Grafton | 183 |
| Royal Porcelain Manufactory | 195 |
| Royal Staffordshire Pottery | 236 |
| Royal Tettau | 216 |
| Royal Tunstall | 234 |
| Royal Vale | 213 |
| Royal Winton | 180 |
| Royal Worcester | 238, 239 |
| Royal Worcester Spode Ltd | 227 |
| Rozane | 262 |
| R S Germany | 210, 211 |
| R S Poland | 210, 211 |
| R S Prussia | 210, 211 |
| R S Tillowitz | 210, 211 |
| Rum Rill | 261 |
| S | 162, 226 |
| S A | 217 |
| S H | 170 |
| S H & Sons | 224 |
| S P | 265 |
| S P Co | 264, 265 |
| S & T | 211 |
| Salem China Co | 263. 264 |
| Salopian | 162 |
| Sampson, Hancock & Sons | 224 |
| Schegelmilch, Erdman | 210 |
| Schegelmilch, Oscar | 211 |
| Schegelmilch, Reinhold | 211 |
| Schoonhoven | 178 |
| Schuler, H | 250 |
| Schwab, W | 250 |
| Sears Robuck & Co | 258 |
| Sebring Pottery | 264 |
| Select | 258 |
| Sevres | 225, 226 |
| Shelley Potteries Ltd | 235 |
| Shield | 158, 161, 173, 179, 183, |

Ceramics, Continued

| | |
|---|---|
| Shield | 185, 186, 201, 206, 220, 234, 235, 238, 239, 264, 266 |
| Ship | 161, 175, 228, 260 |
| Silhouette | 266 |
| Simcoe Street Pottery | 250 |
| Skinner, S | 250 |
| Smith, William & Co | 234 |
| Spode | 227, 228 |
| Square/Rectangle etc. | 157, 179, 184, 193, 204, 206, 212, 219, 226, 227, 228, 229, 255, 256, 263 |
| St Johns Pottery | 246 |
| St Johns Stone Chinaware Co | 250 |
| St Johns Stoneware | 246 |
| Stangl Pottery | 264 |
| Star Pottery | 250 |
| Star/Sun | 172, 180, 183, 186, 192, 205 |
| Sterling China Co | 264, 265 |
| Steubenville Pottery Co | 265 |
| Stevenson Sharp & Co | 170 |
| Stone Chinaware Co | 250 |
| Stubbs & Kent | 168 |
| Sturdi Ware | 264 |
| Sun-Glow | 257 |
| Swan China | 174 |
| Syracuse China Corp | 266 |
| T | 216 |
| T B & S | 161 |
| T & C F | 174 |
| T F | 174 |
| T F & Co | 175 |
| T F Sons | 175 |
| T H | 184, 185 |
| T & R B | 161 |
| T S T | 266 |
| T S & T | 266 |
| Tara Pottery | 250 |
| Taylor, J W | 250 |
| Taylor, Smith & Taylor | 266, 267 |
| Taylorstone | 267 |
| Taylorton | 267 |
| Tettau Porcelain Factory | 216 |
| Thieme, Carl | 173 |
| Tilson, F B | 250 |

### Ceramics, Continued

Tillsonburg Pottery Co ...... 251
Tokay ............... 259
Toronto Pottery Co ........ 251
Triangle ............ 176, 189,
........ 208, 223, 226, 234
Tropico Pottery .......... 255
Triumph .............. 259
Tudor Rose ............ 258
Tujiyam ................ 262
Turner ............... 162

U S P ............... 253
Ultra Dine ............. 265
United States Pottery Co  253, 254

V .................... 176
Vale .................. 213
Vernon China ............ 267
Vernon Kilns ........ 267, 268
Vernon's ............. 268
Vernonware ....... 267, 268
Vitrilain ................ 234

W .................... 238
W & B .............. 231
W & C .............. 235
W & Co .............. 229
W H G .............. 177
W G .................. 176
W M .................. 200
W & R .............. 237
Wacolware ............. 234
Wade & Co .............. 229
Wade, George & Son Ltd .... 229
Wade Heath & Co .... 229, 230
Wade (Ulster) Ltd .... 229, 230
Wagner, Joseph .......... 251
Warner & Co ........... 251
Weber, J B .......... 248, 251
Wedge Wood, John ........ 234
Wedgwood .......... 231, 232
Wedgwood & Bentley ...... 231
Wedgwood & Co Ltd ...... 234
Wedgwood, Josiah .... 231 - 233
Wedgwood, Ralph & Co .... 234
Welding ............... 244
Welding & Belding .... 244, 251

### Ceramics, Continued

Welding, W E ........... 251
Weller ............... 268
Weller Pottery ........... 268
Wells ................. 258
White & Handley ......... 251
Wild Rose ............. 258
Wileman & Co ........... 235
Wilkinson, Arthur J ........ 236
Wilkinson's .............. 236
Willets Mfg Co .......... 159
Wilson, Norman .......... 232
Wiltshaw & Robinson Ltd .... 237
Wood, Arthur ........... 168
Wolfsohn .............. 172
Woodyatt & Co .......... 251
Woodyatt, James .......... 244
Worcester .......... 238, 239
Wright, Russel ........ 260, 265

Zenith Gouda .......... 178
Zuid Gouda ............ 178

### GLASS ............ 99 - 143

Adna .............. 107, 108
Alford ............... 110
Almy & Thomas .......... 110
Argy-Rousseau .......... 104
Art Glass .......... 104, 109
Averbeck Cut Glass Cut .... 110

B ............... 110, 124
B F G Co ............. 122
B G Co ............. 122
B G W ............. 122
Baccarat ............. 104
Beaver Flint Glass Co .. 119, 122
Belleville Cut Glass ........ 115
Bergen ............... 110
Birks .............. 114, 115
British American Glass Works  117
Burlington Glass
    Works ...... 118, 121, 122

C ............... 114, 122
Caledonia Glass Works ...... 118

292

## Glass, Continued

Canada Glass Works . . . . . . . . 117
Canadian Glass Mfg. Co . . . . 121
Clapperton & Sons . . . . . . . . 114
Clark . . . . . . . . . . . . . . . . . . 110
Consumers Glass Co . . . . 118, 122
Cristallerie d'E . . . . . . . . . . 105
Cut Glass . . . . . . . . . . 110 - 115

D . . . . . . . . . . . . . . . . . . . . 123
D G Co . . . . . . . . . . . . . . . . 122
D'Argental . . . . . . . . . . . . . . 104
Daum . . . . . . . . . . . . . . . . 104
Daum Nancy . . . . . . . . . . . . 104
DeLatte . . . . . . . . . . . . . . . . 104
DeVez . . . . . . . . . . . . . . . . 105
Diamond Flint Glass
    Company . . . . 116, 118, 121
Diamond Glass Co
    . . . . . . . . 116, 118, 121, 122
Domglas Inc . . . . . . . . 116, 121
Dominion . . . . . . . . . . . . . . 123
Dominion Glass Co 116, 117, 118,
    . . . . . . . . 120, 121, 122, 123
Dorflinger . . . . . . . . . . . . . . 110

E . . . . . . . . . . . . . . . . . . . . 123
E G Co . . . . . . . . . . . . . . . . 123
Egginton . . . . . . . . . . . . . . 110
Elite . . . . . . . . . . . . . . . . . . 114
Erie Glass Works . . . . . . 119, 123
Excelsior Glass Co
    . . . . . . . . 115, 117, 118, 123

Favrile . . . . . . . . . . . . 107, 108
Foster Bros . . . . . . . . . . . . 117
Foster Glass Works . . . . . . . . 119
Fry . . . . . . . . . . . . . . . . . . 110

G C Co . . . . . . . . . . . . . . . . 114
Galle . . . . . . . . . . . . . . . . . . 105
Glass - Various —
    Trademarks . . . . . . 125 - 143
Gowans & Kent . . . . . . . . . . 114
Gregory, Mary . . . . . . . . . . 109
Gundy - Clapperton . . . . . . . . 114

H G . . . . . . . . . . . . . . . . . . 124

## Glass, Continued

H G Co . . . . . . . . . . . . . . . . 124
H G W . . . . . . . . . . . . . . . . 124
Hamilton Glass
    Works . . . . . . 118, 121, 124
Hawkes . . . . . . . . . . . . . . . . 111
Hoare, J & Co . . . . . . . . . . . . 111
Hobbs . . . . . . . . . . . . . . . . . . 111
Hope Glass Works . . . . . . . . 111
Humphreys Glass Co . . 116, 117
Hunt . . . . . . . . . . . . . . . . . . 111

I X L . . . . . . . . . . . . . . . . . . 123
Irving . . . . . . . . . . . . . . . . 111

Jefferson Glass Co . . . . . . 121

L . . . . . . . . . . . . . . . . . . . . 111
L C T . . . . . . . . . . . . . . . . 108
L C T & Co . . . . . . . . . . . . 108
L G Co . . . . . . . . . . . . . . . . 124
Lackawana Cut Glass . . . . . . 111
Lakefield Cut Glass . . . . . . . . 115
Lalique . . . . . . . . . . . . . . . . 106
Lamont Glass Co . . 116. 121, 124
Laurel . . . . . . . . . . . . . . . . 111
LeGras . . . . . . . . . . . . . . . . 105
Libbey . . . . . . . . . . . . . . . . 111
Libbey-St Clair Inc. . . . . . . . . 121
Loetz . . . . . . . . . . . . . . . . 105
Lotus . . . . . . . . . . . . . . . . 111
Lyons . . . . . . . . . . . . . . . . 111

M . . . . . . . . . . . . . . . . . 112, 124
M T W G Co . . . . . . . . . . . . 112
Majestic Cut Glass . . . . . . . . 112
Mallorytown Glass Works . . . . 118
Manitoba Glass Mfg Co . . . . . . 124
Manitoba Glass Works . . 119, 121
Maple City Glass Co. . . . . . . 112
Mid-West Glass Co . . . . 119, 124
Moser . . . . . . . . . . . . . . . . 105
Mt Washington Glass Co . . . . 112
Mueller . . . . . . . . . . . . . . . . 105

Napanee Glass Works . . . . . . 119
Nash . . . . . . . . . . . . . . 107, 108
New Brunswick Glass Co . . . . 117
Newark . . . . . . . . . . . . . . . . 112

Glass, Continued

North American Glass Co   118, 121
Northwood, John . . . . . . . . 104
Nova Scotia Glass Co . . . . . 121

Ontario Glass Works . . . . . . . . 119
Ottawa Cut Glass . . . . . . . . 115
Ottawa Glass Works . . . . . . . . 117

P . . . . . . . . . . . . . . . . . . . 112
P & B . . . . . . . . . . . . . . . 112
Pairpoint . . . . . . . . . . . . . . 112
Pantin . . . . . . . . . . . . . . . . 105
Parche, P X & Son . . . . . . . . 112
Phillips, George & Co . . . . . . 115
Pitkin & Brooks . . . . . . . . . . 112

Quaker City Cut Glass Co . . . . 112
Queen's Burmese . . . . . . . . . . 104

R . . . . . . . . . . . . . . . . . . . 115
R G Co T . . . . . . . . . . . . . 124
Richards Glass Co . . . . . . . . 124
Rigo . . . . . . . . . . . . . . . . . 124
Roden Bros . . . . . . . . . . . . 115
Rutherford & Co . . . . . . . . . . 124

S . . . . . . . . . . . . . . . . . . . 112
S W . . . . . . . . . . . . . . . . . 104
S & W . . . . . . . . . . . . . . . 104
ST L . . . . . . . . . . . . . . . . . 124
Sandwich & Boston Glass Co . . 109
Schneider . . . . . . . . . . . . . . 105
Signet . . . . . . . . . . . . . . . 112
Sinclaire, H P & Co . . . . . . . . 112
St John's Glass Co . . . . . . . . 117
St Lawrence Glass
    Company . . . . 115, 117, 124
Sterling . . . . . . . . . . . . 105, 112
Steuben . . . . . . . . . . . . . . . 113
Stevens & Williams . . . . . . . . 104
Straus . . . . . . . . . . . . . . . . 112
Sydenham Glass Co . . . . 119, 121

T B . . . . . . . . . . . . . . . . . . 113
T G Co . . . . . . . . . . . . . . . 124
T G D Co . . . . . . . . . . . . . . 108
Taylor . . . . . . . . . . . . . . . . 103

Glass, Continued

Tiffany . . . . . . . . . . . . 107, 108
Toronto Glass Co   119, 192, 124
Tuthill . . . . . . . . . . . . . . . . 113

Unger Bros . . . . . . . . . . . . . 113

Val St Lambert . . . . . . . . . . 105
Van Heusen, Charles . . . . . . 113
Victoria Glass & Bottle Co . . 120

W & W . . . . . . . . . . . . . . . 104
Wallaceburg Cut Glass Co . . . . 115
Walter, A . . . . . . . . . . . . . 104
Webb . . . . . . . . . . . . . . . . 104
Woodhall . . . . . . . . . . . . . . 104
Wright . . . . . . . . . . . . . . . 113

SILVER, CANADIAN . .   5 - 79

A & E . . . . . . . . . . . . . . . . 73
A & J HAY . . . . . . . . . . . . . 8
A B . . . . . . . . . . . . . . . . . 70
A C J & B . . . . . . . . . . . . . 70
A H . . . . . . . . . . . . . . . . . 76
A J R . . . . . . . . . . . . . . . . 71
A K & S . . . . . . . . . . . . . . . 70
A M . . . . . . . . . . . . . . . . . 9
A P . . . . . . . . . . . . . . . . . 11
A PAGE . . . . . . . . . . . . . . 11
A R . . . . . . . . . . . . . . 21, 22
A S H . . . . . . . . . . . . . . . . 8
A S HAY . . . . . . . . . . . . . . 8
A T . . . . . . . . . . . . . . . . . 23
Acme Plate Company . . . . . . 51
Acme Silver Co., The . . . . . . 41
Addison, Charles . . . . . . . . . . 40
Agnew, James . . . . . . . . . . . . 6
Allan, Thomas . . . . . . . . . . 56
Allen, Josiah . . . . . . . . . . . . 12
Amiot, Jean Nicolas . . . . . . . . 74
Amiot, Laurent . . . . . . . . . . 74
Anderson, Robert . . . . . . . . 26
Arms & Quigley . . . . . . . . . . 42
Arnoldi, Charles . . . . . . . . . . 56
Arnoldi, John Peter . . . . . . . . 56
Arnoldi, Michael . . . . . . . . . . 57

Silver, Continued

| | |
|---|---|
| B B E | 16 |
| B E | 16 |
| B ETTER | 16 |
| B H | 18 |
| B HURD | 18 |
| B M CO | 55 |
| B P & B | 12 |
| B P M CO | 54 |
| B W | 6 |
| Baker, T. H. | 36 |
| Barlow, Edouard | 57 |
| BARRY | 6 |
| Barry, John | 6 |
| Baume, Gustave La | 12 |
| Bean, John | 57 |
| Beaudry, Narcisse | 57 |
| BEAVER | 35 |
| Becker & Cornelius | 13 |
| Beemer & Newbury | 34 |
| Beguay, Jean Baptiste | 74 |
| Bell, Wm. | 42 |
| BENEDICT PROCTOR | 54 |
| Benedict Ptoctor Mfg. Co. | 54 |
| Bennett, John B. | 13 |
| Bessonett, J.S.B. | 12 |
| Bewes, Daniel | 74 |
| BILSKY & SON | 69 |
| BIRD | 28 |
| BIRKS 57, 64, 65, 68, | 69 |
| Birks, Henry & Sons . . . . 57, | 64, |
| . . . . . . . . . . . 65, 68, | 69 |
| Bishop, Henry | 25 |
| Black & Parker | 12 |
| Black, Parker & Black | 12 |
| Black, Wm. A & S | 12 |
| Bohle, David | 58 |
| Bohle, Francis | 58 |
| Bohle, Peter | 58 |
| Boivin, Louis Phillpe | 58 |
| Bolton, Thomas | 12 |
| BOOTH | 7 |
| Booth, John | 7 |
| Boure, Narcisse | 74 |
| Braun, F B | 13 |
| Breadner Manufacturing Co. | 55 |
| Breadner, S. . . . . . . . 34, | 55 |
| BREMNER | 61 |

Silver, Continued

| | |
|---|---|
| Brothers, Wm. | 7 |
| Brown & Co., M S. . . . . 13, | 14 |
| Brown, George Stairs | 13 |
| Brown, Michael Septimus . . . . | 13 |
| Brown, T B | 14 |
| Brown, Thomas | 14 |
| Bruff, Charles Oliver | 25 |
| BULL DOG BRAND | 32 |
| Burns, James | 7 |
| Butler, James | 14 |
| | |
| C | 59 |
| C & J A | 69 |
| A & J ALLEN | 69 |
| C A . . . . . . . . . . . 56, | 69 |
| C A O . . . . . . . . . . . 41, | 71 |
| C E R | 71 |
| C O B | 25 |
| Camirand J D & Co. | 58 |
| CAMIRAND LIMITED | 58 |
| Campbell, A | 34 |
| CANADA MFG. CO. . . 42, | 70 |
| Canadian Jewellers Ltd. | 59 |
| Canadian Robers Company | 37 |
| Canadian Wm. A Rogers | |
| Limited . . . . . . . . . 37, | 42 |
| Caron Bros | 58 |
| CARON FRERES | 59 |
| Carter, J F | 34 |
| Christmas, D S | 74 |
| Claringbowl, Fred | 35 |
| COMMUNITY | 40 |
| COMMUNITY PLATE | 40 |
| COMMUNITY SILVER | 40 |
| Cornelius & Co. | 15 |
| Cornelius Becker & Co. | 26 |
| Cornelius, Julius | 15 |
| Couture, Pierre | 74 |
| Crawford, William | 15 |
| CROWN & LION | 53 |
| CROWN SILVER PLATE CO. | 43 |
| Cruickshank, Robert | 59 |
| | |
| D & S | 60 |
| D B . . . . . . . . . . . . 58, | 74 |
| D G | 25 |
| D H W | 24 |

Silver, Continued

| | |
|---|---|
| D L | 9 |
| D M M | 71 |
| D MILLER | 71 |
| D S CO | 33 |
| D SAVAGE | 34 |
| D W  11, | 24 |
| Darling, George | 41 |
| Davis, Henry | 36 |
| Denman & Bohle | 59 |
| DERBY SILVER CO | 43 |
| Desroche, Alfred | 59 |
| Dewey, William | 36 |
| Dingman, James F | 34 |
| DUTCHESS PLATE | 49 |
| Dwight & Savage | 59 |
| Dwight, James Adams | 59 |
| | |
| E  31, | 34 |
| E & T S | 22 |
| E G W & S | 31 |
| E M M | 48 |
| E S | 22 |
| EAGLE BRAND | 43 |
| EAGLE'S HEAD | 29 |
| Eastwood, James | 24 |
| ED BARLOW | 57 |
| 1847 Rogers Bros | 27 |
| Ellis, James | 74 |
| Ellis, James E | 45 |
| Ellis, P. W. & Company | 44 |
| Etter, B B | 16 |
| Etter, Benjamin | 16 |
| EUREKA SILVER CO | 28 |
| | |
| F B | 58 |
| F M | 20 |
| F R | 78 |
| F S | 78 |
| F W S  36, | 72 |
| F W S & B | 72 |
| Fairbanks, Whitcombe | 8 |
| Ferguson & Page | 10 |
| Fletcher, W S | 25 |
| FLEUR-DE-LIS | 26 |
| FORBES PLATE | 27 |
| | |
| G | 45 |

Silver, Continued

| | |
|---|---|
| G B | 70 |
| G G R & CO | 71 |
| G H | 8 |
| G L DARLING  41, | 70 |
| G RODGERS | 50 |
| G S  22, 51, 71, | 79 |
| G S & S | 62 |
| G S B | 13 |
| G SEIFERT  72, | 79 |
| G W | 24 |
| G WARREN | 72 |
| Gano, David | 25 |
| GARD | 8 |
| Gard, Thomas Dapleton | 8 |
| Gatien, M | 75 |
| Geddie, John | 25 |
| Gendron, P | 75 |
| Goldsmith's Stock Co. of Canada  45, | 73 |
| GRIGG | 16 |
| Grigg, William | 16 |
| Grothe, Z. | 75 |
| | |
| H & A S | 72 |
| H & E | 45 |
| H & L  67, | 70 |
| H & P | 17 |
| H B & CO | 69 |
| H C | 60 |
| H G B | 25 |
| H J | 46 |
| H M | 20 |
| H R S & CO | 61 |
| H S M | 71 |
| Hall, George A | 17 |
| Hamman, Thomas | 17 |
| Hanna & Delagrave | 75 |
| Hanna, James | 75 |
| Hanna, James Godfrey | 75 |
| Hardy, Anselm | 76 |
| Harris, E B | 76 |
| Harwood, Arthur | 8 |
| Hay, A & J | 8 |
| HEIRLOOM | 40 |
| Hemming Mfg. Co. | 60 |
| HENDERY & LESLIE | 70 |
| Hendery, Robert | 67 |

Silver, Continued

| | |
|---|---|
| HENRY ROGERS SONS & CO | 61 |
| Herbin, John Frederic | 26 |
| Hersey, John A | 8 |
| Hill & Houghton | 45 |
| HOLMES & EDWARDS | 31, 45, 51 |
| HORSESHOE & DOG | 57, 65 |
| Hosterman & Parker | 17 |
| Hosterman, Thomas | 17 |
| Hull, E Mrs. | 76 |
| Hulsman, Louis | 17 |
| Hunt, William | 17 |
| Hunter, William | 76 |
| Hurd, Benjamin | 18 |
| Hurd, Nathaniel | 18 |
| HUTCHINSON | 8 |
| Hutchinson, Georg G | 8 |
| I A | 74 |
| I A D | 59 |
| I B | 14 |
| I F L | 76 |
| I HURD | 18 |
| I M | 10 |
| I O | 77, 78 |
| I S | 30, 32, 78 |
| I S CO | 31 |
| INDIAN HEAD | 29 |
| Inlaid Silver Co. | 45 |
| INLAID SILVER PATD | 45 |
| Innes, William | 76 |
| INSICO | 30 |
| INTERNATIONAL SILVER CO | 31 |
| Internation Silver Co. of Canada Ltd. | 27, 52 |
| INTERNATIONAL SILVER COMPANY | 30 |
| INTERNATIONAL STERLING | 30 |
| J & B | 7 |
| J A | 6, 12 |
| J A D | 59 |
| J A H | 8 |
| J B | 7, 12, 57 |
| J B W | 72 |
| J C | 15 |
| J C C | 70 |

Silver, Continued

| | |
|---|---|
| J CORNELIUS | 15, 70 |
| J D CAMIRAND & CO | 58 |
| J E | 25 |
| J E E | 45 |
| J E E & CO | 70 |
| J ELLIS | 74 |
| J F | 70 |
| J F C | 35 |
| J F D | 34 |
| J G J & CO | 46, 70 |
| J H | 75 |
| J H J & CO | 70 |
| J HURD | 18 |
| J L | 19, 40, 77 |
| J LESLEY | 40 |
| J LESLIE | 71 |
| J M | 9 |
| J MC | 20 |
| J MUNRO | 10 |
| J R | 48 |
| J R & CO | 73 |
| J R H & CO | 70 |
| J RAMAGE | 35 |
| J W | 53 |
| J W M & CO | 71 |
| J ZIMMERMAN | 72 |
| J FROLAND | 70 |
| Jackson, Henry | 46 |
| JOHN WANLESS & CO | 53 |
| Johnson, Thomas Charles | 18 |
| Joseph, J G & Co. | 46 |
| Judge, Michael | 34 |
| K | 46 |
| K & T | 9, 72 |
| K T | 9 |
| KENT BROS | 46, 70 |
| Kent, Ambrose & Sons Ltd. | 46 |
| KERR & THORNE | 9 |
| KNIGHT'S HEAD | 63 |
| KNIGHT'S HEAD & SHIELD | 29 |
| L & A | 47, 69 |
| L & C | 70 |
| L A | 74 |
| L H | 17 |
| L P B | 58 |

Silver, Continued

| | |
|---|---|
| Labaume, Gustave | 12 |
| Lafrance, Ambroise | 76 |
| Lambert, Paul | 76 |
| Lamontagne, Michael | 76 |
| Landron, Jean Francois | 76 |
| Langford, Jas. I | 19 |
| LASH & CO | 46 |
| Lash, J B | 46 |
| Learmont, William | 60 |
| Lee & Chillas | 47 |
| Lees, George H | 35 |
| LEOPARD HEAD IN SHIELD | 34 |
| Lesley, John | 40 |
| Leslie, John | 71 |
| Lesperance, Pierre | 77 |
| Lido Jewellers Co. | 60 |
| LION | 28 |
| LION & HEAD | 40 |
| Lord, Daniel | 9 |
| Lowe & Anderson | 47 |
| LOWE & CO | 71 |
| Lowe, Wm. G H | 47 |
| Lucas, Joseph | 77 |
| M & B | 71 |
| M A | 57 |
| M B CO | 27, 28 |
| M C | 70 |
| M C D | 20 |
| M COCHENTHALER | 70 |
| M G | 75 |
| M GAGE | 70 |
| M L GURD | 70 |
| M S B | 13 |
| M S B & CO | 13, 14, 70 |
| M S BROWN & CO LTD | 14 |
| Malone, William | 34 |
| MAPLE LEAF | 44 |
| Marks, N M | 40 |
| Marsters, R U | 19 |
| Martyn, John, Mrs. | 77 |
| McCullock, John | 19 |
| McDonald, Daniel | 20 |
| McLaughlin, Samuel | 77 |
| McNaught & Lowe | 47 |
| Melick, James Godfrey | 9 |
| Melrose, George | 20 |

Silver, Continued

| | |
|---|---|
| MERIDEN B CO | 29 |
| Meriden Britannia Co. Ltd. | 27, 52 |
| MERIDEN S P CO | 29 |
| Meriden Silver Plate Co. | 47 |
| Meves, Otto | 60 |
| Meyer & Bolton | 12 |
| Meyer, Franz F | 20 |
| Mignowitz, Henry | 20 |
| MILLER | 61 |
| Miller & Bremner | 60 |
| MONARCH SILVER CO | 31, 51 |
| MONARCH SILVER PLATE CO | 47 |
| MORGAN | 26 |
| Morgan, C P | 25 |
| Morin, Paul | 77 |
| Morphy, Edward M | 48 |
| MUNRO | 9 |
| Munro, Alex | 9 |
| Munro, John | 9 |
| N B | 11, 74 |
| N BEAUDRY | 57, 69 |
| N F NICKEL SILVER 1877 | 40 |
| N F SILVER CO 1877 | 37 |
| N M MARKS | 40 |
| N MARKS | 71 |
| Newman, William Herman | 21 |
| NIAGARA FALLS CO 1877 | 37 |
| Niagara Falls Silver Co. | 37 |
| Niagara Silver Co. | 37 |
| Nordbeck, Peter | 21 |
| NORMAN PLATE | 52 |
| NOVA SCOTIA SILVER C B & CO | 26 |
| O & H | 41, 70 |
| O L | 25 |
| O MEVES | 60 |
| Oliver, Richard Kestell | 48 |
| OLMSTEAD | 71 |
| Olmstead, C A | 41 |
| ONEIDA | 39, 40 |
| ONEIDA COMMUNITY | 39, 40 |
| ONEIDA LTD | 39 |
| Oneida Ltd. | 38 |
| Oneida Silversmiths | 37 |
| ONEIDA SILVERSMITHS | 39 |

Silver, Continued

| | |
|---|---|
| ONEIDACRAFT | 39 |
| Orkney, James | 77 |
| Osborne, Robert | 35 |
| | |
| P A | 56 |
| P B | 58 |
| P E P | 71, 78 |
| P L | 76, 77 |
| P M | 77 |
| P N | 21 |
| P W ELLIS | 44 |
| PAGE BROS | 10, 11 |
| Page Bros | 10 |
| PAGE SMALLEY & FERGUSON | 10 |
| Page, Amos | 11 |
| Page, David | 26 |
| Page, Jacques | 77 |
| Page, Smalley & Ferguson | 10 |
| Page, Thomas | 11 |
| Paradis, Roland | 77 |
| Peacock, Henry | 61 |
| PELTON | 71 |
| PIECES OF 8 | 33 |
| PINE TREE | 33 |
| POST | 48 |
| Post, Jordan | 48 |
| POULIN | 71, 78 |
| Poulin, P E & Co. | 78 |
| Powis, Thomas | 78 |
| | |
| R | 49 |
| R & B | 33 |
| R C | 59 |
| R H | 67 |
| R H TWEEDELL | 26 |
| R HENDERY | 67, 70 |
| R K O | 48 |
| R O | 35 |
| R OSBORNE | 35 |
| R P | 77 |
| R S | 63 |
| R SHARPLEY | 63 |
| R SHARPLEY & SONS | 72 |
| R T | 10 |
| R U MARSTERS | 19 |
| R W & CO | 36, 72 |
| R W & S | 36 |

Silver, Continued

| | |
|---|---|
| Ramage, John | 35 |
| Ranvooyze, Ignace Francois | 78 |
| RELIANCE | 40 |
| REX PLATE | 40 |
| RIDEAU PLATE | 65 |
| Robinson, Joseph & Co. | 48 |
| Roden Bros., Ltd. | 49 |
| Rodgers, G. | 50 |
| ROGERS | 37, 39 |
| Rogers, Henry, Sons & Co. | 61 |
| Rogers, William & Son | 27 |
| Rogers, Wm. A | 37 |
| ROSENTHAL | 41, 71 |
| Rosenthal, A J | 41 |
| Rosenthal, Abraham | 50 |
| Ross, Adam | 21 |
| Ross, J | 22 |
| Round, John & Co. | 73 |
| Russell, Richard | 35 |
| RYRIE | 71 |
| Ryrie Birks | 50 |
| RYRIE BROS. | 50 |
| Ryrie, James | 50 |
| | |
| S | 35 |
| S & A | 52 |
| S & A SAUNDERS | 51 |
| S & S | 63 |
| S A S | 36, 72 |
| S B | 34, 55 |
| S B S | 70 |
| S B W | 72 |
| S C | 52 |
| S H M & CO | 71 |
| S L & C O | 62, 71 |
| S W S | 34 |
| Sargent, S J | 50 |
| Sasseville & Orkney | 78 |
| Sasseville, Francois | 78 |
| Sasseville, Joseph | 78 |
| Saunders, Lorie & Co. | 50 |
| SAVAGE | 62, 71 |
| SAVAGE & LYMAN | 71 |
| SAVAGE LYMAN & CO. | 62 |
| Savage, David | 34 |
| Savage, George | 51, 61 |
| Saxton, John | 51 |

Silver, Continued

| | |
|---|---|
| SCALES & STAR | 79 |
| Schindler, Jonas | 79 |
| SEIFERT | 72 |
| Seifert, Gustavus | 79 |
| Sharpley, Rice | 63 |
| Sharpley, Rice & Sons | 63 |
| SHEFFIELD HOUSE | 79 |
| SILVER METAL | 40 |
| SIMEON L & GEORGE H ROGERS COMPANY | 37 |
| SIMPSON HALL MILLER & CO | 29, 63 |
| Simpson, Hall, Miller & Co | 52, 63 |
| Smith, S. W | 34 |
| SOVEREIGN PLATE | 44 |
| Sovereighn Plate | 51 |
| SPAHN | 6 |
| Spahn, Justin | 6 |
| Spanenberg, Frederick W | 36 |
| Spanenberg, George | 35 |
| Spanenberg, S A | 36 |
| Spike, Edmun Lloyd | 22 |
| Spike, Thomas Daniel | 22 |
| STANDARD "S" CO | 29 |
| STANDARD SILVER CO LTD | 51 |
| Standard Silver Co | 27, 47, 50, 51, 52 |
| Stanley & Aylward Ltd | 52 |
| Stennet, Wm. | 36 |
| Stephanis, Gothelf | 22 |
| Sterling Craft Ltd. | 52 |
| Stern, Samuel | 52 |
| Sterns, Edwin | 22 |
| | |
| T | 73 |
| T A | 56 |
| T A & CO | 56, 69 |
| T B | 23 |
| T B BROWN | 14 |
| T B STEACY | 72 |
| T C J | 18 |
| T C J & S | 18 |
| T C JOHNSON & SONS | 18 |
| T H | 17 |
| T HAMMAN | 17 |
| T S P | 73 |
| Taggart, Frank | 52 |

Silver, Continued

| | |
|---|---|
| TASKER & SONS | 72 |
| THE ACME SILVER CO | 42 |
| THE HIGHLAND BRAND | 29 |
| THE TORONTO SILVER PLATE COMPANY | 53 |
| Thompson, Richard | 10 |
| Toler, Joseph | 23 |
| TORONTO SILVER PLATE CO | 72 |
| Toronto Silver Plate Company | 53 |
| TORSIL | 53 |
| Tracy, William H | 41 |
| Troop, Alexander | 23 |
| TUDOR PLATE | 40 |
| Tully, Henry Wentworth | 23 |
| Tweedell, Richard Henry | 26 |
| | |
| UNCROWNED HEAD | 34 |
| | |
| V & W | 24 |
| Veith & Witham | 24 |
| Veith, William James | 23 |
| VENNING | 10 |
| Venning, J H | 10 |
| Venning, William Norris | 10 |
| VIANDE | 30 |
| VICTOR SILVER COMPANY | 33 |
| VIKING PLATE | 54 |
| | |
| W | 33 |
| W & P M | 72 |
| W A & S B | 12 |
| W B | 7 |
| W BRAMLEY | 69 |
| W C | 16 |
| W C M | 71 |
| W F | 8 |
| W G YOUNG | 72 |
| W H | 76 |
| W H K | 70 |
| W H KEARNEY | 70 |
| W H N | 21 |
| W H NEWMAN | 21 |
| W H S | 71 |
| W H TRACY | 41, 72 |
| W I | 76 |
| W L | 60 |
| W LEARMONT | 60 |

Silver, Continued

| | |
|---|---|
| W R | 39 |
| W S P CO | 32 |
| W S W | 72 |
| W V | 10, 23 |
| W W | 72 |
| WALKER | 72 |
| Wallace & Balcom | 24 |
| WANLESS | 72 |
| Wanless, John | 53 |
| Ware, D T & Co. | 36 |
| Ware, T P & Co. | 35 |
| Warlock, Daniel O L | 11 |
| WATROUS MFG CO | 29 |
| WATSON | 72 |
| WELCH & TROWERN | 54 |
| Whiston, David Hudson | 24 |
| White, T & Son | 54 |
| WILCOX | 30 |
| Witham, George | 24 |
| WM & S BLACK | 12 |
| WM A ROGERS | 37, 42 |
| Wolhaupter, Benjamin | 6 |
| | |
| Y S & CO | 6 |
| | |
| Z G | 75 |
| Z MCN & CO | 47, 71 |
| Zimmerman & McNaught & Co. | 47 |

**SILVER, HALLMARKED 80 - 98**

| | |
|---|---|
| Birmingham | 84, 85 |
| Chester | 86 |
| Dublin | 95 |
| Exeter | 87 |
| Glasgow | 96 |
| Jubilee Mark 1934 /45 | 97, 98 |
| London | 88, 89, 90 |
| Newcastle | 91 |
| Sheffield | 92, 93 |
| York | 94 |

# NOTES